CASTAWAY
IN
PARADISE

October 5, 2003

For Ashley —
Many thanks for your competent
care during my medical emergency.

Jim Simmons

Other Books by James C. Simmons

The Novelist as Historian:
  Essays on the Victorian Historical Novel

Truman Capote:
  The Story of His Bizarre and Exotic Boyhood
  (with Marie Rudisill)

The Secrets Men Keep (with Ken Druck)

Passionate Pilgrims:
  English Travelers to the World of the Desert Arabs

The Big Book of Adventure Travel:
  500 Great Escapes

Americans:
  The View from Abroad

CASTAWAY IN PARADISE

THE INCREDIBLE ADVENTURES OF TRUE-LIFE ROBINSON CRUSOES

James C. Simmons

SHERIDAN
HOUSE

Published by Sheridan House Inc.
145 Palisade Street
Dobbs Ferry, NY 10522

Cover design: Madkat Studio
Book design: Richard Stalzer

Library of Congress Cataloging-in-Publication Data

Simmons, James C.
   Castaway in paradise : the incredible adventures of true-life
Robinson Crusoes / by James C. Simmons.
     p. cm.
   Includes bibliographical references and index.
   ISBN 0-924486-44-9
   1. Castaways.   I. Title.
  G525.S554 1993   93-13882
  910.4—dc20   CIP

Printed in the United States of America

ISBN 0-924486-44-9

Printed on acid-free paper

For Larry Abramson,
Josephine Ciccariello,
Jim Cooper,
Susan Kaye,
Robert Reinke,
and Bob Sundquist

"I know an Island
Where the long scented holy nights pass
   slow,
And there, 'twixt lowland and highland,
The white stream falls into a pool...,
Deep, hidden with ferns and flowers, soft
   as dreaming,
Where the brown, laughing, dancing
   bathers go."

Rupert Brooke

CONTENTS

INTRODUCTION

Of Islands and Men

In August of 1929 Richard Halliburton, that indefatigable traveler and writer whose name had become synonymous with romance, adventure, and freedom, stood on the shores of the tiny Caribbean island of Tobago. He was at the end of a long and exhausting journey around Latin America that he had undertaken for *The Ladies' Home Journal.* He had already walked in the footsteps of Cortez from Vera Cruz to Mexico City, been the first man to swim the length of the Panama Canal, and smuggled himself *into* the notorious French penal colony of Devil's Island.

On Tobago Halliburton determined to live out another of his life's ambitions—to become, if only for a few weeks, a twentieth century Robinson Crusoe. He found a convenient cave near the beach and set up housekeeping there. And from the natives in a nearby village he bought those props he needed for his little drama—some sheepskin garments, a parrot, an old musket, two milk goats, a cat, and a dog. He also purchased the services of a young Negro goatherd to play Friday to his Robinson Crusoe. The two of them set about building a shelter, a lean-to for his goats, and a dugout canoe, which proved too heavy for them to carry to the water. After two weeks Halliburton's schooner returned. Before departing for New York, he gave his animals to Friday, who loaded them into an ancient Ford and puttered happily back to his village.

The figure of the castaway is one of the most powerful in our literary heritage. Whether he is St. Paul shipwrecked on Malta, Ulysses cast up on Nausicaa's beach, Prospero on Bermuda, Gulliver on Lilliput, or the Ancient Mariner adrift on an endless ocean, the castaway figure has maintained a firm grip on our imagination and sympathy.

In the figure of Robinson Crusoe, the English novelist Daniel Defoe gave Western civilization one of its seminal myths. Crusoe went on to join the exclusive company of Faust, Don Juan, and Don Quixote, other literary figures who were apotheosized into myth. By the end of the nineteenth century *Robinson Crusoe* had appeared in at least 700 editions, translations, and imitations, not to mention a popular eighteenth century pantomime and an opera by Offenbach.

The story of Robinson Crusoe alone on his island with its palm-fringed beaches, deprived of all assistance from his fellow men and yet against all odds able to look after himself and prosper, continues to enthrall readers of all ages. The popularity of Defoe's epic of the triumph of individual enterprise and survival cuts across all cultural boundaries. A century ago a newspaper in Greenland published a serial translation of the famous novel into one of the Eskimo languages. One of the illustrative plates showed Friday prostrating himself before his master to build a fire on the shore. Friday is naked except for a scanty loincloth. Crusoe is bundled tightly in furs as any true Eskimo, a harpoon nearby, while palm trees wave above dense undergrowth on a low hill, the side of which is partly covered with snow. As in all great works of the imagination, the inner vision has become more significant than external facts.

To all of us who feel alienated from desk-bound lives, the story of Robinson Crusoe on his little island with its palm-fringed beaches offers a powerful and continuing appeal. That unprofaned sanctuary, an island removed from the haunts of man where we may dwell in tranquility, happiness, and security amidst a closeness to nature, has for centuries proven an ideal that exerts an enormous attraction over our imagination. The beachcomber's life on his idyllic island offers the promise of freedom, the opportunity to indulge our own caprices, work out our own salvation, and find pleasure in the simple life. Thoreau had done it once at Walden Pond, to be sure. But how much more enticing would such an existence be on the tropical island of our dreams?

The myth of Robinson Crusoe is bound inseparably with the age-old fascination with islands. On an island he has become a timeless symbol. Would we remember Crusoe today had he come ashore on a deserted stretch of Florida beach?

To the popular imagination islands are transcendental, magical places, capable of magnifying and transforming experiences and emotions beyond the norm of mainland reality. Thoreau observed in *Walden*, "An island pleases my imagination, even the smallest, as a small continent and integral part of the globe."

At deeper levels the island represents both the Garden of Eden and the Womb. Here, surrounded on all sides by a protective moat, one is insulated from the grosser absurdities of an irrational world, from the wearisome conflicts of a restless society. The island offers once more the great prize of passionate individualism. It is no wonder that the possession of an island is one of the central fantasies of man's dreams. In actual fact, for these true-life Robinson Crusoes some islands offered paradise, others hell.

Island dwellers, too, quickly learn their dependence upon nature, a lesson that is the beginning of wisdom for us all. "An island is close to nature," James Michener has written. "The sea is omnipresent. The birds come and go. The stars hang low in the sky. The blazing sun of noonday is imperative. And when the wind begins to howl and the waves rise, there is always the possibility that a hurricane will send water sweeping across the entire land."

The successful castaway on his small, deserted island must always become the perfect environmentalist. His success will depend upon his ability to become a part of the ecological harmony of his little kingdom and not to succumb to the temptation to upset it through imprudent exploitation.

For the Utopian, an island offers that rare opportunity to create a world of one's own choosing. As one island-dweller noted some years back, "This is probably the unspoken promise that draws twentieth-century man to islands—not that he wants to run ahead of the rest of the human race, but quite the contrary, to run back to the beginning and make certain that the same mistakes are not repeated. This is the true lure of islands, whether they are large or small."

And always at the heart of the popular fantasy of the island is the alluring figure of the beachcomber, that happy-go-lucky rascal in paradise with his outrigger canoe parked on a white sand beach in front of his simple thatched-roof hut and a couple of dusky-skinned island women in tow—an image that continues to exert a powerful appeal to those of us who are alienated from our nine-to-five jobs. Indeed, any traveler today through the remote island clusters of the Pacific will find them on the far-flung atolls: former machinists, sailors, accountants, and adventurers, who have succumbed to the seductive siren-song of the tropical islands.

Island living has a primitive appeal that is powerfully seductive. We all feel, sooner or later, the irresistible call of the islands stirring in our blood. How often do we weary of civilization and experience the urge to get away from it, especially during times of severe anxiety and personal disappointment when life on those faraway shores in the tropical climes seems peaceful and serene. There time stands still and cares melt like a chip of ice in the noonday sun. Climate is a special attraction of the South Seas and means tropical fruits, semi-nakedness, and indolence.

Novelist Paul Theroux is another traveler and author who temporarily fell under that spell after the collapse of his marriage. He set off on a solo journey by plane, ship, and kayak through the island groups of the Pacific. At one point, like Richard Halliburton before him, he set himself up as a Robinson Crusoe on the deserted island of Pau in the Vava'u group of Tonga. This was the idyllic life of many a would-be beachcomber's fantasies: camped on a white sandy beach, watching the lazy breakers curling over a distant reef and swimming in the quiet waters of a palm-fringed lagoon. But reality soon intruded rudely upon his fantasy. As he confessed later in his book, *The Happy Isles of Oceania*, he was too enamored of his creature comforts to endure for long as a beachcomber on the island of his dreams.

> I had a taste of what it was to be a beachcomber on a happy empty island. It was mostly purely idleness, with the invented urgencies of having to carry out various duties. And then I came to believe in these fictions, and so the day was filled. It meant being alone and self-sufficient. It meant that I got plenty of sleep and perhaps a bit too much sun and more mosquito bites than I had ever known. It meant keeping close track of my food and eating coconuts whenever possible. Most of all, because I had very

little fresh water for washing, it meant a perpetual
state of being sticky and salty.

What finally ended his stay was a jarring discovery.
Theroux remembered the passage from Defoe's novel in
which Robinson Crusoe comes upon the print of a man's foot
in the soft sand on his shore and realizes he is no longer
alone on his sanctuary:

> I had an identical experience, except that it was
> dark—the tide had ebbed all afternoon, I looked up
> from my meal and saw footprints everywhere. They
> led down the beach and into the woods; up to the
> cliffs, along the shore, across the dunes, all around the
> camp, desperate little solitary tracks.
>
> There were hundreds, perhaps thousands of
> footprints, suggesting vast wandering mobs of idle
> strangers, and what frightened me—what eventually
> impelled me to break camp soon afterward and head
> for the nearest inhabited island, where I was assured
> of a welcome—and what sent a chill through me, was
> the thought that every single footprint, every urgent
> little trail, was mine.

Castaway in Paradise explores the reality in the myth
through the stories of a variety of castaways. Because of shipwrecks, perfidious sea captains, or simple choice, they found
themselves true-life Robinson Crusoes. Their adventures
were sufficiently extravagant to make those of Defoe's hero
seem almost commonplace by comparison.

All of us who have traveled the oceans of the world have
wondered how we would react if we were stranded as castaways on a remote shore. What if our ship wrecked on a tropical reef, and we found ourselves cast upon a strange shore?
How would we survive? From the safe comfort of our arm-
chairs, it is easy to believe that we would react well, even
heroically.

But would we? Would we really know enough to stay

alive, keep others alive, keep going? Most of us don't know. And, fortunately, few of us ever have to find out.

These are stories of survival. All these men and women showed sufficient courage, practical intelligence, self-discipline, and mental balance to overcome their difficulties. Each had the ability to endure the pressures of isolation and solitude. Most castaways find themselves leading animal-like lives after a few months ashore, sinking into degradation and madness. But these men and women all exhibited those virtues of will power, common sense, and a decisiveness that are important to our culture. They made a virtue out of their necessity. And their experiences tell us powerfully that isolation can be the beginning of a new realization of the potential of the individual.

CHAPTER ONE

Alexander Selkirk:

The Monarch of the Juan Fernández Islands

It is the first day of February in 1709. Two small British privateers cautiously approach Más á Tierra Island in the Juan Fernández group, an uninhabited scrap of land 400 miles off the coast of Chile, fearful lest they find Spanish warships in the vicinity. Badly battered by storms while rounding the Horn, their crews are sick with scurvy and exhaustion and in no condition to fight an enemy force no matter how small. The ships sail warily into a bay and drop anchor. That night they spy a signal fire ashore burning brightly in the darkness. Woodes Rogers, the captain of the expedition, assumes the worst and prepares for a fight he doubts he can win.

But the next morning the British force can discover no other ships. At noon a heavily armed landing party goes ashore. They return a few hours later with an extraordinary discovery—a man half-British, half-savage. Rogers and his crew stare in wonder at the heavily bearded castaway clothed in a cap, breeches, and coat, all crudely fashioned from goatskins, who climbs aboard their ship.

"He looked wilder than the first owners of them," Rogers notes in his journal for that day. "At his first coming on board us, he had so much forgot his language for want of use, that we could scarce understand him, for he seemed to speak his words of by halves."

That wild man clothed in animal skins was Alexander Selkirk. Back in London, he would enjoy a brief moment of fame before receding into the shadows of history. But he would find immortality under another name, Robinson Crusoe, the Prince of Castaways. For Selkirk's extraordinary survival for four years and four months on Más á Tierra Island served as the model for Daniel Defoe's greatest creation and, as such, the inspiration for one of the seminal myths of Western civilization.

Born Alexander Selcraig in 1676 in Largo, a small fishing village on the east coast of Scotland, he was the seventh son of a prosperous tanner and shoemaker. We know more than usual about his youth because he was a spoiled and unruly boy who was often in trouble with the church authorities. His name crops up unfavorably in the preserved minutes of the monthly church meetings at which the minister and the church elders passed judgment on the wayward actions of their parishioners. When he was thirteen, for example, he and an older brother led a protest demonstration. An unpopular minister had raised funds for the poor but failed to distribute them. "This Sabbath the minister, being obstructed in his duties, was kept out of church by a great mob, headed by John and Alexander Selcraig," the Kirk-Session minutes reads. (Soon afterwards the minister in question did distribute the funds, which suggests strongly that the Selcraigs were in the right.) These and other incidents suggest a youth who was quick tempered, impulsive, and often insubordinate, traits which would stay with him into adulthood and eventually lead to his being marooned on an uninhabited island in the Pacific.

His father wanted to apprentice the boy to the family business. And indeed he had spent several years dutifully learning his father's trade of shoemaker. But his mother held to the Scottish superstition that seventh sons were blessed with foreknowledge of future events and destined to fame and fortune. She encouraged her son to disregard his father's wishes and go to sea. His parents bickered continuously about his future. Finally, in 1695 young Selcraig decided the issue himself by running away and joining a ship's crew. At this time he changed his name to Selkirk, perhaps an additional sign of youthful rebellion. Virtually nothing is known of this voyage. He remained away for six years and returned home an officer. This rapid rise suggests the unruly young Scotsman submitted without complaint to the harsh discipline of sea life and learned quickly the various skills of navigation and seamanship necessary to be an officer.

Selkirk returned to his hometown in 1701 and found himself caught up almost immediately in the family quarrels. When his brother for a joke substituted a cup of salt water for fresh, the quarrel turned so violent that the church elders of his church once again cited him to appear before them. The church minutes for November 29 read:

"Alexander Selcraig, scandalous for contention and disagreeing with his brothers, called, compeared, and being questioned concerning the tumult that was in his house, whereof he was said to be the occasion, he confessed that, having taken a drink of salt water, his brother Andrew laughing at him for it, he did beat him twice with a staff. He confessed also that he had spoken very ill words concerning his brother John, and particularly he challenged him to a combat of fists, which afterwards he did refuse and retract; whereupon the session appointed him to compear before the face of his congregation for his scandalous carriage."

But Selkirk had had enough of domestic life ashore. Soon afterwards he fled Largo for London to seek a berth on another ship. On May 1702, the War of the Spanish Succession broke out. The Spanish empire, although considerably shrunken from its sixteenth century boundaries, still cast a formidable shadow over Europe. Spain was allied with France, and vessels of both nations were now fair game. The British Crown began commissioning privateers to raid Spanish shipping in South American waters. There was a rush of applications from ship owners for letters of marque and reprisal to sail against the enemy.

As every schoolboy knows from a reading of *Treasure Island*, the great days of privateering and piracy were the days of exploration, conquest, and colonization—the seven-

teenth and eighteenth centuries. Legalized privateering flourished then as an expansion of naval power by seafaring nations. The major incentive for private businessmen to send
their merchantships off to war was, of course, the share of
the booty they could expect after raiding enemy shipping and
coastal towns. And given the unsettled conditions that prevailed on many seas, the merchant vessels of the day were
built and armed like men-of-war.

The distinction between pirates and privateers was supposed to operate under certain terms
of engagement. The Crown was entitled to a one-tenth share
of the prize value and the Admiralty a fifteenth. The ship's
owners collected up to fifty percent. The crew all signed on
without pay, agreeing to a policy of "no purchase, no pay,"
meaning they were paid only if the voyage was successful.
However, generous rewards were often given to the first
sailor to sight an enemy ship and the first to board her.

The distinction between pirates and privateers was more
easily made in theory than practice. The pirate was a seago-
ing robber who owed allegiance to no government, but op-
portunistically preyed upon all ships that came within range
of his cannons. The privateer, on the other hand, was legally
commissioned by a government to wage war on its behalf
and therefore could claim, in the event of capture, all the
rights accorded proper prisoners of war. In actual practice,
the distinction between pirates and privateers was often im-
precise. "The conduct of all privateers is, as far as I have
seen, so near piracy that I only wonder any civilized nation
can allow them," Lord Nelson complained in 1804.

In London Selkirk met Captain William Dampier, then
in the midst of organizing a two-ship privateering squadron
to operate against the Spaniards in the Pacific. From the ac-
cession of Charles I to the death of Queen Anne, there were
no English voyages of discovery comparable to Dampier's or
any travel books as valuable to later sea captains as his. His
wind map of the Pacific was the first of its kind ever published and an important contribution to the science of hy-
drography. England's greatest navigator at the time, he was
one of the few Englishmen to sail around the world and
would do so three times within fifteen years. A portrait of
him in the National Portrait Gallery shows a man in middle

age with brown hair, deep blue eyes, prominent nose, round chin, and jutting lower lip.

Dampier was unusual in that he had few of those obvious characteristics we generally associate with great discoverers of the likes of Captain James Cook. There was little of the swashbuckler about him and a great deal of natural modesty. Early in his travels he began a habit of writing a daily journal. He delighted in describing every detail of his adventures and was a keen observer of the local flora and fauna. In 1697 he published *A New Voyage Round the World*, an account of a twelve-year-long sea voyage with pirates that began in 1680 and involved a confusing number of ships and captains. He returned to London with nothing to show for his time but his journal concealed in a hollow length of bamboo and a slave boy whose body was covered from head to foot with elaborate tattoos, a gift from one of his sea captains. He quickly sold the boy to some London investors, who put him up for view to the public, for an admission price. A second lengthy cruise to Australia led to the discovery of New Britain and many lesser islands. He was the first Englishman to set foot on the Australian continent. But on his return he was court-martialed by the Royal Navy for "many irregularities and undue practices." He was found guilty, ordered to forfeit all his pay, and declared "not a fit person to be employed as commander of any of his Majesty's ships."

Although his government would have nothing to do with him any longer, Dampier quickly learned that his experience and expertise as a navigator put him in great demand by the British merchants, eager for a captain to lead a privateering expedition against the Spanish forces in South America. In the excitement of the moment they overlooked the fact that Dampier had no previous experience as a captain.

Dampier was given two ships, fully equipped. His flagship was the *St. George*, a 230-ton vessel carrying 26 guns and a crew of 120. Supporting her was the *Cinque Ports*, a small ship of 90 tons, 16 guns, and 63 crew. Selkirk enlisted and was made the sail master, the third in command, on the second vessel, a position of trust in which he could display the high qualities of a skilled mariner.

Exaggerated reports had filtered back to England of the

fabulous wealth to be had with little risk by privateers bold enough to attack the poorly protected Spanish towns and ships. Dampier convinced his investors that he would return them a hundredfold for their money by raiding Spanish treasure galleons and sacking rich towns along the Pacific coast of South America. His scheme was incredibly optimistic. First, they would sail up the Rio de la Plata to Buenos Aires. There he hoped to capture the two or three Spanish treasure galleons, which his sources reported were usually stationed there. If they succeeded in obtaining £600,000, then they would return to England. Otherwise, they would cruise off the Pacific coast, raiding towns and seeking one of the great Manila treasure galleons said to be worth up to fourteen million pieces-of-eight.

The expedition sailed on April 30, 1703, and quickly proved a disaster from the first. Dampier was an excellent navigator but an inept captain. He quarrelled with his popular second officer on the *St. George* and cruelly marooned him with just his sea chest, clothes, and a servant on one of the Cape Verde Islands, a course of action he had learned, no doubt, from his years spent with pirates. This demoralized the entire expedition. Then the captain of the *Cinque Ports* died suddenly of a tropical fever, and Dampier replaced him with his lieutenant, Thomas Stradling, a sullen, irascible, incompetent, and unpopular leader. In January of 1704 the expedition rounded the Horn (only the second British ship in history to do so) and sailed into the Spanish lake, as the British then called the Pacific. The crews on both ships were in a state of near mutiny.

A few days later the expedition dropped anchor at Más á Tierra, the largest of the Juan Fernández Islands located some 400 miles off the coast of present-day Chile. Discovered by the Spaniards in the third quarter of the sixteenth century, this tiny oasis of some fifty square miles became a favorite stopping-off place for scurvy-ridden sailing ships, especially those of seventeenth century privateers, who, unlike the Spanish, had no home ports in that part of the globe. Dampier had visited the island on his earlier cruise and knew that there he could hide from the Spaniards and find a safe anchorage in Cumberland Bay along with an abundance of goat meat, fruits, and water.

Más á Tierra Island is a cluster of rugged wooded volcanic peaks, some over 3,000 feet high, and sloping valleys, measuring fifteen miles by five. It was a perfect site for a colony. But the Spaniards had never maintained a permanent settlement there. Streams of clear water tumble down the mountain sides into the bay. The climate is temperate and delightful. The valley beyond Cumberland Bay is filled with lush semi-tropical vegetation. An officer with Lord George Anson's expedition, which visited there in the spring of 1741, wrote about the island in effusive terms:

> The shade and fragrance of the contiguous woods, the loftiness of the overhanging rocks, and the transparency and frequent falls of the neighbouring streams, presented scenes of such elegance and dignity as are but rarely paralleled in any other part of the globe. It is in this place, perhaps, that the simple production of unassisted nature may be said to excel all the fictitious descriptions of the most animated imagination.

Dampier hoped to repair his ships, rest their crews, and take on fresh food and water. He had visited the island in 1684 with Captain John Cook and told his officers a curious story about a Miskito Indian, named William, who had been marooned on the island for four years. The Miskito Indians from the Caribbean coast of present-day Nicaragua were a resourceful people, fierce warriors, superb hunters, and great haters of the Spanish. They often enlisted in pirate crews. William had arrived at Más á Tierra Island in 1681 with a Captain John Watling and gone ashore with several other men to hunt goats. Suddenly, Spanish ships appeared on the horizon. Watling collected all his men except for the Indian and hurriedly sailed out to sea. William found himself stranded with only his gun, a knife, some shot, and a small horn of powder. By notching his knife, he made a saw and cut his musket barrel into pieces. Out of these, he fashioned harpoons, lances, fishhooks, and another long knife. He built a wooden hut and lined it with goatskins. When his own clothes wore out, he wrapped a hairy goatskin about his loins. On several occasions Spanish ships called at Cumberland Bay and put sailors ashore, but he eluded capture in the thick forests of the upper valley.

When William saw Cook's ship approach the harbor, he quickly determined it was a British vessel and set about preparing a welcome. As the longboats approached his beach, he ran down to congratulate them on a safe arrival and invite them up to his house for a feast. He had killed three goats, dressed them in wild cabbage, and cooked them English style as a treat for the crew. Four years in solitude on the island had not roughened his manners at all. He was the perfect host.

Dampier was also touched by a remarkable coincidence. The first man ashore was another Miskito Indian named Robin who immediately recognized William as a friend. He commented later:

"Robin threw himself flat on his face at [William's] feet, who helping him up and embracing him, fell flat with his face on the ground at Robin's feet, and was by him taken up also. We stood with pleasure to behold the surprise and tenderness and solemnity of this interview, which was exceedingly affectionate on both sides."

Will was the most Crusoesque of Selkirk's predecessors, but he was not the last. The Captain John Cook who took him off in 1684 was himself succeeded on the same ship by Edward Davis, who two years later returned to Más á Tierra Island and, at their own request, put ashore five English pirates and four blacks and then sailed off. Dampier reported how the nine men defended themselves successfully against the Spanish who came to take them, how because of disagreements and personality conflicts the group had lived apart from one another, how one went over to the Spanish, and how the remaining eight were rescued three years later by another British ship.

Dampier set about taking advantage of the resources of Más á Tierra Island. His men refitted both ships, cut wood, and filled the water casks. Hunting parties supplied them with fresh meat from the goats which roamed the island in great numbers, the descendants of a small herd left behind in the 1570s by the island's discoverer, Juan Fernández. These they boiled with the tops of cabbage palms to give themselves a welcomed respite from their monotonous shipboard diet of salt pork and hard tack. The seals and sea lions carpeting the beach around Cumberland Bay provided both food for their stomach and oil for their lamps. They proved an easy enough quarry. William Fanning, Dampier's mate, left us a detailed description of the slaughter:

> They are very much afraid of a man; and so soon as they see him anything near, they will make to the water, for they never go far from it. If they are hard pursued, they will turn about and raise their body up with their fore-fins and face you, standing with their mouth wide open upon their guard. So that when we wanted to kill one, to make oil, we used commonly to clap a pistol just to his mouth, as it stood open, and fire it down his throat. But if we had a mind to have some sport with him, which we called lion-baiting, usually six, seven, or eight, or more of us would go with each a half pike in his hand, and so prick him to death, which commonly would be a sport for two or three hours before we could conquer him.

Some of these animals were of enormous size. They killed one old bull that measured twenty-three feet in length and fourteen feet around the body and had a layer of blubber seventeen inches thick. He provided an entire barrel of oil for their lamps. Young seals proved a favorite food source; they were cooked in a variety of ways. Flanning noted they tasted well to those who were hungry and had no better food at hand.

During this time a violent quarrel broke out between Captain Stradling and his crew. Forty-two of them went ashore, determined not to return on board. For two days the *Cinque Ports* rode at anchor, quite deserted, while the captain and crew argued over their future. We do not know which side Selkirk took up. But he almost certainly used his time ashore to acquaint himself with the island and its attractions. In time Dampier succeeding in reconciling the crew with their captain, and they returned to their ship.

Suddenly, on February 29 a strange sail appeared on the

horizon and headed toward Cumberland Bay. The crews returned to their ships so quickly that they left on shore six of
their number along with the spare sails, extra anchors, and
other supplies. The *St. George* and *Cinque Ports* were under
sail and out of Cumberland Bay before the stranger spotted
them. As soon as she did, she tacked and headed out to sea
with the English vessels in pursuit. The chase continued into
the late afternoon. When Dampier drew alongside the enemy,
he discovered she was a French merchantman of about 400
tons, mounting thirty cannons. At daybreak the two ships
began exchanging cannonades. The battle lasted for seven
hours without either side gaining advantage. Dampier had
nine men killed and many of his crew injured. Then he broke
off the fight, much to the consternation of his men.

Dampier ordered both the *St. George* and the *Cinque
Ports* back to Más á Tierra Island to collect the men and supplies abandoned there a few days before. They arrived at
Cumberland Bay on March 3 only to discover two French
South Sea vessels of 36 guns each anchored there. Dampier
knew at once they were too great a force for his small ships
to engage. He called a council of his officers. They agreed to
sail on toward the coast of Peru and leave their men to their
fate and the stores to the enemy. The French captured six of
the crew and all the supplies; the other two sailors escaped
by hiding in the forests and were picked up later when the
Cinque Ports returned.

The two ships split company, each going off in search of
targets of opportunity. The *St. George* cruised the coast off
Peru, while the *Cinque Ports* headed north toward Mexico,
raiding Spanish coastal towns. The campaign was poorly executed, and the expedition suffered numerous casualties. It
was during these months that a violent disagreement began
to build between Selkirk and Captain Stradling.

One night Selkirk had a dream in which he watched his
ship, the *Cinque Ports*, break up and sink with all hands during a violent storm. As the seventh son gifted in foreknowledge, he never questioned the truth of his dream. He resolved
to leave the vessel at the first opportunity.

The lack of provisions and proper supplies at last forced
Stradling to return to Más á Tierra Island. He hoped to recover the men and the stores left there several months be-

fore. Soon after his arrival at the island he learned from the two crewmembers who had successfully eluded capture that the other six sailors and all the supplies had been captured by the French.

The *Cinque Ports* remained a full month in Cumberland Bay undergoing repairs. Selkirk made a careful inspection of the ship, saw leaking seams badly in need of caulking and planks honeycombed with marine-worm borings, and decided she must be careened and thoroughly repaired or she would sink long before she returned to England. Stradling disagreed and ordered the ship to sail.

Selkirk then made up his mind to risk a lifetime of solitude on Más á Tierra Island rather than certain death on the *Cinque Ports*. He requested to be put ashore. The captain agreed, happy to be rid of an officer he saw as mutinous. Selkirk took ashore all his earthly belongings: the clothes on his back, a sea chest, a musket, a pound of gun powder, a bag of bullets, a flint and steel, several pounds of tobacco, a hatchet, a knife, a kettle, a Bible, and several books of devotional writing and navigational treatises. He landed on the beach a man much richer in this world's goods than William, the Miskito Indian who had been stranded there years before.

The longboat deposited Selkirk on the beach in October 1704. Suddenly, as the boat started back through the surf, he had a change of mind. "His heart yearned within him, and melted at the parting with his comrades and all human society at once," it was later written. In a paroxysm of terror, he ran down the beach and splashed into the sea. The oarsmen briefly stopped in their stroke. Selkirk begged to be taken back on board. But Stradling mocked him and left him standing there in the surge.

Selkirk returned to the beach and sat down next to his small pile of belongings. He watched in despair, as the *Cinque Ports* unfurled her sails, slipped out of the harbor, and slowly disappeared over the horizon.

The despair lasted for eighteen long months, as Selkirk kept to his beach, paralyzed by his predicament. The futility of his situation became apparent to him the moment he had stepped ashore from the longboat. There he was, an Englishman in the midst of the "Spanish lake," where there were no other British ships and none likely to venture in again for many years. Ahead was an uncertain future on an unknown island. But for a sailor used to performing his duties in the midst of bustle and fellowship, the solitude of the remote island offered up the greatest terrors. Selkirk simply went to pieces.

For many days, he sat on his sea chest on the beach, scanning the horizon and hoping his ship would return. He ate only when driven to it by hunger. "He grew dejected, languid, and melancholy, scarce able to refrain from doing himself violence, till by degrees, by the force of reason, and frequent reading of the Scriptures, and turning his thoughts upon the study of navigation, after the space of eighteen months, he grew reconciled to his condition," wrote Richard Steele, who interviewed Selkirk after his return to London.

Selkirk finally moved into a shallow cave along the edge of the beach. But he still refused to explore the interior, fearful he might miss a ship. His diet consisted largely of shellfish that he collected along the shore during low tide. He found that what he missed most were salt and bread.

One night he was awakened by a strange chorus of unfamiliar animal sounds. In the early light of dawn he discovered that hundreds of seals and sea lions had come ashore to whelp and breed. At first he was fearful. Then he realized that the flesh of the young seals offered him a pleasing change from his monotonous diet of shellfish. He waded into the herds, wielding his hatchet, taking only what he needed for his food. The sea lions proved too fat and oily to eat. But he discovered another use for them. "The hair of their whiskers was stiff enough to make exceedingly fine toothpickers," he told Steele.

The annual migration of seals and sea lions to Más á Tierra Island changed Selkirk's life in other ways. He could no longer pass his days moping on the beach, lost in self-pity. Now that he had been evicted, he began to explore the interior of the island. Each day he went farther afield, finding more and more about his island that fascinated him. In the valley behind his beach he discovered all sorts of wonders— lush forests, running streams, numerous herbs growing wild, also acres of turnips, cabbage palms, wild peppers, and, best of all, black plum trees that yielded fresh fruit in season and dried prunes for the rest of the year. Everywhere he saw wild goats. Slowly, Selkirk began to pull out of his despair over being marooned and take control, first of himself, and then of his situation.

As the winter season approached, Selkirk began construction on a more permanent habitation. In the foothills near a stream he built two huts of sandalwood and thatched them with long grass. The larger one served both as his sleeping quarters and chapel. He furnished it with a bed, chair, and table he had crudely fashioned. Over the years he carved wooden ornaments to hang on the walls.

In the smaller hut he made his kitchen and built a fireplace. Realizing that his flint and steel would soon wear out, he taught himself to start a fire Indian fashion by rubbing two sticks together. A small herd of tame goats browsed about his huts, animals he had captured while young, and lamed, but not enough to injure their health, so that he might have a food supply nearby in the event of serious illness or injury.

Selkirk's food supply steadily improved as he discovered new additions to his diet—lobsters, some weighing ten pounds, went into his kettle, as did the flesh of wild goats, turnips, cabbage palms, watercress, and radishes. With an abundance of food and a pleasant climate, he recovered his peace of mind and reconciled himself to his situation.

Once Selkirk had provided for all the necessities of his life, he found himself with ample leisure to spend as he wished. At first, he whiled away the hours aimlessly whittling ornaments. He soon learned a basic truth about the daily existence of a castaway—the long periods of unrelieved monotony. He became bored and sought more substantial activities, finding them in the small library he had brought ashore. He began a diligent study of mathematics and navigation. But he found the Bible to be his salvation. He read the Scriptures regularly and returned to a routine of morning and evening prayer services, speaking his devotions aloud for the satisfaction of hearing a voice, even if it was only his own. To celebrate the Sabbath, he kept an exact account of the days of the week and month during his four years on the island. "I was a better Christian while in this solitude than ever I was before, or that, I am afraid, I should ever be again," he admitted after his rescue.

After he had built his shelters and secured his food supply, Selkirk's major problem became the hordes of rats that overran his island and threatened his existence. At night he could look beyond his fire and see scores of red eyes glowing in the dark and hear the rustling of countless other rats waiting for him to bed down before they moved into his camp. While he slept, the rats fearlessly gnawed at his feet and clothes.

Selkirk solved this problem rather easily. He captured and tamed several dozen of the wild cats common on the island, descendants of ships' cats that had made it ashore from earlier visits. These quickly put the rats to flight and became themselves the companions of his leisure hours. He then added several young goats to his collection of household pets. He amused himself by teaching his animals to dance to the tunes of sea chanteys and Scottish folk songs: "I never danced with a lighter heart or greater spirit any where to the best of music than I did to the sound of my own voice with my dumb animals."

In time Selkirk exhausted his supply of bullets and gun powder. Now if he wanted fresh goat meat, he would have to find other means. He immediately began conditioning his body, so that he might have both the stamina and speed to run the goats down. At first, he could overtake only the kids. But soon his strength and speed improved to the point where he could chase down any goat with ease in a few minutes, toss the struggling animal over his shoulder, and bring it back to his shelter.

Selkirk now became familiar with all the obscure nooks and crannies of his valley. He would bound from crag to crag and slip down any precipice with confidence in his pursuit of goats. He later told Rogers that he had run down and killed over 500 goats during his stay on the island and caught as many more for the sheer sport of the chase, notching the animals' ears before releasing them. Rogers was skeptical and asked Selkirk to capture some goats for the crew's dinner. "He ran with wonderful swiftness through the woods and up the rocks and hills," Rogers wrote in his journal later. "We had a bulldog, which we sent with several of our nimblest runners, to help him in catching goats; but he distanced and tired both the dog and the men, catched the goats and brought them to us on his back."

Selkirk told Rogers that his agility at catching goats had almost cost him his life. One day he pursued a goat with such eagerness that when he got hold of it on the edge of a cliff, he lost his balance and they both slipped over the edge. He recovered consciousness several hours later. The goat lay crushed beneath his body. An entire day went by before he could muster the strength to crawl back to his hut a mile away. It was ten days before he could go out again.

The close call made him more pensive about his own death. He began to worry that if he should die alone in his hut, there would be no one to supply his cats with food and his body would be devoured by those very animals which he at present nourished for his convenience. He took to carving on tree trunks his name and the date of his arrival. Thus, in the event of his death some future visitor would learn from these rude memorials that Alexander Selkirk had lived and died on this island.

As the months passed, Selkirk's clothing wore out and had to be replaced. After the rats had eaten his shoes, he simply went barefoot and within a few weeks had so toughened his soles that he could walk anywhere without pain. He dried the skins of goats, cut them into proper shapes, sewed them with slender thongs of leather, using a sharp nail for a needle. In that way, he made for himself a cap, jacket, and short breeches. He next made shirts, using some linen cloth he had brought from the ship, sewing them with his nail and using the threads of his worsted stockings which he un-twisted for that purpose. His beard grew to chest-length.

One day, while walking along the beach of Cumberland Bay, Selkirk discovered to his joy several iron hoops left behind from an earlier vessel that had called there. They proved a richer treasure to him than gold or precious jewels. He fashioned them into knives; one with a two-foot long blade and a goat's horn handle became his machete.

On several occasions Selkirk saw the sails of ships on the horizon, but only two anchored in the shallow waters of the bay where he lived. Once he skirted close to the beach to spy on a landing party that had put ashore. He discovered his vis-itors were Spanish. They saw him and gave chase, firing several shots. He made good his escape, and the Spaniards soon returned to their ship. "Their prize being so inconsiderable, it is unlikely they thought it worth while to be at great trouble to find it," he remarked later. "Had they been French, I would have submitted; but I chose to risk dying on the island, rather than fall into the hands of Spaniards in these parts, because I apprehended they would murder me or make me a slave in the mines."

Selkirk was fully aware of the Spanish policy never to allow an Englishman to return to Europe after he had gained knowledge of the Pacific. The officials were determined to keep their ocean Spanish.

By now Selkirk's existence on Más á Tierra Island had become something of an idyll. All his basic needs were met. He had reconciled himself completely to the solitude of his life. He was in better health than ever before. The weather was pleasant throughout the year. Through his own skill and ingenuity, Selkirk had managed to fashion a paradise from his hell.

Selkirk had conquered his island by becoming at one with it. He did not dwell on those advantages of civilization which were denied him. "He now took delight in every thing, made the hut in which he lay, by ornaments cut down from a spacious wood, on the side of which he was situated, the most delicious bower, fanned with continual breezes and gentle aspirations of wind, that made his repose after the chase equal to the most sensual pleasures," Richard Steele wrote after Selkirk's return to London. "Life grew so exquisitely pleasant, that he never had a moment heavy upon his hands; his nights were untroubled, and his days joyous, from the practice of temperance and exercise."

Selkirk's establishment of himself on Más á Tierra Island was essentially an act of creation. The island became his little kingdom and his adventure one of individual enterprise. His four years there were a declaration of human independence. Those virtues of courage, practical intelligence, forbearance, and a stolid self-sufficiency allowed him to survive and prosper. His story is singularly unheroic. He never did explore the whole extent of his island, only his valley. He was not an adventurer in a traditional sense. By the reassuring method of hard work, not epic action, he fashioned for himself a profoundly domestic, ultimately familiar world. And this became the key to his survival.

On the afternoon of February 1, 1709, Selkirk visited, as he did every day, his observation post to scan the sea for ships. Suddenly, he saw far off the sails of two ships approaching his island. When they came closer, he ascertained they were English. They were the *Duke* and *Duchess*, privateers sailing under the command of Captain Woodes Rogers. Ironically, William Dampier was along as the chief navigator. The desire to return home, long repressed, now welled within Selkirk. He gathered a great quantity of wood and prepared a bonfire. As soon as darkness fell, he lit his signal fire and kept it burning through the night. He was much too agitated to sleep. Instead he killed several goats and prepared a feast for his guests.

Selkirk's fire caused great alarm on the ships, for Rogers and his officers knew Más á Tierra Island to be uninhabited and feared the signal came from Spanish sentries stationed on shore. Because the British crews were in desperate need of fresh water and provisions, they made ready to engage in combat that next morning.

The following day an excited Selkirk watched as a longboat approached his beach. He ran joyfully from cover to meet the boat, waving a crude flag to attract attention. He soon found himself among heavily armed Englishmen and hearing new voices for the first time in over four years. He was overcome with emotion and rendered speechless.

Captain Woodes Rogers possessed in abundance those qualities of effective leadership that were lacking in Dampier. In addition to courage and physical toughness, he displayed a keen sense of humor that frequently helped him through difficult situations and a broad tolerance for those whose opinions differed from his. For example, he held Anglican religious services regularly on board, but insisted that the religious minorities among his crew keep their own worship as they desired. He readily gained the confidence of his sailors and quickly established the discipline necessary for a lengthy sea voyage. From 1708 to 1711 he commanded one of the most successful privateering expeditions in British maritime history. His bestselling book, *A Cruising Voyage Round the World*, exerted a profound influence on British naval thinking and was indispensable reading for any captain contemplating a circumnavigation.

Born in 1678, the son of a Bristol sea captain, Rogers at a young age became an apprentice sailor. After several voyages the young man married the daughter of Admiral Sir William Whetstone, who had commanded a small squadron in the West Indies during the outbreak of the War of the Spanish Succession. Between 1705 and 1707 Rogers captained two small privateers in the English Channel. These did not prove profitable. But his reading in books about privateers, including Dampier's *A New Voyage Round the World*, convinced him that in the Pacific he could make his fortune. He drew up plans for an ambitious voyage into the Pacific by way of the Horn; he would attack shipping and coastal towns along Peru, and then head north to the region of present-day Baja California in Mexico in the hopes of intercepting a Manila treasure galleon. About this time Queen Anne announced that the Crown was forfeiting its ten percent share to encourage the owners of more merchantships to take up privateering. The enemy this time was France allied with Spain.

Rogers easily persuaded the leading merchants of Bristol to finance his proposed expedition. They were well experienced in backing such voyages in the Caribbean, but competition among British privateers in that region was fierce and Spanish prizes few. The Pacific, on the other hand, was unexploited. And the merchants had all heard stories of the legendary Spanish treasure galleons—slow moving, heavily armed, and exceedingly rich—that transported hundreds of tons of precious cargoes each year from Manila Bay to the port of Acapulco on the Mexican coast.

The syndicate provided Rogers with two three-masted ships. Both were small by modern standards, the recently constructed *Duke* at 320 tons with 30 guns and 117 men and the *Duchess* at 260 tons with 26 guns and 108 men. The largest cannons were only six-pounders, which proved a source of weakness later when it came to serious action. Both ships were double-sheathed in their hulls to protect them against boring shipworms. And they carried letters of marque and reprisal which allowed them to pursue, attack, and seize enemy ships in the Pacific.

The ships carried twice the normal complement of officers both to compensate for deaths in battle and to have extras on hand to man the Spanish vessels they hoped to capture. Rogers' younger brother John sailed on the *Duchess*. But his greatest coup, so far as his Bristol backers were concerned, was the hiring of William Dampier as his South Seas pilot. Dampier stood alone among British navigators in his knowledge and experience in the Pacific, a part of the world that had been virtually closed to British shipping. Twice he had sailed around the world, a feat no other living Englishman could claim.

The crew were a rough group with so few experienced sailors among them that Rogers complained in his journal that most were "tinkers, tailors, haymakers, peddlers, and fiddlers." However, he was optimistic, adding: "With this mixed gang we hoped to be well manned as soon as they have learnt the use of arms and got their sea legs, which we doubted not soon to teach them and bring them to discipline."

The small squadron sailed out of Bristol Harbor on August 2, 1708, for Cork where additional recruits for the voyage were hired. On September 1 they left Cork for Madeira. Within a few days Rogers had his first mutiny. He dealt with it swiftly and effectively, clapping the guilty sailors in irons and ordering their leader publicly lashed by several of his followers. "This method I thought best for breaking any unlawful friendships amongst themselves, which, with different correction to other offenders, allayed the tumult."

Scurvy, which afflicted any voyage of more than a month at sea, was an even greater risk than mutiny to the success of the expedition. The lack of vitamin C caused the gums to soften, teeth to fall out, black blotches to appear on the skin, and a stupor to set in. Far more British sailors (some 800,000) succumbed to scurvy in the seventeenth and eighteenth centuries than to the enemy. Rogers had researched the problem and discovered that in 1593 Sir Richard Hawkins had used lemon juice to cure his crew of scurvy. As a result, he carried a supply of lemons on his ships, a reform the British Navy did not adopt until 1795.

Soon afterwards the two ships crossed the Tropic of Cancer. This was the occasion for traditional festivities. "According to custom we ducked those who had never passed the tropic before," Rogers noted in his journal. "The manner of doing it was by a rope through a block from the main-yard, to hoist 'em above half-way up to the yard and let 'em fall at once into the water, having a stock crossed through their legs, and well fastened to the rope that they might not be surprised and let go their hold. This proved of great use to our fresh-water sailors, to recover the colour of their skins which were grown very black and nasty."

The expedition proceeded to the Brazilian coast which they sighted on November 14, where they made a stop, and then down the coast toward Cape Horn. They rounded the tip of South America just after the New Year and found themselves overtaken by a fierce gale which drove them farther south toward the Antarctic Peninsula. All the men and their belongings were soaked, while the outside temperatures dropped below freezing. On both ships men began to drop from scurvy—the supply of fresh lemons had been exhausted— and nine men died.

But the squadron finally reached the Pacific. Only twice before had Englishmen successfully rounded Cape Horn traveling in a westerly direction, Captain John Cooke in the *Bachelor's Delight* in 1684 and Dampier with the *St. George* and the *Cinque Ports* in 1704.

The men were desperate for landfall. The situation on board was quickly becoming critical. On January 26 Rogers noted gloomily in his journal: "We are very uncertain of the latitude and longitude of Juan Fernández Island, the books laying it down so differently that not one chart agrees with another; and being such a small island we are in some doubts of striking it."

On January 31 the expedition finally arrived at Más á Tierra Island. Strong head winds kept the two ships outside Cumberland Bay. In the late afternoon Rogers ordered a longboat ashore to bring back fresh water, which his crews desperately needed. The men were rowing toward the land in the failing light, the island looming up dim and mountainous before them. Suddenly, Rogers and his officers observed a signal fire among the trees. They immediately concluded that Spanish ships were about and fired a cannon to recall the longboat. At that point of the voyage drinking water was in such short supply that they knew they would have to fight the next morning whatever forces were on the island.

At daybreak Rogers saw no sign of other vessels. He ordered one boat manned by heavily armed sailors to go ashore to investigate. They returned loaded with fresh lobsters and carrying a man clothed in goatskins who introduced himself to Rogers as Alexander Selkirk, late of the County of Fife in Scotland.

The ships anchored just off the beach, landed their sick, mainly sailors with scurvy, and set up a tent camp made from the sails. The patients recovered rapidly on a diet of fresh meat, pure water, and plenty of wild vegetables. Most of the other crew also went ashore to live. Selkirk provided the group with fresh meat from the goats he ran down. Other sailors kept the crew supplied with fresh fish and lobsters. Sails were mended. A blacksmith forge was set up on the shore. The ships were cleaned and refitted.

Rogers had a small tent made for himself. He noted in his journal that their situation on Más á Tierra Island was quite agreeable. " 'Twas very pleasant ashore among the green pimiento trees, which cast a refreshing smell." They remained there until February 12.

They shared the beaches with hundreds of seals and sea lions. Of the seals, Rogers observed in his journal: "They lined the shore very thick for above half a mile of ground all round the bay. When we came in, they kept a continual noise day and night, some bleating like lambs, some howling like dogs or wolves, others making hideous noises of various sorts; so that we heard them abroad, although a mile from the shore. Their fur is the finest that I ever saw of the kind, and exceeds that of our otters."

The enormous sea lions especially impressed Rogers. He ordered some slaughtered. "We boiled up about 80 gallons of sea lions' oil. We refined and strained it for use in our lamps and to save our candles, although sailors sometimes used it to fry their meat, when straitened for want of butter. The men who worked ashore on our rigging ate young seals, which they preferred to our ships' victuals, and said it was as good as English lamb."

With all his hard-won knowledge of Más á Tierra Island, Selkirk proved most helpful to his rescuers during their short stay there. Dampier recommended Selkirk highly to his captain as the finest officer on the *Cinque Ports*. Rogers quickly appointed him to the post of second mate on his ship, the *Duke*. Later he noted in his journal that Selkirk was an excellent officer "of great skill and conduct; who, having had his books with him, had improved himself much in navigation during his solitude."

Selkirk's adjustment to the busy life of a ship's officer was not without difficulties. For many weeks he lived on a diet of hard tack and water, his system unable to tolerate the salt pork after four salt-free years. For the same reason he refused all rations of rum. From the confirmed habit of living alone for so long, he was reserved and taciturn, a frame of mind that continued throughout the rest of his life. As an officer, he was required to wear shoes, and they gave him great discomfort when he first came aboard. He had been without them for so long they made his feet swell and crippled his movements. But this wore off by degrees, and he once more became accustomed to their use.

There were other changes, more subtle, that provoked Rogers to philosophical speculation in the privacy of his journal. "Selkirk's story may instruct us, how much a plain and temperate way of living conduces to the health of the body and the vigour of the mind, both which we are apt to destroy by excess and plenty, especially of strong liquor, and the variety as well as the nature of our meat and drink," he observed. "For this man when he came to our ordinary method of diet and life, though he was sober enough, lost much of his strength and agility."

After their sojourn on Más á Tierra Island, the crews of the two British ships were now ready for their expedition's chief purpose. They were refreshed and toughened and eager to get on with the business at hand of raiding Spanish shipping and coastal towns. The entire coast of South America from Panama to the southern tip of Chile beckoned to them. Rogers knew the Spanish authorities were not yet aware that British ships had sailed into their "lake." He decided to forego the temptation of many smaller towns, so that they would have the element of surprise on their side when they mounted an attack on the rich prize of Guayaquil. Along the way they captured several small vessels and converted them to auxiliary privateers. One was christened the *Increase*, and Selkirk was appointed her commander.

But it was the capture of the *Asunción*, a tiny 16-ton trader with a crew of eight, that most interested Selkirk. From the ship's captain he finally learned the fate of his former ship, the *Cinque Ports*—and that his dream had indeed been a vision. Caught in a sudden storm off Colombia while sailing perilously close to uncharted reefs, the *Cinque Ports* was blown onto a coral reef and sank within five minutes with 51 crew members. Captain Stradling and six hands alone made it to shore. The next day they were captured by Spanish authorities and transferred to the prison in Lima. Rogers assured Selkirk that "being prisoners for four years at Lima, they have lived there much worse than ever you did on your Island."

On April 15 the English force attacked a ship from Lima, and Rogers' twenty-year-old brother John was killed as he tried to board her. Rogers had little time to grieve. He had to put aside his "unspeakable sorrow" to begin preparations for the assault on Guayaquil.

The town of Santiago de Guayaquil sits thirty miles up a tidal estuary. Then, as today, it was the only port for the present-day country of Ecuador. Though not one of the largest Spanish cities in that part of the world, it was important, poorly defended, and obviously rich. The town was the only port along the entire Pacific coast of the Spanish empire where ships could be drydocked for repair. Several times in the past pirates had successfully attacked the inhabitants.

On April 22 five longboats with 110 heavily armed men slowly made their way up the Guayaquil River to the town. They lost the element of surprise when an Indian spotted the boats shortly after dawn and spread the word. The small Spanish garrison fled into the nearby jungle at the first word of an attack, leaving their commander alone to deal with the advancing English force. Rogers opened negotiations with the governor for a ransom. A sum of 50,000 pieces-of-eight was demanded, but the town could only raise 25,000 and stalled on the delivery. Rogers then broke off the negotiations, ordered his ships up the estuary, bombarded the town, and landed a force of seventy men and several cannons. "We landed and fired, every man on his knee at the brink of the bank, then kept firing, loading, and firing very fast," Rogers noted later in his journal. The English met only token resistance and quickly captured the town. Rogers ordered the Union Jack raised from the church tower. The governor promptly paid the ransom.

The English invaders were surprised to find little valuable booty in the town. Reports came in that the wealthier residents had withdrawn upriver for the duration of the occupation. Rogers dispatched a small party under the command of Selkirk to see what they could obtain. He wrote later in his journal:

"The houses up the river were full of women, and particularly at one place there were above a dozen handsome genteel young women, where our men got several gold chains and ear-rings, but otherwise were so civil to them that the ladies offered to dress them victuals and brought them a cask of good liquor. Some of their largest gold chains were concealed and wound about their middles, legs, and thighs, but the gentlewomen in these hot countries being very thin clad with silk and fine linen, and their hair dressed with ribbons very neatly, our men by pressing felt the chains with their hands on the outside of the lady's apparel, and by their [interpreter] modestly desired the gentlewomen to take them off and surrender them. This I mention as proof of our sailors' modesty and in respect to Mr. Selkirk who commanded this party."

Afterwards Rogers and his officers estimated a rough total for their plunder. Gold, plate, and jewels amounted to about £20,000 and captured merchandise to another £60,000. An additional 15,000 pieces-of-eight were raised when they ransomed the 180 prisoners they had captured aboard the vessels seized at sea. Their privateering expedition thus far had met with reasonable success.

The English fleet of four ships sailed north along the coast of Central America, and on November 1 arrived at the southern tip of Baja California, a 1,000-mile long peninsula that appeared on all Spanish charts of the day as an island.

They were searching for the ultimate prize, a Manila treasure galleon. Only once before had an Englishman succeeded in capturing one of these richest of all prizes. In 1587 Thomas Cavendish plundered the poorly armed *Santa Ana*. The formidable armament and massive size of the galleons made them virtual floating fortresses. And the vast reaches of the Pacific meant that only by sheer luck could an enemy vessel hope to encounter one.

These galleons lay at the heart of the Spanish trade with the Orient. The first made the annual crossing in 1566, the last in 1815—a 250-year endurance record no other line of ships has equaled. Only four were captured in that entire stretch of time. Once a year they sailed eastward from Acapulco, their holds filled with hundreds of chests of silver pesos which bought the rare and exotic products of the Far East. (The Spanish silver peso was so common in the Orient that it was the preferred medium of exchange everywhere.) As valuable as the westbound ships were, it was the eastbound galleons that lay at the heart of every privateer's fantasy. As historian James Poling has written, "The eastbound galleons carried everything of worth produced in the Far East: gold and silver plates and goblets, pearls and rubies, priceless jades and delicate porcelains, ivory fans, jewel-studded sword hilts—even brass toothpicks, copper cuspidors, and alligator teeth capped with gold to be sold as good luck charms. Surprisingly, though, silks and spices were the treasure ships' most valuable cargoes. These were so rare and considered such a luxury in the European market that they were practically worth their weight in gold."

Rogers' fleet began patrolling the waters off Baja California searching for a Manila galleon. For three weeks they saw only empty ocean. And then suddenly late on December 21 a lookout called out the good news—a sail on the horizon. The *Duke* and *Duchess* immediately set off in pursuit. As they closed, Rogers saw through his spyglass that she was indeed a Manila galleon. The crews on both ships were jubilant. "I ordered a large kettle of chocolate to be made for our ship's company (having no spiritous liquor to give them)," Rogers wrote in his journal, "then we went to prayers, and before we had concluded were disturbed by the enemy firing at us."

Rogers in the *Duke* closed in first and fired several broadsides, while the *Duchess* raked the enormous galleon from the bows. The fight was brief but intense. Rogers' masterly seamanship made a mockery of the enemy's superior firepower. And then, to their surprise, the Spanish captain struck his colors. The 500-ton *Nuestra Señora de La Encarnación Disengano* was now theirs. Only two men on the *Duke* were injured, an Irishman shot through the buttocks and Rogers himself. It was a serious wound. "I was shot through the left cheek, the bullet struck away a great part of my upper jaw and several of my teeth, part of which dropped on the deck." The injury effectively prevented him from speaking, and he had to issue his orders in writing.

When the English boarded the Spanish ship, they discovered she was the smaller of two ships that had sailed in tandem across the Pacific. But she was still a very rich prize, indeed. Her cargo consisted of 48,698 pounds of silk, 4,310 pairs of silk stockings, 24,289 pieces of chintz, 7,200 bolts of Chinese satin flowered with gold and silver, and hundreds of uncut gem stones. Rogers renamed the Spanish galleon *Bachelor* and put an English crew on her. Selkirk was sent on board as the master.

The squadron sailed on January 10, 1710, for Guam with all the crew on short rations. The daily rations consisted of five ounces of bread, a fragment of salt pork, and three pints of water. Dampier had made the crossing twice before, and so the voyage proved uneventful. The passage took fifty-nine days, the best day's run being 168 miles. They arrived at the harbor in Guam on March 11. Rogers had to be tied to a chair and lifted down from his ship. Ashore he made a gift to the Spanish governor of two Negro slave boys, whom he had outfitted in scarlet cloth from the galleon. In return, on the next day, the governor sent Rogers sixty hogs, ninety-nine fowls, twenty-four baskets of corn, fourteen bags of rice, and hundreds of baskets of yams and coconuts.

From Guam they sailed to the Javanese city of Batavia (now Djakarta) in the Dutch East Indies, stopping at several islands and suppressing several mutinies along the way. The ship's doctor performed operations at regular intervals on Rogers' mouth and throat to remove pieces of broken jaw bone and metal from the shattered ball. At Batavia they sold their fourth ship, the leaky *Marquis*, to an English trader. Now they were down to three ships—the *Duke*, the *Duchess*, and the captured Spanish galleon. The squadron sailed across the Indian Ocean for the Cape of Good Hope. At the Cape, they waited from December 29, 1710, to April 5, 1711, and then joined with the regular Dutch convoy for Holland and England. Finally, on October 14 about noon the three ships sailed up the Thames River and dropped anchor in London. For Selkirk, it had been eight years, one month, and three days since his departure.

Rogers' epic-making voyage was finally at an end. He and his people found themselves heroes in a jubilant England. London was agog at the sight of a Spanish galleon rolling gently at anchor. As a testimony to Rogers' extraordinary leadership, he brought home to England both his original ships and the prize galleon, while losing no more than fifty men on the whole voyage. The expedition had returned its investors £170,000 as against an original cost of £14,000. Selkirk's share of the captured booty was £800 (over $100,000 in today's values).

In the spring of 1712 Selkirk returned to his hometown of Largo, cutting a striking figure in a new suit of elegant gold-laced clothes. For a few days he was happy to be home among his family and friends. The British novelist Anthony Trollope was to observe 150 years later, "Though the life of a Robinson Crusoe or a few Crusoes may be very picturesque, humanity will always desire to restore a Robinson Crusoe back to the community of the world." But Selkirk soon found himself uncomfortable in society and gradually withdrew, spending most of his days alone wandering and meditating in the secluded valleys nearby.

The former castaway was overcome with a nostalgic melancholy for his life on Más á Tierra Island. There were pathetic attempts to recapture his previous existence. He fashioned a small cave in a hillside above town and passed long hours there, looking out to sea. He tried to teach his brother's two cats to dance and perform the antics of his own cats back on the island. He bought a small boat and made short excursions alone, fishing for lobsters because they reminded him of those back on his beloved island. His relatives often found him in tears. "I am now worth 800 pounds, but shall never be so happy, as when I was not worth a far-thing," Selkirk told them.

Still, Selkirk found time to court a young girl from a nearby neighborhood. He had first spotted her while on one of his wanderings. She was alone in a pasture, tending her parents' cow. Her solitary occupation and innocent looks made a deep impression upon him. Hidden from sight, he watched her for hours, as she amused herself by making gar-lands of wild flowers and singing sad songs. At last after viewing her from a distance for several days, he worked up the courage to approach her. She gave her name as Sophia Bruce. The couple fell in love and soon afterwards eloped to London.

Little is known about this period of Selkirk's life. Apparently, Sophia lived only a few years and died some time around 1718. He married a second time soon after-wards. In December of 1724 a woman named Frances Candis appeared suddenly in Largo and claimed the property left to Selkirk upon the death of his father. She produced docu-ments to prove both the marriage and her husband's death. These were accepted by the local magistrate. The estate was paid to her, and she left Largo a few days later. Neither of his two wives had any children by him, as far as is known.

The publication of Rogers' book, *A Cruising Voyage Round the World*, gave Selkirk a passing fame. The writer Richard Steele interviewed him at length in London in 1713 and then wrote an account of his remarkable survival on Más á Tierra Island for his paper, *The Englishman*. "There was a strong but cheerful seriousness in his look and a certain dis-regard to the ordinary things about him, as if he had been sunk in thought," the writer observed. "The man frequently bewailed his return to the world, which could not, he said, with all its enjoyments restore him to the tranquility of his solitude."

There has always been speculation that the writer Daniel Defoe sought out Selkirk after the publication of Rogers' book with its lengthy account of his survival on Más á Tierra. He had taken a keen interest in Rogers' expedition. In several tracts he had advocated the importance of a British presence in the Pacific region. In late 1718, eager to raise money for his daughter's dowry, Defoe started what he hoped would prove a profitable new venture—a lengthy work of fiction. The next year on April 25 he published *The Life and Strange and Surprising Adventures of Robinson Crusoe,* a title that obviously failed to foresee the needs of modern movie theater marquees.

Defoe's book changed the course of English literary history. He created both a new literary genre and a new reading public. Before *Robinson Crusoe* there was no English novel worth the name, and no book (except the Bible) widely accepted among all classes of English and Scottish readers. But Defoe's novel created a sensation. "There is not an old woman that can go to the price of it, but buys *Robinson Crusoe* and leaves it as a legacy . . . to her posterity," commented one mid-century observer.

Defoe made substantial changes in Selkirk's story of survival as a castaway. He shifted the setting from the Pacific to the Caribbean. Then he added cannibals, a shipload of mutineers, and the man Friday. He kept his hero on his island a full twenty-four years longer than Selkirk had spent on Más á Tierra. But in the many practical details of his survival and in his religious preoccupation, Robinson Crusoe was simply Selkirk's story amplified.

Selkirk finally returned to the sea and enlisted in the Royal Navy. In 1720 he was appointed the master mate of H.M.S. *Weymouth,* bound for West Africa with orders to attack slave traders and pirates. The following year a tropical fever swept through the ship, killing many of the crew and officers. Selkirk was one of the few officers to survive, but not for long. A second fever erupted, and the *Weymouth*'s log for December 13, 1721, reads simply: "Alxr. Selkirk, Deceased."

Selkirk died in obscurity and probably never knew that 30 months before, a struggling London writer had fashioned his story of survival on Más á Tierra Island into a best-selling novel. Even as Selkirk's body was shrouded in canvas and hurriedly buried at sea somewhere off West Africa, his spirit had found its apotheosis in the story of Robinson Crusoe.

CHAPTER TWO

Captain Charles H. Barnard:

The American Robinson Crusoe

The Crusoes of fiction are almost invariably cast upon tropical islands where the sand is white and the waving fronds of palm trees throw cool, dark shadows on the luxuriant undergrowth. But, as likely as not, the Crusoes of history found themselves on rocky islands where the wind pierces to the marrow and vegetation is almost non-existent. They counted themselves lucky to get ashore with the clothes on their backs. If they were marooned, they had only the items in their sea chests to sustain them.

Their fictional counterparts always fared much better because their generous authors conveniently provided for them just offshore a wrecked ship overflowing with riches to ease their survival in the wilderness. For thirteen days Crusoe paddles a makeshift raft back and forth to his stranded ship to salvage an incredible wealth of supplies. His bonanza includes a wide assortment of tools, barrels of foodstuffs, a large collection of weapons with plentiful powder and shot, a cache of European gold and silver coins, piles of canvas, several spyglasses, considerable rope and twine, bedding, numerous books, and the ship's dog along with two cats.

One of the most remarkable sagas of survival in American maritime history concerned Captain Charles H. Barnard, a sealer from New York City, who was treacherously marooned in April of 1813 on the desolate Falkland Islands without any of the necessities of life. Few castaways had the inner resources to triumph over such harsh conditions as those he faced.

Barnard's story first attracted public attention in 1827 when the British sealing captain James Weddell published his book, *A Voyage Towards the South Pole.* In 1821 he had dropped anchor at New Island in the Falkland group. An American sealing brig *Charity* under the command of Barnard was there on her way to the uncharted South Shetland Islands. The two seafarers exchanged stories. Weddell found himself fascinated by the American's tale of survival on that same island a few years earlier and he devoted five pages in his book recounting it. The two of them visited the stone house Barnard had built during his years as a castaway.

"A particular account of this residency on an uninhabited island would not fail of being considered almost as wonderful as the celebrated fiction of Robinson Crusoe," Weddell noted in his book. He had urged the American captain to write an account of his terrible ordeal. His advice must have struck a responsive chord, for in 1829 a New York publisher brought out *A Narrative of the Sufferings and Adventures of Capt. Charles H. Barnard.* The book sold a few hundred copies. And soon afterwards Barnard disappeared from the historical record. Nothing about his later life is known.

Barnard's early years, like his later ones, including the dates of his birth and death, are totally unknown. One of his ancestors settled on Nantucket Island in the 1660s; most of his descendants were seafarers. In the late seventeenth century the family moved to the mainland on the Hudson River. The family members were all Quakers. One of the few surviving historical references to Barnard is by the clerk of the New York Monthly Meeting. The minutes for January 1805 record that he was disowned by his church for marrying a woman outside his religion.

In his book Barnard wrote of his beginnings only, "From my boyhood I have loved and pursued a seafaring life and have performed many voyages to various parts of the world." We can assume that his career followed the traditional pattern beginning with an apprenticeship as a cabin boy and a progression up through the ranks to that of captain in charge of his own ship.

In early 1812 Barnard was engaged by the New York City firm of John B. Murray and Son for an expedition to the southern seas to collect seal skins and oil. They had recently "purchased the brig *Nanina*, of one hundred and thirty two tons, had her completely fitted and amply supplied with provisions and stores, and every necessary article; with the frame of a shallop of twenty tons, all that would be required to complete her for service after we should have arrived at the islands, I performed my stipulation of putting on board the brig, a full and efficient crew."

The *Nanina* was a sturdy ship built of virgin oak constructed in 1804 at Pittsburgh where a small shipyard flourished in the first decade of the century. Her first captain undoubtedly took advantage of the spring runoffs to sail her down the Ohio and Mississippi rivers to the sea.

In 1812 war fever was building in America. Great Britain was engaged in a desperate war with Napoleon, who had successfully closed off most of the European markets. President James Madison allied America with the French. The American people were outraged when the ships of the Royal Navy repeatedly violated the country's territorial waters and stopped American vessels in international waters to impress their sailors. On June 12 Congress declared war. But on April 4 the talk was of an embargo, which would have temporarily closed American ports. Barnard ordered the *Nanina* out of New York Harbor to Sandy Hook which lay safely beyond the control of the port officials.

The contract called for John B. Murray and Son to get 52 percent of the profits, while Barnard was to receive the remaining 48 percent. Out of his share, he would pay his crew. His plan was to head to the South Atlantic waters, collect fur seal skins and elephant seal oil on the subantarctic islands, and then sail around the Horn to the Chinese port of Canton.

There is much too strong a temptation to think of the history of man's involvement in Antarctica almost exclusively in terms of the heroic accomplishments, often of epic proportions, of such early explorers as Scott, Amundsen, and Shackleton, who traveled there from a selfless desire to expand the boundaries of man's knowledge. But most of the men who braved the hazards and the discomforts of those southern seas were impelled by different motives, lured there by the promise of the huge fortunes to be made from the exploitation of the vast multitudes of whales, fur, and elephant seals which made the Antarctic one of the most lucrative hunting zones in the history of the world.

Captain James Cook was one of the first to explore the subantarctic region. The Englishman was searching in the mid-1770s for *Terra Australis Incognita*, a continent which many cartographers believed lay at the southern pole. Instead he found a series of islands which encircle the frozen continent like a loose-fitting necklace. Repelled by landscapes he found "savage and horrible" and convinced "no one would ever be benefited by the discoveries," Cook failed to reckon with the British and American sealers and whalers who read with keen interest his descriptions of one of the greatest concentrations of wildlife yet discovered, "whales blowing at every point of the compass" and rocky beaches "loaded with sea lions, seals, geese, shags, and penguins." To an industry already worried about declining catches from overhunting, there could be no better news than these accounts of a magnificent hunting zone in the South Seas where there were millions of seals and whales simply for the taking.

The sealers were the first to arrive. With the aid of Cook's charts they had no difficulty in locating the remote islands. The large island of South Georgia located 800 miles east of the Falkland Islands was by 1800 the major destination for fur sealers. Captain Edmund Fanning, an American sealer, arrived early but was soon joined by seventeen other ships. Together they secured in a single season more than 112,000 fur seal skins, half of which were taken by Fanning's people. His backers reaped an immense profit and the figures of the season's catch indicate the size to which the industry had grown in a mere twenty-five years after Cook's voyage through the region. Those same figures also foreshadowed the rapid decline of sealing, which lasted less than four decades, owing to the extermination of the species.

In their orgy of greedy exploitation the sealers killed without restraint or discrimination. Once on shore the crew rounded up the slow-moving seals, clubbed them to death, and skinned them. No attempt was made to cull the herds so as to leave adequate breeding stocks for the future. Whole populations were eliminated in short order. An expert sealer, it was reported, could skin up to sixty animals an hour.

As the populations thinned out, the custom of landing small parties of men on scattered beaches prevailed. The lives of the sealing gangs were hard and monotonous. They hunted in all kinds of weather and were often cold, hungry, and wet most of the time. Contemplating a residence of several months on those forbidding shores, sealers erected flimsy huts and spars and canvas and kept pigs, sheep, poultry, and goats to vary the monotonous local diet of fish, seal, shellfish, and penguin.

For most of these men the subantarctic islands were but the first stop on a long voyage around the world to Canton, the most profitable market for these skins. In 1750 a Chinese merchant discovered a process for removing the coarse outer hairs of the pelts, leaving behind the soft undercoat. For more than sixty years this process was a closely kept secret, unknown to western furriers, so that the majority of all skins ended up in the Chinese markets. The demand among wealthy Chinese appeared insatiable. They not only made the skins into elegant coats, but also adorned their walls and floors with them and used them for insulation. A shipload of fur seal skins could bring upwards of $15,000. This money was, in turn, invested in spices, tea, silk, lacquer ware, and other rarities of the Orient which brought top prices back in Boston and New York. Sealing was a lucrative trade for both the shipowners and the crews.

Within fifty years of Cook's visit to the southern Atlantic islands, the fur seal was virtually extinct there. When the fur seals were exhausted, the next generation of hunters turned to the elephant seals. These enormous animals sometimes reached a length of twenty feet and a weight of five tons and yielded up to three barrels of high-grade lubricating oil. After 1850 a visit to one of the subantarctic islands became a regular feature of a whaling expedition that might last three years. The common practice was to land a shore party on a promising beach and leave them there for many months to collect the oil to be picked up later when the ship returned from a whaling cruise in the lower latitudes.

Even more than fur sealing, elephant sealing was hard, brutal, backbreaking work. The creatures were driven to the water's edge and dispatched with musket balls fired through the roofs of their mouths. The huge rookeries of penguins were decimated as hundreds of thousands of the birds were butchered for their skins which provided the fuel for the roaring fires beneath the large cauldrons, called try-pots, in which the chunks of elephant seal blubber were rendered into oil.

The greedy search for new rookeries triggered the greatest period of sea exploration the world has known. As the better known islands and coastal stretches of South America were swept free of fur and elephant seals, the sealing ships were forced into the unknown regions off the charts in their search for islands as yet unvisited. In their continued hunt for new rookeries, where seals had lived for centuries unmolested by man, these mariners became the nomads of the sea. In 1820 an American sealing captain discovered the Antarctic continent while collecting skins on the hazardous shores of the South Shetland Islands 500 miles south of Cape Horn. But for the most part their discoveries went unannounced. Secrecy was the essence of successful sealing, as captains returned year after year to their favorite hunting grounds.

When Captain Barnard finally sailed the *Nanina* on April 6, 1812, away from the New York coast toward the Falkland Islands in the South Atlantic, he and his crew of eleven were just one more American sealing vessel participating in the "Great Southern Fur Rush." But within months he would find himself engaged in an epic struggle for survival unique in American maritime history.

"To those who have been educated to the sea, and who derive all their support from navigating its surges, . . . the ocean is their element, their home, almost a part of themselves," Barnard wrote in his book. "And it matters not to them whether skies are bright, or tempests rave, so long as they are wafted on its bosom to the haven they are seeking."

Thirty-five days after departing the American coast, the *Nanina* arrived at the port of Boa Vista in the Cape Verde Islands. There Barnard bought salt for curing the seal skins, filled his water casks, and took on board a plentiful supply of fresh fruits and vegetables. Because of unfavorable weather, the sea voyage to the Falkland Islands took three months. Finally, on September 7 the *Nanina* dropped anchor in Hooker's Harbor off New Island, at the far western edge of the archipelago.

Barnard noted prophetically in his journal the bleakness of the place: "It presented nothing but darkness and desolation to the eye; woe to the unhappy warrior whom contending winds dash against this inhospitable region, for here he will find deliverance from the waves to be only a prelude to a more lingering and awful death."

Set deep in the South Atlantic some 400 miles off the tip of South America, the Falkland Islands closely resemble in physical appearance and climate the western islands of Scotland. They have a cool oceanic climate dominated by strong western winds. Overcast is typical. The islands experience fewer than three weeks of sunshine a year. The two main masses of East and West Falkland have formidable cliffs, stacks, and bluffs. Another 340 islands or islets lie scattered in the seas beyond. The most common vegetation is a long, coarse, and hardy tussock grass. Trees are nonexistent because of the frequent gale-force winds.

The English navigator, John Davis, was the first European to visit the islands, when his ship, the *Desire*, was driven among them in August 1592. Captain John Strong of the *Welfare* made the first recorded landing in 1690. Richard Simson, a member of that voyage, was chiefly impressed with the abundance of wildlife there, much of it unfearful of man because of an absence of onshore predators. He wrote:

The inhabitants, such as they were, were exceedingly numerous. The penguins . . . gave us the first reception. Being mustered in infinite numbers on a rock, upon some of our men landing, they stood, viewed, and then seemed to salute them with a great many graceful bows, with the same gestures, equally expressing their curiosity and good breeding. As for other creatures, there were eagles, hawks, which although they had long wings, suffered themselves to be taken up by our men. The island, if it were not quite destitute of wood, would make a noble plantation.

Other ships trickled in over the years. On January 28, 1684, William Dampier visited there briefly, followed by Woodes Rogers' two ships, the *Duke* and *Duchess*, on December 23, 1708. Rogers went ashore and named the island group Falkland's Land. Later both the French and Spanish in turn established small settlements. In time these were abandoned. The publication of Captain Cook's book on his explorations in the region soon led to a rush of sealing expeditions to the Falklands. In 1784 the American vessel *States* spent several months there and collected some 13,000 fur seal skins. When Captain Edmund Fanning called at the islands in 1792, he found forty vessels, mostly American and British, working the beaches.

From 1806 to 1820 the Falklands were uninhabited and became a haven for sealers and whalers, the same vessels returning year after year to the now familiar beaches. They set pigs loose on many small offshore islands to insure themselves future supplies of fresh meat. To conserve their supplies of salt pork and hard tack, the crews lived almost entirely on eggs, geese, and pigs.

The *Nanina* arrived at the Falkland Islands in the early austral spring. Barnard ordered the ship's longboat lowered. Christened *The Young Nanina*, the boat was quickly outfitted for a cruise among the western Falkland Islands in a quest for seals. Barnard next set up several shore stations where the men could stay and harvest the seals. The breeding rookeries were densely populated. Several thousand seals often bunched together on just a few acres.

Then in early January of 1813 the sealing vessel *Hope*, also from New York, arrived at New Island. Its master, Obed Chase, informed Barnard that the United States Congress had voted a declaration of war against Great Britain. He also handed him a letter from his partners, advising him to abort the voyage and return home immediately, as British sealers might seize the *Nanina* as a prize of war. Barnard refused. His men were enjoying great success in harvesting the seals. If they returned early, there would be little profit in the long voyage. He decided to seek a more remote harbor and continue filling his ship's hold with the seal skins.

Over the next several months the crew of the *Nanina* collected several thousand fur skins. A hunting party kept the crew well supplied with the wild hogs and fowls found in abundance on all the larger islands. On one rocky beach covered with elephant seals, the crew set up the great try-pots and began killing the animals, boiling down their blubber into oil, and filling numerous barrels.

One day in April 1813, as Barnard cruised off the east coast of West Falkland Island, he spotted heavy smoke columns rising from a small island group in the distance. He hurried to investigate, thinking they might be signal fires set by shipwrecked sailors. A dozen people, including a woman, suddenly appeared on shore, two in the uniforms of British marines. Barnard dispatched a boat ashore to bring them on board.

The British castaways informed Barnard that their ship, the *Isabella*, had gone aground several months previously. They described vividly the terrors of their life on the barren island. They had all resigned themselves to death with the approach of winter.

The first group of survivors guided Barnard to the rest of their party, some 33 men, women, and children, all of whom had been bound from Australia to England when the disaster overtook them. They had managed to scavenge all that was useful from their ship, which sat partially submerged on a rocky ledge just offshore. With some planks and canvas, they built several temporary huts on a bluff above the beach and raised a tattered Union Jack above their settlement. Their provisions were limited to what they had saved from the *Isabella*, and these were rationed out at the rate of two pounds of bread and two pounds of salt pork per person per week.

Barnard met with the British officers in charge and generously agreed to take the entire group to the nearest South American port. He then advised the officers that war had broken out between their two countries, "lest they suspect us of having base motives." He asked the British survivors to sign an agreement that they would act as if their two nations were at peace and would make no attempt to seize his ship. The group eagerly agreed. Barnard himself had no misgivings about his generous action. "I felt assured that by rendering them this assistance I would bind them to me by the strongest ties of gratitude." This misjudgment of human nature would haunt him for the rest of his life.

A winter gale kept them in the Falklands an additional two weeks. When the skies cleared and the seas calmed, Barnard took four men, one American and three British sailors, to a small island nearby to shoot some wild hogs and geese for the long trip back to the South American mainland. That evening they sailed their small boat back to their anchorage and discovered to their horror that they had been betrayed. The *Nanina* was nowhere to be seen.

Barnard now realized the truth. The British officers had seized his ship and marooned him and his companions on the island with none of the necessities needed to survive. "That they who had so recently felt so acutely the horrors of their own situation should betray and abandon me during the very time I was actually engaged in providing subsistence for them proves how corrupt human nature can become when it is the slave of its own passion."

Barnard immediately surveyed their situation. Nothing more precarious could be imagined. They had their boat, the clothing on their backs, the ship's dog Cent, their knives, a single blanket, and little else. Winter was quickly approaching. The surrounding terrain was desolate. They were far from the normal shipping routes. Survival appeared hopeless.

The next day Barnard ordered his men to row through heavy seas to a larger island. They hauled their boat out of the water and turned it over to make a shelter, as a winter gale settled over the Falklands. They used some of their precious firewood to cook several pieces of pork they had brought with them. The next morning they awoke to find eight inches of fresh snow on the ground. Their supplies of fresh water and firewood were soon exhausted. The crew was in despair.

Barnard refused to concede defeat. Exploring the beach, he discovered a frozen pond of fresh water and killed several small elephant seals whose blubber provided them with much needed fuel. "The tender providence of Heaven is never known to leave us so desolate, without sending counter-balancing blessings to keep us from sinking," he wrote later.

Nonetheless, providence did not provide a bountiful table. Starvation became such a real possibility that Barnard took to calling their temporary settlement "Pinch-gut Camp." For a time the five of them lived solely off rancid elephant seal blubber and the tough meat of skuas, the large scavenger birds that hung around the camp fighting with the men for scraps of food. Later they turned in desperation to the roots of the tough tussock grass. But this new addition to their diet brought extreme dizziness and vomiting. Then when matters seemed hopeless, they clubbed one seal, two foxes, and three geese. The foxes, in particular, proved a challenge to eat. "I ate some of their flesh, but it is so very strong that nothing but the sauce of extreme hunger could force it down."

Barnard's own cheerful optimism lifted the spirits of the other four men. ("What a blessed thing it is that captains and commanders are often supported, sometimes with almost superhuman fortitude, to soothe down the murmurs and complaints, and unite the jarring tempers and interests of the men who are placed under them.") Against all odds, the small party survived the first difficult days. Barnard proved to be a consummate leader, one able to weld four disparate personalities into an effectively functioning unit, capable of withstanding the severe stresses of their abandonment.

Barnard soon began to take note of the strengths and weaknesses of the men with him. These were a black American whaler, Jacob Green, a veteran of numerous whaling voyages from New Bedford, and three British sailors, James Lauder, Joseph Albrook, and Samuel Ansel.

The first three proved reliable. But Barnard quickly saw that Ansel would be trouble. A twenty-six-year-old illiterate bully and coward, Ansel showed his true colors one day when he admitted that he was a fool to have volunteered to go with Barnard that fateful day, as he had been privy to the plot to seize the ship. Barnard was greatly distressed when he heard this and told Ansel, "Then you are just where you ought to be."

When the weather improved, the group loaded their provisions into their small boat and rowed farther west to New Island which promised better conditions for survival. First, they built a rude stone shelter to protect them from the elements. Bleached whale ribs were laid across the top and then thatched with tussock grass to provide a waterproof roof.

Barnard assigned duties. One man was to cook and keep watch. Two men daily scoured the island with the dog in search of food. The other two cut and stitched seal skins into jackets, trousers, vests, caps, shoes, and blankets. "We were fortunate enough to have sail-needles and a ball of twine, and when that was expended, we took a cloth out of our mainsail, ravelled it, and thus procured a good substitute for the twine." They exchanged duties daily, so that each man performed his full share.

Life on New Island slowly fell into place. They made beds from the rough tussock grass and later improved them by sewing seal skins together to make bed sacks which they then filled with feathers shed by the thousands of lowland geese which nested on the islands. Seal blubber provided them with fuel. Shells ingeniously became spoons. An old adze found on a remote beach was fashioned into an invaluable hatchet. Barnard started keeping a detailed journal on the back of pup elephant seal skins. He mixed charcoal and sticky plant juice for ink and fashioned pens from goose quills.

The five lived off wild pigs, shellfish, and edible plants. They fashioned a snare and became skilled at catching geese. Cent, their dog, proved vital to their survival. They made a leash out of strips of seal skin and took their dog on all their hunting expeditions, finding in him a formidable ally, especially useful for killing wild pigs.

The winter weather moderated. Then another unexpected threat to their survival appeared. Rats! They were everywhere. They ate the castaways' provisions as fast as these could be collected. Barnard ingenuously solved this problem by lashing three oars together to form a tripod, suspending the food from the apex, and greasing the oars with seal blubber to keep the rats from climbing them.

Spring arrived. With it came the vast populations of albatrosses, penguins, geese, herons, and other fowl that make the Falkland Islands their summer nesting area. Some sixty-three species breed there, and another eighty-four have been sighted on a regular basis. The numbers of some species are staggering, even today. One colony of black-browed albatrosses has been calculated at well over a million birds, a figure probably exceeded at several Rockhopper penguin rookeries. The men feasted on scrambled eggs, fried eggs, and omelets.

Everything fell into place. They had gone to the brink. But Barnard's strength and wisdom as a leader had brought them back from the precipice. They were survivors.

Then, unexpectedly one day in October, Barnard's world collapsed. He had set out to search for elephant seals. As he returned to camp, he spotted his four companions rowing the one boat away from the shore. Without warning, they had abandoned him, taking everything he needed to survive.

Barnard acted quickly. First, he had to have fire. He checked the cold ashes in the fire pit, discovered one solitary ember, and kindled a blaze. "Thus, I surmounted one of the most serious difficulties in which their inhuman desertion had involved me."

Barnard took a fresh accounting of his situation. It was clear that his companions, by depriving him of every necessary article for his survival, wished him dead. He gazed at the sail of their boat growing smaller in the distance and shouted in their direction, "Go then, for you are all bad fellows." He guessed that Ansel had somehow imposed his will on the other three.

Characteristically, Barnard wasted no time in recriminations or self-pity. Instead he set about anew to fashion a semblance of life from his bleak surroundings. He had only a club, knife, and steel to see to all his needs. Lacking a flint for fire-starting, he tested hundreds of stones on the nearby beaches until he found one from which his steel blade might strike sparks. He also discovered a peat deposit, which provided him with a ready source of fuel. One day on the beach at low tide he found the remains of an old tin pot without its bottom. He fashioned it into a frying pan for cooking his eggs. He marked the passage of time by notching a pole and thus managed to keep track of the days.

Each day Barnard climbed a high hill to scan the horizon for ships. Always the same vista presented itself, the empty horizon of the ocean on one side and a string of dark, uninhabited islands on the other. His thoughts dwelled increasingly upon his counterpart of the previous century, Alexander Selkirk, who enjoyed a wealth of riches compared to what he now had. Atop his hill and alone in his world, Barnard recalled the mournful first stanza of William Cowper's famous poem about Selkirk:

I am the monarch of all I survey,
    My right there is none to dispute,
From the center all around to the sea,
    I am lord of the fowl and the brute.
O, solitude! where are the charms
    That sages have seen in thy face?
Better dwell in the midst of alarms,
    Than reign in this horrible place.

Once again Barnard's faith sustained him. "I was now a Robinson Crusoe again; but began to be more reconciled to my hard fate, and determined, with the divine aid, if it should be my destiny to continue here for the remainder of my days, that I should in no case despair, but that, cheered by the recollection of having endeavored to perform the duties of my station, I would with the calm surface of the oceans of eternity in view, say, 'God's will be done.'"

Within a month Barnard had taken care of his most immediate needs. But then another, more insoluble problem presented itself. "I began to feel very solitary, and time moved so slowly on leaden wings, that bad as they were, I wished for the return of the men," he admitted later.

Barnard had been correct in his reasoning. Ansel had been the instigator of the treachery. His plan was to return to the wreck of the *Isabella* and salvage all they might need to live comfortably, Robinson Crusoe-style, on a nearby island until they were rescued. He insisted upon being the leader and demanded the other three choose between him and Barnard. His plan seemed plausible to the others, desperate to improve their situation. To bind them to him, Ansel forced them to swear a blood oath of loyalty, cutting their arms and mingling their blood together.

Three weeks later they arrived at the wreck and found to their bitter disappointment little of value to salvage, only a few pieces of waterlogged canvas and some old newspapers. A disappointed Ansel took out his anger on his depressed and frightened followers, bullying them viciously and threatening to kill them when they objected. Their situation under Ansel's leadership deteriorated rapidly. Soon the other three looked back on their time with Barnard as almost a life of luxury.

Finally, after several months of sheer hell the group decided to return to Barnard's encampment and seek forgiveness. They piled their belongings into their boat and sailed to New Island. The captain was cooking some eggs in front of his hut when he looked up and spotted the boat round a point half a mile away and head toward him. He walked down to the beach to greet them. They looked at one another in a long silence, while the boat bobbed just off shore. Barnard was the first to speak.

"Do you wish to come ashore?"

"Yes, we wish to live with you again and we hope you will forgive us," answered a repentant James Louder. "But we are fearful that we have so offended you that you do not want us to rejoin you. We have put a hog ashore for you on the point, with some old newspapers that I picked up at the wreck, as I had often heard you wish that you had some books or papers to read."

"I can get my living alone as well as with company," Barnard told them. "If you desire to remain here, I am agreed. But I do not wish to control you. Neither shall I refer to what is past, unless you raise the subject."

The four cheerfully agreed and came ashore. True to his nature, Barnard readily forgave them. Though he had quickly promised to reform his bad character, Ansel soon reverted to his true nature. On December 28 the other three advised their captain that Ansel was "in a sulky, malicious mood, planning some scheme of revenge; and they were positive he would attempt the execution of it before many days." They urged Barnard to let them put the bully ashore on nearby Swan Island with sufficient food and supplies for survival. He agreed. Several days later the four sailors took the boat to Swan Island under the pretext of hunting seals. At the beach they sent Ansel off to collect some driftwood and then rowed out to sea, stranding him.

The removal of Ansel boosted the group's morale. "We were now freed from apprehensions for our personal safety," Barnard wrote later, "and tried to make ourselves as comfortable and cheerful as our situation allowed." They began to make long-range plans for their survival. The three crewmembers set off in the boat to visit the wreck of the *Isabella* to look for pieces of plank, boards, old nails, and rope for oakum to mend their boat which had fallen into disrepair.

Barnard passed the time while they were away on hunts for wild pigs, accompanied by the ship's dog Cent. The procedure was always the same. Cent would track down and corner the pig, distracting it with his barking, while the castaways closed in on the animal, spears and clubs at the ready. The dog's body bore dozens of scars from other battles in which the sharp tusks of the boars had ripped him from head to tail. Once he lost an eye to a particularly vicious animal. But in spite of his injuries Cent never held back from a hunt. Indeed, the sailors had to make him a leash to prevent him from running too far ahead whenever he picked up the scent of a wild pig. The dog had become critical to their survival.

"No one can judge how serviceable Cent was to us," an appreciative Barnard wrote later. "And we were more sensible of it when he was wounded, for then we had but a very scanty subsistence, which consisted of fowl, which we luckily killed by throwing our clubs at them, but in this we did not often succeed. We would then go, at low water, to the rocky beach, and turn over the loose flat stones, in whose beds we sometimes found a small fish about the size of an anchovy."

Barnard's three companions returned from the wreck on January 26, 1814, their boat filled with small items they had scavenged. A few days later they set off with a stack of fur seal skins and some supplies to Swan Island to check on Ansel's condition. They found him near a crude hut he had fashioned from tussock bogs. The sailor had lost considerable weight and was in a state of despair. He fell to his knees in front of Barnard and begged to be allowed to rejoin the group. The captain was deeply moved:

> I saw that he was almost reduced to a skeleton, having . . . become almost incapable of procuring his daily subsistence and was entirely indifferent about life. I told him that it was not our intention to take him off. [Rather] he must exert his courage, and endeavor to procure his living, for that he was much better provided with the means than I was, when left alone. But he did not know how to live in that state, as he had no energy or dependence on himself, no new resources on the failure of old ones.

Barnard forgave Ansel on the spot. He persuaded the others to accept him back into the group on the condition that if he lapsed into his former ways he would be immediately returned to Swan Island. This did not prove necessary. The terrors of solitude kept Ansel in line.

A second winter was quickly approaching. The men built a larger stone house, this one with walls three feet thick and five feet high to keep out the bitterly cold winds they knew to expect. They were pleased with the results. "Our house was now completed to the extent of our materials," Barnard observed. "The roof proved to be perfectly tight, and the chimney carried off the smoke very well." As the days shortened, they spent most of the time stitching their fur skins into clothes and blankets.

Louder, Albrook, and Green expressed a desire to return to the wreck to collect another boat load of articles. Barnard agreed. Weather and sea conditions were worsening. Everyone knew the trip might take several weeks. Barnard reviewed the contingency plan about where they were to go if they found they could not make it back to New Island. Ansel stayed behind. The two passed their days hunting geese and pigs, their nights in their shelter, making wooden plates, spoons, and forks by the light of burning wicks immersed in elephant seal oil. Ansel carved a flute and surprised his captain by being a rather good musician.

There was yet another activity to fill the empty hours. Barnard taught Ansel how to read, using the scraps of newspapers salvaged from the *Isabella* earlier. "This was a great source of gratification to him, and some amusement to me. I have heard him, when he did not suspect that I was within hearing, holding dialogues with himself on the subject of his acquirements. Fancying himself at home, he would begin with 'Mother, have you got a newspaper?' 'No, what do you want with a newspaper?' 'I want to read it.' 'Pooh! you can't read.' 'Can't I? Send to the Bell and borrow one. I will read it.' I would come in and ask him, 'Well, Sam, what did the old woman say?' He would laugh and reply she would be frightened and say, 'Sam, who learned you how to read?' And [then he would tell her], 'Why, that American captain I was so long with.'"

After many weeks, the other three finally returned on October 6, having "suffered everything but death." It had taken them five weeks to reach the wreck and the small settlement where the British castaways had lived. Once again they had filled their boat with pieces of boards, ropes, canvas, nails, and other items certain to be useful to their survival. Louder handed Barnard a pair of glasses he had found in the ruins of the British officer's hut. This they intended to use to focus the sun's rays in order to kindle fires.

Rescue finally came on November 25, 1814, eighteen months after the five had been marooned. Barnard, Louder, and Albrook had climbed a high hill to gather some herbs and fill a keg with fresh water from a small pond they knew to be nearby. Barnard suddenly heard a scream from Louder. He saw Albrook turn, go pale, nearly fall, and then start to cry. "The first thought that struck me was that they had both gone mad, and that it was occasioned by our diet," he recalled. Albrook finally managed to stutter, "Two ships! Two ships!" and pointed to the bay. Barnard turned and saw two brigs sailing into the harbor. The three men broke down and wept.

Barnard tracked the ships from his vantage point and saw where they anchored. That afternoon the castaways launched their little boat for the last time. Barnard had put on his last remnant of a shirt: "I observed that on this joyful occasion I could afford to wear a shirt."

The two ships were British whalers, the *Asp* and the *Indispensable*. They had had come to the Falkland Islands to secure fresh water and meat and to hunt the fur seals. On the afternoon of November 25, the two captains were engaged in a conference below on the *Indispensable*. Suddenly, a loud knock on the cabin door interrupted them. A dumbfounded mate urged them to come on deck immediately. A most unusual thing has happened. Five men have just boarded the ship, castaways, he told them.

The two captains hurried on deck. There they found an astonishing sight, "a being who had more the appearance of a savage than a native of an enlightened and Christian country." A thick beard eight inches long hung down his chest. His clothes and shoes had been stitched from the skins of fur seals. The four men with him also looked as if they had just stepped from the pages of *Robinson Crusoe*.

After the captains had learned some of the details of their ordeal, they wanted to know from Barnard how his men had behaved under those difficult circumstances. They knew that sometimes in cases of accident or shipwreck, the sailors would often treat their commanders improperly and prove insubordinate. Fearful that the British captains would order Ansel back on the island if they learned the truth about his actions, Barnard lied. "I told them that was not the case here, for that generally they had been as attentive and obedient as in the ship; and that they had exerted themselves to render our situation as comfortable as the severity of our sufferings allowed."

Four days later, as Barnard and his four companions sailed away from the Falklands, their incredible adventure at an end, British authorities in Plymouth, England, declared the brig *Nanina* a legitimate prize of war and put her up for sale.

CHAPTER THREE

Stove by a Whale:

The Ordeal of the Crew of the *Essex*

In 1884 a German ship put in at the English port of Falmouth with three British castaways picked up in the South Atlantic. They were the captain, Tom Dudley, and two crewmembers of the yacht *Mignonette*, which had sunk within five minutes of floundering during a storm. For twenty-four days they had drifted in an open boat. They had no fresh water whatsoever, and their only food consisted of two cans of turnips. A fourth survivor of the sinking, a seventeen-year-old boy named Richard Parker, had been killed and eaten by the others. Captain Dudley was perfectly candid about what had happened. The boy had been dying anyway; by hastening his death, the others were able to survive. Dudley insisted that he had acted responsibly and was so confident of his rectitude that he regarded a judicial inquiry as a mere formality.

Instead, Dudley and the mate, Edwin Stephens, were brought to trial on a charge of murder on the high seas, while the third member of the party, Able Seaman Ned Brooks, turned prosecution witness. The trial was a curious one, since the defendants had the full sympathy of the public and even of the authorities, who were only concerned to get a ruling into the law books that eating people is wrong. Dudley and Stephens were found guilty and then immediately pardoned by Queen Victoria, on the condition that they serve a token six months in prison.

We generally think of castaways in terms of remote islands and shores. And yet many times after a calamity at sea, the survivors took to open boats, and the ensuing drama played itself out in the vastness of the great oceans. Lieutenant William Bligh's epic voyage across the Pacific Ocean after Fletcher Christian led the mutiny on the *Bounty* is the most celebrated voyage of this sort. But the American crew of the whaleship *Essex* went the British one better in 1820 after a giant sperm whale sank their ship in the South Pacific. They would quickly learn that distance and chance are cruel hereabouts, and the Pacific was made not for men, but for far-ranging whales and seabirds.

Like Selkirk's survival on the Juan Fernández Islands, that of the crew of the *Essex* achieved a measure of immortality because it was recast into a literary masterpiece. The story of a rogue whale sinking a ship had become so legendary by 1850 when Herman Melville started work on his classic novel, *Moby Dick*, that many questioned whether the story was fact or fiction. But the young Melville on a whaling cruise had heard the story from the son of the first mate—how an enormous sperm whale had rammed and sunk the ship, forcing the crew into three small boats, which then sailed 4,500 miles to safety. It was a tale of unmatched valor and endurance under the severest stress imaginable, rendered all the more horrible because the handful of survivors resorted to cannibalism to save their lives.

By 1820 whaling was the great American industry. Nantucket was synonymous with whaling and boasted a rapidly growing fleet of seventy-two ships. (The British fleet, by way of contrast, had entered into a steep decline.) Whale products were as ubiquitous in the society of the day as petroleum products are today. Whale oil lamps and spermaceti wax candles lighted the homes of the nation. Sperm oil was critical in the manufacture of paints and soaps, the tanning of hides, and the lubrication of industrial machinery. Thousands of workers fashioned whalebone into umbrella ribs, buggy whips, canes, corset stays, hoop skirts, and dozens of other products. Ladies of fashion dabbed on perfumes made from ambergris, a valuable substance coughed up from the stomach of diseased whales.

In the seventeenth century whaling had been limited to offshore ventures from the island of Nantucket. After the War of 1812 Yankee whalers found themselves in a new world. Industrialization proceeded swiftly. The demand for their products mushroomed. In 1791 the first American whaling vessel rounded the Horn, sailed into the Pacific, and discovered along the coasts of Chile and Peru vast numbers of sperm whales for the taking. In 1818 whalers began cruising into the open Pacific beyond the Galápagos Islands. While the mountain men explored the unknown wilderness of the American West, their counterparts at sea were the New England whalemen who became pathfinders in the uncharted Central Pacific. (Melville in *Moby Dick* likened the Pacific Ocean to the great American prairie.) The area quickly became the richest of the world's whaling grounds and drew the greatest number of ships. One visitor to Hawaii in 1852 counted 131 whaling ships at anchor in the harbor of Honolulu. The waste was appalling. Contemporary estimates were that two of every three whales killed either sank or drifted away. Yet huge fortunes were amassed.

The heroes of Nantucket society were the successful captains, and its lords were the owners of the ships and wharves. Pacific island artifacts decorated most homes on the island. Delicate shells, tapa cloth, shark-tooth swords, ceremonial masks, models of elaborately carved canoes, and even the dried heads of Maori chiefs from New Zealand ended up on the mantles in whalers' homes.

"And thus have these naked Nantucketers, these sea hermits, issuing from their ant-hill in the sea, overrun and conquered the watery world like so many Alexanders, parcelling out among them the Atlantic, Pacific, and Indian oceans," Melville wrote in *Moby Dick*. "The Nantucketer, he alone resides and riots on the sea; he alone, in Bible language, goes down to it in ships, to and fro plowing it as his own special plantation. *There* is his home."

Herman Melville was born in New York City on August 1, 1819. Eleven days later the whaleship *Essex* sailed from Nantucket Harbor under the command of Captain George Pollard with Owen Chase as his first mate. His destination was the hunting grounds of the Central Pacific Ocean, a region that was then but poorly explored. The *Essex* carried a crew of twenty along with provisions for thirty months at sea.

The twenty-eight-year-old Pollard on his first voyage of command was a young, untested captain. He was engaged in no metaphysical quest, like Captain Ahab of Melville's novel. Sperm whale oil was his sole object. Two months before he had married Mary C. Riddell. He had apparently served as a first mate on the *Essex* during a previous whaling voyage. Little else is known about his early years.

We know considerably more about Chase, first mate, for whom this was his third whaling cruise. He had been born on Nantucket on October 7, 1796, into a family of eight children. The five surviving sons all sought their life at sea and by their late twenties had become whaling captains. One contemporary shipping document describes Chase as five feet ten inches tall, with brown hair and a dark complexion. Earlier that spring he had married Peggy Gardner and she had become pregnant a few months later. (A baby girl was born on April 16, 1820, while the *Essex* was cruising the waters off the coast of Chile.) At twenty-three Chase was mature beyond his years and had already demonstrated the important qualities of endurance and leadership on his previous voyages.

Almost all the crew were from Nantucket Island. Most were young, under twenty-one. Seven were black, Negroes forming an important element in the New England whaling society where they found true equality and sometimes rose to the rank of captain. The cabin boy was Owen Coffin, Pollard's sixteen-year-old nephew who was like a son to him. He was on his first ocean voyage.

The *Essex* was a rather typical square-rigged whaling ship of her day. She had been constructed in 1799. The original register describes her as having "two decks and three masts; and her length is eighty-seven feet, seven inches, her breadth twenty-five feet, her depth twelve feet six inches, and she measures two-hundred -thirty-eight tons; she is square-sterned and has no gallery and no figure head."

Pollard ordered the *Essex* to sail due east to the Azores Islands and then straight south to the Cape Verde Islands off the coast of West Africa. At each port he bartered for an ample supply of fresh fruits and vegetables. The trade item was the same in each place—whale oil. In the Cape Verde Islands he traded some one and a half barrels of dried beans for thirty hogs, most so thin that their bones seemed ready to burst their skins. The crew welcomed the taste of freshly butchered pork after their steady diet of salt pork and hard tack, but the animals were almost too much trouble for the pleasures of eating them. They often got mixed up among the crew's legs and tumbled them over. The decks had to be washed clean two or three times a day, otherwise the stench became unbearable. But the pigs were history by the time the *Essex* rounded the Horn and sailed into the Pacific Ocean. Her first stop was the Juan Fernández Islands where the crew replenished their supply of wood (for the galley stove), fruits, vegetables,and, of course, goats. They also noted that the beaches were empty of fur and elephant seals, a consequence of the ferocious overhunting in the past decade. Pollard then cruised north toward the hunting grounds off northern Chile and Peru, where he knew he could count upon large numbers of sperm whales.

"I will have no man in my boat who is not afraid of a whale," insists Starbuck, Ahab's chief mate in *Moby Dick*.

The sperm whale was both the most lucrative and most dangerous of the cetacean species. Its huge head (up to forty percent of its boxlike body) and the telltale foward angle of its spout—all other whales spout straight up into the air—make it the most easily recognized whale species. Fifty thick, conical eleven-inch teeth line the underslung lower jaw and fit into sockets in the toothless upper jaw. At twenty pounds, its brain is the largest on earth. The sperm whale has a distinctive dorsal hump located about two-thirds of the way back from the tip of the snout. Immediately behind the hump is a series of knuckles along the midline, which are clearly visible when the animal arches its tail before beginning a dive. The huge forehead holds an enormous amount of oil. This may help give a neutral buoyancy in deep dives, which often reach depths of 5,000 feet as the animal hunts for giant squid, its chief food source. Sperm whales generally live in pods of several females led by one bull. In the nineteenth century the most important hunting grounds for the sperm whales were the coastal waters of Chile and Peru, the Hawaiian Islands, the Galápagos Islands, and along the equatorial belt leading to eastern Australia and New Zealand.

Whalers highly prized the sperm whale's oil. It burned with a bright, clear flame and without the disagreeable odor of ordinary whale oil. And it yielded the purest and finest candles, which were vastly superior in both brilliance and fragrance to the tallow candles.

Nineteenth century whalers held the sperm whale in awe. "The mouth of the sperm whale is a wonderful-looking affair, being covered, from the end of his long jaw to as far as one can see down his throat with a shining white membrane, like satin," observed Nelson Halley, the chief harpooner on the *Charles W. Morgan* from 1849 to 1853. "The teeth, however, do not look so pretty," he added as an afterthought. But the teeth made prized trade items on Fiji and some other islands in Melanesia. "Ten small teeth will purchase outright any woman or girl," he insisted.

The *Essex* enjoyed solid success off the coasts of Peru and Chile, obtaining some 800 barrels of whale oil. The cry "T-h-e-r-e s-h-e b-l-o-w-s" from the masthead alerted the crew that the lookout had spotted "the low bushy spouts" indicating a pod of resting sperm whales. The crew rushed to the four boats that hung from wooden davits. Built from light cedar boards less than half an inch in thickness, they were sharply pointed at both ends. For speed, stability, and buoyancy in rolling seas, no boats in the world were their equal at the time. Twenty feet long, they had seats for four oarsmen and a platform at each end for the steersman and the harpooner. Set in the middle of each was a tub which held a spirally coiled rope, two-thirds of an inch thick and almost 1300 feet long, one end of which was fastened to a harpoon.

Once whales had been sighted, the crew leaped into the boats while Pollard and his mates seized the steering oars. And off they went toward the whales, often two miles away. When the whales came up for air after a dive, the whaleboats were waiting. As the unsuspecting whale relaxed on the surface to take a fresh breath of air, the crew rowed toward it at full speed, the boats competing with each other to be the first to sink a harpoon in the whale's side. After the harpoons thudded in, the crew rowed frantically to the stern to get away from the whale's tail that smashed down dangerously. Then the whale took off across the sea's surface, towing the whalemen behind on what they called a "Nantucket sleigh ride." In time it would weaken, rolling from side to side in pain and exhaustion. Then the boats would close in for the kill. The whale's most vital spot was just behind its giant head where the arteries bunched up around the lungs and the protective layer of blubber was thin. One deep thrust of the lance there, and blood flooded into the great lungs, suffocating the animal within a few minutes.

Pollard's crew accepted the enormous risks in whaling. After two months they suffered their first casualty, a stove boat. A large sperm whale suddenly erupted under Chase's boat, smashing the bottom and sending the six men flying into the air. Miraculously, no one was hurt. "We are so much accustomed to the continual recurrence of such scenes as these, that we have become familiarized to them, and consequently always feel that confidence and self-possession, which teaches us every expedient in danger and inures the body as well as the mind to fatigue, privation, and peril," Chase wrote later in his book on the voyage.

Once the whale was killed, the men cut a hole in its head and slipped a rope through. Then the men of the whaleboats rowed together and slowly pulled the great mass back to their ship and tied it fast with chains. A large hook, weighing perhaps 125 pounds, was lowered and fastened into the blubber just behind the whale's eyes. While a man cut away the blubber in a continuous strip, the hook was slowly pulled upwards, rolling the whale around and around until the last of the blubber was removed to be boiled down to oil in the try-pots. The sea around the body churned with dozens of sharks thrashing around in a feeding frenzy.

The head was hoisted on the deck whole. This was the most valued part of the whale. The crew split open the forehead to expose the spermaceti, the highest grade animal oil known to man. A large whale might yield upwards of 500 gallons. The butter-thick liquid hardened to a pearly white after exposure to the air.

After three days all that was left of the leviathan was the thickening oil filling several rows of wooden casks carefully packed below. Then the crew scrubbed the rails, paint work, and decks clean of any trace of the whale.

After several months of successful whaling in the coastal waters off South America, Pollard ordered the *Essex* on a western course toward the Galápagos Islands where they spent seven days anchored off Hood Island. They stopped a leak and brought on board some 300 tortoises, each weighing close to 100 pounds. They were easy creatures to catch. Two crewmen simply walked up to an animal, seized its shell, and flipped it over onto its back, a move which rendered the animal quite helpless. The turtle was then dragged to a boat, ferried back to the ship, and hoisted aboard. Soon turtles were jammed between the decks and in the hold, while the others had the freedom of the deck.

"These turtles are a most delicious food," a grateful Chase wrote later. "With these, ships usually supply themselves for a great length of time and make a great saving of provisions. They neither eat nor drink, nor are the least pains taken with them. They live upwards of a year without food or water."

On their last day on Hood Island Thomas Chappel, the English crewmember, decide to play a joke on his fellow mariners and set a fire in the dry brush to surprise them while they gathered food. The blaze quickly got out of hand and burned for many days after they had left.

"There can be no estimate of the destruction caused by this fire to the animal creation," Thomas Nickerson wrote over fifty years later. "On my return to this place many years afterwards the ruin was still visible. Wherever the fire raged, neither trees, shrubbery, nor grass have since appeared. And judging from the extent of desolate ground, there must have been thousands upon thousands of turtles, birds, lizards, and snakes destroyed. "

The *Essex* departed the Galápagos Islands and headed westward across the Central Pacific, a vast watery wilderness where few whaling ships had ventured before. Charles Darwin crossed the Pacific in 1835 and observed: "It is necessary to sail over this great ocean to comprehend its immensity . . . . Accustomed to look at maps drawn on a smaller scale, where dots, shading, and names are crowded together, we do not rightly judge how infinitely small the proportion of dry land is to the water of this vast expanse."

On November 20 the *Essex* was just below the equator in longitude 119° west. The lookout in the masthead saw the telltale forward spout marking a group of sperm whales and sung out once again, "There she blows." Within minutes three boats were quickly launched. Chase's boat was the first on the scene. A whale surfaced just ahead. He flung his harpoon, saw it sink into the blubber, and then ordered his crew to reverse direction. It was too late. The whale lashed out with its flukes and smashed a hole in the boat's side, opening up a serious leak. Chase grabbed the hatchet and cut the line, saving his boat from almost certain destruction. By stuffing their jackets into the holes, the men managed to stop the leaks. The other two boats chased after the wounded whale. But Chase ordered his boat back to the *Essex* for quick repairs. While they worked on deck, an enormous bull sperm whale, eighty-five feet in length, surfaced nearby. He spouted several times and then disappeared, to reappear a few seconds later and then rush the ship.

The seventeen-year-old Nickerson was at the helm. "I looked up on the windward side of the ship and saw a large whale approaching us," he recalled years later. "I called out to the mate to inform him of it. On his seeing the whale he instantly gave me an order to put the helm hard up and steer toward the boats. I scarcely had time to obey the orders . . . when the whale with a tremendous crack struck the ship with his head directly under the larboard forechains at the water's edge with such force as to shock every man upon his feet."

The whale passed directly under the ship and came up alongside of her to the leeward to lie quietly on the surface. The crew looked at one another in stunned disbelief, as the *Essex* slowly began to settle in the water. Chase ordered pumping to start immediately. A few minutes later the whale surfaced again, rolling about in convulsions and "smithing his jaws together, as if distracted with rage and fury." Suddenly, he turned once again, lifted his head out of the water, and charged the crippled ship a second time, striking near the bow and completely caving in the hull. Water poured in. Chase saw at once that the ship was lost. He ordered the spare boat launched. Crewmembers hastily collected a few supplies—two quadrants, two compasses, the chartbook of Pacific navigation, and Pollard's and Chase's trunks. They leaped into the boat and pushed off, just as the *Essex* rolled over on her beam ends and settled into the water. The entire time between the first attack and the sinking of the ship was less than ten minutes.

The men sat dumbfounded in their boat, bobbing alongside the wreck. "The shock to our feelings was such I am sure none can have an adequate conception," the mate wrote later. "We were dejected by a sudden most mysterious, and overwhelming calamity . . . . We were more than a thousand miles from the nearest land, and with nothing but a light boat, as the resource of safety for myself and companions."

Soon the other two boats arrived, unaware of what had happened, only that the *Essex* had suddenly disappeared.

"My God, Mr. Chase, what is the matter?" Captain Pollard demanded.

"We have been stove by a whale," Chase replied quietly. He gave a full account of the tragedy. For several minutes they were all stunned, unable to take action.

Finally, Pollard ordered his crew back on the floating hulk of the *Essex* in a desperate attempt to get additional supplies, food, and water. Using small hatchets from their whaleboats, they cut away the masts. The ship rose up on an even keel. They then cut through the hull and entered her. Before the day was out, Pollard and his crew had salvaged 65 gallons of fresh water, 600 pounds of bread, several turtles, and a selection of miscellaneous supplies, including a musket, two pistols, a small sack of gun powder, two pounds of nails, and some tools. Chase's sea chest, saved earlier, held such valuable items as fish hooks, a knife, extra clothes, some twine and sail cloth needles, a pencil, and some sheets of paper. He began almost immediately to keep "a sort of journal."

For three days the boats remained alongside the stricken ship hoping that another whaler would appear. But none did. The men lay in a state of shock in their boats, contemplating their condition. "How many long and watchful nights are to be passed?" Chase thought to himself. "How many tedious days of partial starvation are to be endured before the least relief or mitigation of our sufferings can be reasonably anticipated?"

The crew managed to save some cedar boards, poles, and canvas. They built up the sides of their whaleboats to give them some protection against swamping and fixed each boat with a mast and sail. Pollard called a council of his officers to determine the best course to take and decide upon the "best means for our security and preservation." They were twenty men in three boats. With their boats loaded to the gunwales with supplies, they felt in better spirits. On the other hand, they all realized that a whaleboat was an extremely fragile thing, built for speed rather than punishment.

"Now for the first time did the horrors of our situation fall fully before us," Nickerson recalled. "Now it was that we could realize the slender thread upon which our lives were hung."

Pollard held a conference with the officers in his boat. They studied the Bowditch chartbook of the Central Pacific. Which direction to take? There were no accurate charts of the sea around them in 1820. Few whalers or merchantmen had crossed the Pacific, and the ocean was largely unexplored. The *Essex* had been one of the first ships from Nantucket to enter the area.

The Hawaiian Islands lay 2,500 miles to the north. Fearful of the typhoons that were thought to rage through the area at that time of year, they ruled them out. The Galápagos Islands lay to the east, but the winds and currents were unfavorable for a direct sail there. Tahiti lay less than 1,000 miles to the southwest. But knowing nothing of the natives there and fearful they might be cannibals, Pollard and the officers refused to consider them for refuge.

Information on the Pacific islands was sparse in 1820, and the crew of the *Essex* did not know that for twenty years Christian missionaries had lived in Tahiti and the island was entirely safe for ships. Thus, they unwillingly found themselves victims of one of the supreme ironies in maritime history: Sailing east to escape cannibals, they themselves would become cannibals.

Pollard and the two mates finally decided upon a course of action—south for 1,000 miles to catch the trade winds and then east for another 3,000 miles to the Chilean coast. It was a wild throw of the dice. But under the circumstances they thought it was their best hope. Pollard ordered the provisions distributed equally among the three boats. Each mate received a firearm and some powder.

On November 24 the three small boats hoisted their sails and set off, determined to keep together. Chase had the oldest, most patched boat, so it carried only six men while the others held seven. Pollard calculated they had enough provisions to last sixty days. Each man was to receive as his daily rations one biscuit of bread, weighing perhaps a pound, and half a pint of water.

Within a few days the calm seas gave way to rough ones. Heavy waves swamped the boats, wetting the precious supplies, and springing a bad leak in Chase's boat. They were able to patch it up, but serious damage had been done. ("Were we at home we would not feel safe to go ten miles in her," observed Nickerson.) Salt water had soaked the boat's supply of biscuits. The crew dried out the wet bread and ate it first, before it spoiled. After several days the men realized that the salt left behind on the bread parched their throats and gave them an extreme thirst. Several men started drinking their own urine to survive. And yet no one complained when the captain refused to increase their daily ration of water. Chase noted approvingly in his journal: "The most perfect discipline is still maintained in respect to our provisions."

The small flotilla made good time. One night several flying fish landed in the boats. They were eaten, fins and all, within minutes. Then one crewmember discovered small clams growing on the bottoms of their boats. Eagerly, the men scrapped these off and ate them by the handful until there were no more.

On the eleventh day Chase proposed they kill one of their turtle. The suggestion was taken up enthusiastically. They kindled a fire in the shell and cooked the meat as best they could. They ate the turtle, entrails and all, and rationed out the fresh blood, which they gulped eagerly. This "exquisite banquet" lifted their spirits considerably, but a week later when a storm overtook them, their strength was ebbing. Rain poured from the skies, but they had nothing to catch the water in. The waves built to a fearful height. It looked as though none of the boats could possibly survive.

Chase remembered: "The appearance of the heavens was dark and dreary, and the blackness that was spread over the face of the waters dismal beyond description. The heavy squalls, that followed each other in quick succession, were preceded by sharp flashes of lightning that appeared to wrap our little barge in flames."

The men lay down below the gunwales and let the boats run before the storm. "To an over-ruling Providence alone must be attributed our salvation from the horrors of that terrible night," Chase wrote later. Despite the violence of the storm the three boats had stayed together, a tribute to the seamanship of the Nantucket whalemen. The next morning the storm abated. None had had any sleep, yet in spite of their exhaustion they managed to set a double-reefed mainsail and jib in each boat and once again took command of their direction.

Their condition steadily weakened, as dehydration and hunger took their toll. They longed for fresh meat. Schools of porpoises swam nearby and tantalized them, but all efforts to catch one failed. Their bodies wasted away to mere skeletons. The hot tropical sun seared their exposed skin. Their lips became cracked and swollen, and their thirst so intense they could scarcely talk. Each knew that unless relief came, they would soon perish. "The privation of water is justly ranked among the most dreadful of the miseries of life," Chase mused. "The violence of raging thirst has no parallel in the catalogue of human calamities."

A modern traveler may look at a map of the Pacific with the hundreds of atolls and islands scattered across its surface and wonder how men could sail so far and yet encounter no landfall. The explanation, of course, is that islands are much easier to find on a map than from the deck of a ship and almost impossible from the plank seat of a tiny whaleboat bobbing in the waves. No less an authority than Herman Melville would describe in detail in *Mardi* almost thirty years later the claustrophobic world of a whaleboat:

Unless the waves, in their gambols, toss you and your chip upon one of their lordly crests, your sphere of vision is little larger than it would be at the bottom of a well. At best, your most extended view in any one direction, at least, is in a high, slow-rolling sea; when you descend into the dark, misty spaces, between long and uniform swells. Then, for the moment, it is like looking up and down in a twilight glade, interminable; where two dawns, one on each hand, seem struggling through the semi-transparent tops of fluid mountains.

Their thirty-first day at sea, December 20, dawned. "This was a day of great happiness and joy," Chase noted in his journal. They had suffered through a trying night of heavy seas and little sleep. The men sat dejected and listless in their boats, drifting with the current. Suddenly, one of the seamen in Chase's boat cried out, "There is land!" They all looked leeward. "There was the blessed vision before us," Chase wrote. "We shook off the lethargy of our senses . . . . It appeared at first as a low, white beach and lay like a basking paradise before our longing eyes."

The whalemen had come upon remote Henderson Island, a low, flat island about eight miles in circumference and covered with trees and brush, located some 100 miles northeast of Pitcairn Island. Except on the northern end, steep cliffs about fifty-feet high eroded into deep caves circled the island. Within an hour the crew of the *Essex* had landed safely on a beach made up entirely of small broken pieces of coral and shells. They stumbled ashore and collapsed, sprawling across the hard packed coral fragments while they recovered their strength. But thirst and hunger soon drove them to explore their refuge. They split up and went off in different directions seeking a source of fresh water.

Musket in hand, Chase walked along the rocky shore and suddenly spotted a large fish swimming in the shallow water close to shore. He speared it with his ramrod and tossed it up on the beach. Within ten minutes he and his companions had eaten the fish, everything—meat, skin, bones, and scales—in their own feeding frenzy. Then they set about ex-

ploring the interior. Interlacing shrubs covered the ground
with a covering so dense it was impossible to see the holes in
the coral below. One false step meant a snapped ankle or broken leg. Progress was so slow and difficult they soon turned
back toward the beach.

The island was uninhabited. On the trunk of a pandanus
tree they found carved the word "Elizabeth," the name of the
British whaler which had discovered the island just a year before.

The castaways found no fresh water. But food there was,
if not plentiful. Colorful tropical birds nested in the perch of
trees, so tame they could be plucked along with their eggs
with bare hands from their nests. Small crabs scurried across
the beach. Chase brought out his fish hooks and lures and
managed to land several fish. They also found several clumps
of eatable peppergrass. That afternoon they built a fire and
managed a splendid feast of roasted fish, birds, eggs, and
boiled peppergrass. "Perhaps no banquet was ever enjoyed
with greater gusto or gave such universal satisfaction,"
Nickerson recalled in later years.

The next day they set out on another search for signs of
water. Their dehydration was now so acute that simple
speech was difficult and painful. That afternoon they discovered a small spring flowing from a crevice in a flat rock a
quarter mile up the beach from their boats. One by one they
took their fill. Afterwards they brought up their water kegs
and filled those, finishing just as the high tide flowed in and
submerged their spring.

The castaways celebrated a bleak Christmas on Henderson Island and then faced up to the problem of setting out
to sea again. Pollard and Chase realized the island lacked sufficient water and food to support all twenty of them for long.
They discussed their options. Twelve years before one of
their Nantucket neighbors, a whaling captain by the name of
Mayhew Folger, had happened upon Pitcairn Island and discovered there the descendants of the *Bounty*'s mutineers. But
the small island was not marked on Pollard's chart, and he
knew they had little chance of reaching it in the vastness of
the ocean without some precise information as to its location.

After a week on Henderson Island the castaways decided

to sail again. The three boats had been repaired, as best as possible under the circumstances. Each boat was stocked with a flat stone and two armfuls of wood, to make a cooking fire should they catch some fish or seabirds. Pollard wrote up an account of the sinking of the *Essex* and placed it in a tin can nailed to the trunk of a tree near the beach.

At the last minute three of the crew—William Wright, Seth Weeks and Thomas Chappel, the crew's lone Englishman—decided to remain on the island rather than confront the dangerous uncertainties of a lengthy open boat voyage to the coast of South America. The three had built a crude shelter and had every confidence they could survive indefinitely on sea birds, eggs, fish, and peppergrass until the arrival of another ship. The separation was hard on all involved. "There was a desperate instinct which bound us together. We continued to cling to each other with a strong and involuntary impulse," Chase observed later.

The three boats put to sea in mid-morning. Their destination was Easter Island, over 1,000 miles to the east. But after several days they realized that the winds and currents were carrying them to the south. So Pollard and the officers decided to try instead for the Juan Fernández Islands and the coast of South America, another 2,000 miles farther east.

On January 10 the party suffered its first death. Matthew Joy, the second mate, died of dehydration and hunger late in the afternoon. The next morning they tied a cooking stone to his feet and consigned him "in a solemn manner" to the ocean. His death left them depressed for several days. The next day a gale overtook them. The storm blew throughout the night. Lightning flashed across the sky. The rain came down in torrents—yet once again they lacked any containers to catch it. The next morning Chase and his crew discovered to their horror they were alone. The other two boats were nowhere in sight. They were in latitude 32° 16' south and longitude 112° west. The loss of this companionship weighed heavily upon them all. "I found it on this occasion true, that misery does indeed love company," Chase wrote. "We lost the cheering of each other's faces, that which strange as it is, we so much required in both our mental and bodily distresses."

Chase reduced their rations sharply. They were now eating just one and a half ounces of bread each day and a quarter pint of water and were all too weak to do much sailing. "Our bodies already debilitated seemed no longer able or willing to act in concert with the mind," Nickerson wrote. During the day they sprawled in the bottom of the whaleboat, covered themselves with some canvas to protect their bodies from the intense sun, and let the easternly winds blow them toward the distant coast of South America. One night Chase caught one of the crew stealing extra bread from the locker, the first such incident since the sinking of the *Essex*. He put a cocked pistol to the man's head, and the bread was returned with the promise not to steal again.

On January 15 a large shark began following their boat, circling in close, snapping at the steering oar, and even attacking the stern post. The creature stayed with them for hours. Chase thought it manifested "fearless malignity" in its persistence. They had a harpoon in the boat, but were all too weak to do any injury to the shark's tough skin.

On January 20 a second crewman, the black deckhand Richard Peterson, died and his body was quickly committed to the sea. "We were now in a most wretched and sinking state of debility, hardly able to crawl around the boat and possessing but strength enough to convey our scanty morsel to our mouths," Chase wrote. At night the first mate was tormented by dreams of splendid feasts—tables groaning beneath the weight of roast fowl, steaming slabs of beef, tempting tureens of soup, serving bowls heaped to overflowing with fresh vegetables, and pies just out of the oven. "Just as I was about to partake of it, I suddenly awoke to the cold realities of my miserable situation," he recollected sadly. "Nothing could have oppressed me so much." Once he found a small piece of cowhide in the bottom of the boat and chewed on that, but it had no substance and only exhausted his already weakened jaws.

Chase calculated they had only enough bread to last several more days. Their condition steadily deteriorated. Boils erupted on their bodies. Their cracked lips began bleeding heavily.

"Our sufferings were now drawing to a close," Chase wrote on February 8. "A terrible death appeared shortly to await us. Hunger became violent. Our speech and reason were both considerably impaired. Nothing but the slight chance of meeting with a vessel remained to us now. We gave ourselves wholly up to the guidance and disposal of our Creator."

That day a man went mad. Isaac Cole was sprawled in the bottom of the boat with the rest. Suddenly, he sat up and in a firm voice demanded a glass of water and a napkin. The others watched him in silence, while he kept repeating his request. In the late afternoon he went into violent convulsions and died soon afterwards.

The next morning the men slowly set about preparing Cole's body for disposal. Chase checked the food reserves. They were down to three days' supplies of bread. Then Chase voiced the thought on each man's mind. Should they eat the flesh of their dead companion and thus buy themselves an extra two weeks of life? The suggestion was accepted immediately and eagerly by the others.

"We set to work as fast as we were able," Chase reported. "We separated his limbs from his body and cut all the flesh from the bones, after which we opened the body, took out the heart, and then closed it again—sewed it up as decently as we could and committed it to the sea."

They quickly ate Cole's heart first and then some of his flesh. The rest they cut into small strips and hung them out to dry in the sun. But the next day the flesh started to turn green and putrid, so they made a fire on the stones from Henderson Island and roasted the flesh to preserve it. "In this manner did we dispose of our fellow sufferer," Chase noted. And thus they restored some strength to their starved and enfeebled bodies. By the fourteenth they had strengthened enough to take turns at the steering oar and managed to "make a tolerable good course."

On the fifteenth the three survivors consumed the last of the flesh and the next day they ate the final portion of the bread. Chase judged they were still at least 300 miles from the nearest landfall. Their only hope lay in a strong westernly wind that continued unabated through the night. In the darkness as he slept, Chase dreamt he saw a ship passing in the distance. He made a tremendous effort to attract the attention of the crew, but the vessel sailed past them without stopping. He awoke angry, bitter, and disappointed. The fact that thus far in the voyage they had not seen another ship was dramatic testimony to how few ships were crisscrossing the Pacific in those early days of whaling.

"Death seemed truly to be hovering over us and staring broadly in our faces," Nickerson recalled in later years. "But upon a consultation we agreed that let whatsoever would come we would never draw lots after our food had quite gone for each other's death but leave all with God."

Early the next morning while two of them slept, the man at the steering oar suddenly sung out, "There's a sail!" The others quickly stood up and saw a ship seven miles away heading in their direction. Soon the British brig *Indian* under the command of Captain William Crozier came alongside. Its crew stared down in silent amazement at the three men in the small boat with their "cadaverous countenances, sunken eyes, and bones just starting through the skin, with the ragged remnants of clothes stuck about our sunburnt bodies."

Chase had brought his men to within 300 miles of the Chilean coast in their little twenty-seven-foot whaleboat, drifting and sailing a distance of 4,500 miles in a quarter of a year, a feat as impressive as the legendary voyage of Lieutenant William Bligh in 1789.

On February 25, the *Indian* arrived at Valparaiso where the three survivors were landed "in utter distress and poverty," as Chase described it.

Five days later Pollard's boat with just two survivors was picked up by the American whaler, the *Dauphin*, off the Chilean coast. He told the stunned captain his account of their survival, a horror story that was destined to be repeated hundreds of times on other ships in later years.

After separating from Chase's boat during the fearful storm on the night of January 12, the other two boats headed on a southeastern course toward Juan Fernández some 2,000 miles away. Pollard had four men in his boat, while five were with the third mate.

Their meager supply of food gave out entirely before the

death of the first man, Charles Shorter. The others knew then what had to be done. Shorter's body was divided between the two boats.

"We had no other alternative but to live on his remains," Pollard admitted later. "These were roasted to dryness by means of fires kindled in the ballast sand at the bottom of the boats. When this supply was spent, what could we do? We looked at each other with horrid thoughts in our minds, but held our tongues."

A second crewmember died, and his body, too, was eaten. Finally, on the night of January 28 heavy seas caused the two boats to separate. The third mate's boat was never seen again. In the captain's boat there were now four men remaining alive—Pollard, his nephew Owen Coffin, Charles Ramsdell, and Brazilla Ray. On February 1 they ate the last of the flesh. The survivors then settled upon an awful alternative. One would be killed, so that the others might live.

"I am sure that we loved one another as brothers all the time," an anguished Pollard recalled later. "But our looks told us plainly what must be done."

They drew lots.

Owen Coffin, Pollard's beloved young nephew, drew the short stick. A few minutes later in the second round Charles Ramsdell drew the executioner's lot.

Pollard quickly offered himself up in Coffin's place. Then Ramsdell, himself a teenager just a couple of years older than Coffin, insisted that he be the one to die. But Coffin demanded they all stick to their original contract. As Pollard told the story later:

"I started forward instantly and cried out, 'My lad, my lad, if you don't like your lot, I'll shoot the first man who touches you.' The poor emaciated boy hesitated a moment or two; then, quietly laying his head down on the gunwale of the boat, he said, 'I like it as well as any other.'"

Ramsdell then quickly shot the youth through the head. His flesh kept them alive another ten days. "But I can tell you no more!" the captain cried some years later, as he recounted the experience. "My head is on fire at the recollection."

Brazilla Ray died on the morning of February 11. Pollard and Ramsdell ate his flesh for twelve days. After that they began to weaken once again, losing what little strength they had regained, drifting in and out of consciousness. A few days later they were picked up by the Nantucket whaling ship *Dauphin*. The stunned crew of the rescue vessel looked down in disbelief at the horrors in the small boat. "They were ninety-two days in the boat and were in a most wretched state," the captain wrote in his journal and then added a grim detail. "They were unable to move when found [and were] sucking on the bones of their dead mess mates, which they were loath to part with."

A week after their rescue, Pollard and Ramsdell arrived in Valparaiso where they had an emotional reunion with the three other survivors. Commodore Charles Goodwin Ridgely, commanding the U.S. frigate *Constellation*, was in the harbor, and the five men from the Essex were taken to his ship for medical treatment. He noted in his official account that the bones of Pollard and Ramsdell pressed through their skin, their legs and feet were shrunken, and their skin was "one ulcer." The local American and British communities took up a collection for the castaways and raised $400 to satisfy their immediate needs and buy them passages back to Nantucket.

Ridgely contracted with Thomas Raine, the British captain of the *Surrey* on her way to Australia with 15,000 bushels of wheat in the hold, to effect a rescue of the three castaways on Henderson Island. On April 8, 1821, the trio were stunned to hear the sound of gunshots. They hurried from their shelter and saw the *Surrey* just offshore. They had been on Henderson 111 days, even today an occupational record for the island. Their condition had become desperate within just a matter of days after the three boats headed out to sea. The birds grew fearful and departed their nests. The land crabs disappeared. And worst of all, they lost their spring of fresh water. Their sole source of fresh water became small pools of rainwater left in the hollows of the rocks after a squall had passed over the island.

Throughout that time the trio had constant reminders of how perilous their situation actually was. In their explorations they found in a nearby cave eight human skeletons, one of them a child, side by side as though they had laid down together and died. The three *Essex* survivors all assumed they were castaways, like themselves, who had come ashore earlier to find an entirely different fate awaiting them.

(In 1958 the Pitcairn islanders, who visit regularly Henderson Island to collect miro wood for their carvings, rediscovered the skeletons. A medical examination showed they were all Caucasian, confirming they were indeed the remains of the shipwrecked crew and passengers from an unidentified ship. They did not have the necessary survival skills. Their probable cause of death was a lack of water. In 1966 the skeletons were given a final burial in coffins in a corner of the cave. The Pitcairn islanders erected a six-foot cross at the entrance of the cave.)

That evening Raine set sail for Pitcairn Island and arrived there on the afternoon of the next day. Only the seventh ship to call there, the crew of the *Surrey* received such a warm welcome they decided to stay two days among the descendants of the *Bounty* mutineers. The visiting crew thought they had stumbled on paradise. The island's women were beautiful, the men handsome. All were hospitable, almost to a fault. They feasted their guests on roast pig and numerous island delicacies, including a homemade whiskey the guests pronounced excellent. Most of the crew slept overnight in the little village. John Adams, the sole survivor of the original mutineers, talked to the visitors at length and at their urging narrated once again the story of the famous mutiny. The islanders, in turn, had a message for the officers of the *Surrey*. They sought their help to recruit a missionary who might teach their children.

The islanders also put on for their guests a demonstration of a water sport they called "sliding." Captain Raine was much impressed and wrote a detailed account in his journal, thus providing the first description of surfboarding:

> The women and the men amused themselves
> with *sliding*, as they term it, one of the strangest, yet
> most pleasing performances I ever saw. They have a
> piece of wood, somewhat resembling a butcher's tray,
> but round at one end and square at the other, and

having on the bottom a small keel. With this they
swim off to the rocks at the entrance [to the little
harbor], getting on which they wait for a heavy surf,
and, just as it breaks, jump off with the piece of wood
under them. And thus with their heads before the
surf, they rush in with amazing rapidity, to the very
head of the bay; and although amongst rocks escape
all injury. They steer themselves with their feet,
which they move very quickly.

It is unlikely that the three survivors from the *Essex*
went ashore for the festivities. They would have been much
too weak from their ordeal. On June 1 seven weeks after the
Surrey departed Pitcairn Island, the ship anchored in Sydney
Harbor, Australia. The two American castaways worked
their way to London and eventually arranged their passage
back to Nantucket. Soon after his return to England in June
of 1823, the third crew member, Thomas Chappel, was interviewed by a writer from the Religious Tract Society, which
published the following year an account of his shipwreck and
survival.

Some twenty years later a young aspiring American
writer, Herman Melville, was on board the whaling ship
Acushnet in the Central Pacific when she rendezvoused with
another Nantucket whaler. The fate of the *Essex* had been a
constant topic among the crew in their forecastle conversa-
tions. To the American's surprise, who should be on board
the other ship but Owen Chase's sixteen-year-old son.
Melville sought him out and questioned him at length about
his father's ordeal. Chase excused himself, went to his sea
chest, and brought back a copy of his father's book, *A
Narrative of the Most Extraordinary and Distressing Shipwreck of the Whaleship Essex*.

Melville borrowed the book. It changed him profoundly.
"The reading of this wondrous story upon the landless sea
and close to the very latitude of the shipwreck had a surpris-

ing effect upon me," he recalled later. Like the irritating grain of sand inside the oyster that eventually becomes a pearl, the story of the *Essex* was to lodge in Melville's imagination and slowly developed over the years into the world's greatest sea novel, *Moby Dick*.

The *Essex* was not the only ship rammed and deliberately sunk by a whale. On August 20, 1851, the American whaling ship *Ann Alexander* was struck just after dusk by a large bull sperm whale in the Central Pacific near the spot where the *Essex* had gone down. The captain and crew scrambled into boats, as water filled the hold. They were able to salvage only a few objects and no food. As they sat there in their boats, they must have thought of the *Essex* and the terrible events that followed her sinking. But this was 1851, not 1820, and the Central Pacific swarmed with whaling ships. Two days later they sighted a ship and were rescued. Five months later the New Bedford whaler *Rebecca Simms* harpooned and killed the whale. He was old and diseased. In his head they found buried large splinters. And embedded in the blubber on his side they discovered the metal heads of two harpoons, both bearing the initials of the *Ann Alexander*.

In November of 1851 copies of *Moby Dick* appeared in the bookstores. The newspapers had recently carried stories of the sinking of the *Ann Alexander*. A friend wrote the author about the remarkable coincidence. Melville replied: "I [have] no doubt it *is* Moby Dick. Ye Gods, what a commentator is this *Ann Alexander* whale." And then he added: "I wonder if my evil art has raised the monster."

Of the five survivors of the *Essex* who had been in the boats, all returned to the sea again, and died in old age. The effects of the ordeal, however, were never really shaken by two of the men.

Pollard's reputation was in no way tainted by either the sinking of the first ship he commanded by a whale nor the subsequent cannibalism. The mother of Owen Coffin, however, broke off all relations with him afterwards. Within a few months of his return to Nantucket, he was in command of another whaling ship, the *Two Brothers*, the same ship that had carried him back from Valparaiso. He sailed from Nantucket on November 12, 1821. Five months later he was in the Hawaiian Islands where the ship ran aground a coral reef and sank. Once again Pollard found himself in an open boat. Fortunately, another whaling ship, the *Martha*, rescued him and his men just a few days later. This second accident marked the end of his career at sea. He was 31 years old. "Now I am utterly ruined," he told those who would listen at Honolulu. "No owner will ever trust me with a whaler again, for all will say I am an unlucky man."

Pollard returned to Nantucket on April 27, 1825. Able to find employment only as a nightwatchman, he stalked the dark, fogbound streets of his town, a ghostly figure harboring a tale too fearful to endure. He died on January 7, 1870, at the age of seventy-eight. The site of his grave is unknown. No portrait of him survives.

An obituary in the local paper summed Pollard up thusly: 'He was still a young man when he retired from the sea and closed the strange, eventful part of his life. For more than forty years he has resided permanently among us; and now leaves the record of a good and worthy man as his legacy to us who remain."

Only one incident in his later life has been saved. In July of 1851 Melville visited Nantucket, curious to meet the captain whose story had done so much to shape his novel, *Moby Dick*. They conversed together quietly in Pollard's home. Later Melville wrote in the margin of his copy of Chase's book: "To the islanders he was a nobody—to me, the most impressive man, tho' wholly unassuming, even humble, that I ever encountered."

Owen Chase, Pollard's first mate, went on to become the historian of the tragedy of the *Essex*, perhaps hoping to earn some money for his distressed family. Within months of his return to Nantucket, he had penned an account of the ship's sinking and the ordeal at sea afterwards. (Or more likely he told his story to a ghostwriter.) A New York publisher brought out the slim volume later the next year. The book was not reviewed and disappeared almost immediately.

After bearing Chase a son and a daughter, Margaret Gardner died in 1824. A year later Chase married Nancy Joy, the widow of Matthew P. Joy, the second mate of the *Essex* and the first of the crew to die. He captained a Nantucket whaling ship, the *Winslow*, from 1825 to 1830. Then he became the captain of the *Charles Carroll* in 1833. His second wife died after giving birth to two more children. In 1836 Chase was married for the third time; his wife, Eunice Chadwick, was considerably younger than he. On August 30, 1836, Chase set off on another whaling voyage, one that would keep him at sea for three and a half years. Sixteen months later Eunice gave birth to a son. Chase received the news while at sea and, upon his return, he sued for divorce on the grounds of adultery. His wife did not contest the suit, and Chase was awarded a divorce on July 7, 1840. In 1863 he announced his retirement. By that time he was quite prosperous, having invested successfully in several stock ventures and some Nantucket real estate.

In the final years of his life the ordeal in the whaleboat after the loss of the *Essex* came back to haunt Chase. Fantasies of starvation tormented him mercilessly. He demanded that all food for his kitchen be purchased in double quantities, and he hid the extra in his attic. Chase died on March 7, 1869.

Shortly after the turn of the century a young woman, curious about the *Essex*, approached a daughter of Benjamin Lawrence, one of the survivors. The old woman listened patiently to her request for details concerning her father's experiences in Owen Chase's whale boat. Then, after a silence, she said quietly:

"Miss Molly, here in Nantucket we never mention the *Essex*."

CHAPTER FOUR

William Mariner:

The Boy Chief of the Tonga Islands

Ever since Ferdinand Magellan made his epic voyage of discovery through the Pacific in the early sixteenth century, the European immigrant has played a major role in the cultures of the South Seas islands. The historians have concentrated on the traders, missionaries, and colonial officials while largely ignoring the importance of the beachcombers, who were the first of these immigrants to settle on the Pacific islands. An exception is the Australian scholar H.E. Maude who in his study, *Of Islands and Men*, wrote of the early Pacific beachcombers: "One has to remember that conditions in the islands at the time were those of the frontier . . . and the beachcombers were the spearhead [of European culture], the first pioneers, the counterpart of Turner's Indianized hunters, trappers, and squaw-men living beyond the pale of Western civilization."

Like the legendary mountain men of the American West, the early beachcomber survived and prospered in part because of his ability to slough off his own cultural identity in favor of adopting the customs, dress, and language of his hosts. For example, the American sailor James O'Connell, shipwrecked on Ponape for three years in the early 1830s, gained high status in the island society and married the chief's daughter after he allowed his body to be elaborately tattooed in the native fashion. Beachcombers, thus, stood in sharp contrast to missionaries, government officials, and other later arrivals who considered themselves culturally superior to the islanders with whom they dealt.

Beachcombing in the South Seas is as old as Pacific exploration itself. History records the first beachcomber as Gonçalo de Vigo, who in 1522 deserted from Magellan's ship, the *Trinidad*, on an island in the Marianas group. A group of islanders befriended him and took him along on a 450-mile passage to Guam. There he lived for four years until he was discovered by the astonished crew of a Spanish ship.

The true heyday of beachcombing in the Pacific did not arrive until the advent of commercial shipping in the late eighteenth century. Then began a period of Pacific history that for violence, adventure, and colorful characters was only equalled many years later by the American Wild West. The first wave of beachcombers consisted entirely of sailors. Some of these were victims of shipwrecks, but by the 1830s hundreds of sailors each year were deserting British and American whaling ships in the Pacific. Some deserted because they could not stand the prospect of another year or more aboard a ship in the vastness of the Pacific. Others were forced off by cruel captains and wretched living conditions. Many were enticed by the beauty of the islands, the ease of life there, and the sexual freedom of the Polynesians, what novelist James Michener has called the "erotic mist" that hangs over the Pacific islands.

The island communities of Polynesia historically were highly receptive to the assimilation of foreigners and welcomed the European beachcombers. Many island societies regarded the first Europeans to reach them as supernatural beings, an identification often facilitated by preexisting myths and legends concerning the return of gods or ancestral spirits.

When Captain Samuel Wallis of the *Dolphin* discovered Tahiti in June 1767, he ordered the ship's cannons fired after hundreds of islanders sailed out to meet him. They fled in terror, crying out *"E Atua haere mai,* It's the god that's come." Later they described the British vessel as a floating island inhabited by a supernatural order of beings at whose directions the lightning flashed, the thunder roared, and the destroying demon slew, with instantaneous but invisible strokes, the bravest of warriors.

On Tonga the islanders called the first Europeans to land there *"ko e vaka no papalangi,"* which translates loosely as "men who burst from the sky." And in some of the southern islands in the Society group, the natives believed that the whites were the long-lost, fair-skinned children of their god Tangaroa, whose return had been prophesized for many generations.

Perhaps nowhere is this more dramatically apparent than in the death of Captain James Cook on Hawaii on that fateful day of February 14, 1779. His death marked an end to the first great phase of Pacific exploration. However, he may have died as a ritual sacrifice of a god to assure a bountiful harvest. In a series of religious celebrations before the killing, the Hawaiian priests put the English captain through the customary rites of welcome to Lono, their god associated with natural growth and human reproduction. As Marshall Shalins has argued brilliantly in *Islands of History:* "As the priest Koa'a and Lt. King held his arms outstretched and the appropriate sacrifices were made, Cook indeed became the image of Lono, a duplicate of the crosspiece icon (constructed of wood staves) which is the appearance of the god. . . . [His] death at Hawaiian hands just a few weeks later could be thus described as the ritual sequel. . . . Cook was transformed from the divine beneficiary of the sacrifice to its victim."

By the end of the eighteenth century the islanders had discovered that Europeans were people, like themselves. But they had also learned to value them as expert artisans and craftsmen who possessed such marvels as metal tools and the skills to use them in amazing ways.

The early beachcombers who claimed these skills quickly ingratiated themselves with Pacific societies and became indispensable political and economic assets. They alone had the skills to repair and maintain the precious guns and to fashion into useful tools such trade items as nails, spikes, and hoop-iron. They were also expected to expound at gatherings large and small on the nature of the white man's country, his customs, religion, economic system, and technology.

In addition, beachcombers often acted as intermediaries between visiting ships and the local island communities. When the American naval captain, David Porter, of the frigate *Essex* spent considerable time at the Marquesas Islands in 1813, he found an English beachcomber named Wilson who became invaluable as a go-between. After ten years on Nuku Hiva, he was fluent in the local language and well acquainted with Marquesan customs. He had also allowed his entire body to be covered with elaborate tattoos. At first Porter was shocked at the sight of a white man who had gone so completely native, but he soon concluded he was "an inoffensive, honest, good-hearted fellow, well disposed to render every service in his power. He became indispensably necessary to us, and without his aid I should have succeeded badly on the island. His knowledge of the people, and the ease with which he spoke their language, removed all difficulties in our intercourse with them."

The early beachcombers profoundly affected the Pacific island societies. Maude observed, "When the Europeans first arrived, the islanders had little knowledge of the use of any article not forming part of their own material culture, much less how to mend or make them. It was mainly the beachcombers who first taught them the manual arts and left as their legacy innumerable skilled craftsmen able to turn their hands to anything from building a boat to mending a gun lock."

Archibald Campbell lived in the Hawaiian Islands for over a year in 1809-10 and was amazed at the impact of several European beachcombers on that society in just a few years:

> It is astonishing how soon they acquire the useful arts from their visitors. Many of the natives are employed as carpenters, coopers, blacksmiths, and tailors, and do their work as perfectly as Europeans. In the king's force there are none but native

blacksmiths; they had been taught by the armorer of a ship, who quitted the island when I was there.

Sometimes beachcombers filled niches in island society in unexpected ways. In the 1830s when Queen Pomare on Moorea learned of the Jewish dietary laws, she appointed a Jewish sailor named Solomon from an American ship to be her Royal Keeper of the Pigs. This was a position comparable to the American Secretary of the Treasury, for pigs functioned then as the chief measure of a person's prestige and power in Tahitian society. Two years later Solomon married the queen's daughter and founded a family that has continued to be a major force in Tahitian society to the present day.

Island chiefs often tempted sailors to desert their ships, using local girls to seduce them ashore and hide them until the ship had sailed. If a captain made a fuss, the chief made a show of searching for the fugitive while actually warning him to stay hidden deep in the bush. Sometimes the beachcomber had little choice but to cooperate with his hosts. "The oven," a Fijian chief once remarked, "is a great persuader."

The political impact of beachcombers on Pacific societies was also far-reaching. On their own, the Pacific islanders had achieved a balance between defensive and offensive warfare that largely precluded the formation of any large-scale political units. European firearms quickly changed all that, radically modifying the way islanders waged war on one another. Beachcombers played a critical role in this modern warfare, maintaining and often firing the guns in the service of their island chiefs.

The mutineers from the *Bounty* established King Pomare's ascendancy in two battles fought in 1790 on the island of Tahiti. In that same year King Kamehameha seized several muskets and a cannon from the ship *Fair American*, kidnapped several sailors to operate them, and within a short time had brought all the Hawaiian islands under his control. In Fiji in 1809 the beachcomber Charles Savage, using guns salvaged from two ships wrecked on a nearby reef, established the ascendancy of the Fijian chief Mbau over the other islands.

Sometimes a chief found his need for Western weapons and metal goods so acute that he would kidnap sailors from a visiting whaling vessel and hold them for ransom. In the Tongan Islands in July of 1823 a sailor from the whaler *Fanny* was seized by natives and ransomed for "6 muskets, 3 cutlasses, 1 grind stone, 1 carpenter's vice, 20 bags of powder, and 100 musket balls," according to the ship's log.

The beachcombers were invariably men. One exception was Elizabeth Morey, an American woman whose ship, the *Duke of Portland*, was seized by natives from one of the eastern Fiji islands. The crew was killed and eaten, but Morey was spared. She became the wife of a local chief and lived with him until September 30, 1804, when she saved the American ship *Union* from being captured and so effected her escape.

By the mid-nineteenth century the missionary, trader, and government official had driven the beachcomber out of all the major island groups. He had ceased to be an influential figure in Pacific society, except on the most remote islands. By the end of the century, the beachcomber was regarded as little more than the hobo of the Pacific.

But as a figure of popular imagination, the beachcomber has loomed large in myth and fantasy. For over a century he has inspired countless thousands of travelers to go to the Pacific in search of their own Isle of Dreams, that unprofaned sanctuary, an island removed from the haunts of man where one may dwell in tranquility, happiness, and security amid a closeness to nature.

The American writer Robert Dean Frisbie, who in 1924 settled on Pukapuka in the northern Cook Islands, perhaps best summed up the perpetual faith of the beachcomber when he wrote: "Everything is dreamlike here. The island itself is a dream come true, so that romanticists who are patient enough and adventurous enough may see vindicated their faith in lonely lands beyond the farthest horizons."

In 1816 London booksellers began displaying a two-volume set with the unwieldy title, *An Account of the Natives of the Tonga Islands in the South Pacific with an Original Grammar and Vocabulary of Their Language.* Opposite the title page was an engraved portrait of the author, a handsome young warrior, his body draped in a classic Polynesian sarong, his right hand clutching a vicious barbed spear. He had been a powerful chief, a celebrated warrior, and an influential landowner in Tongan society. But what was most remarkable was that he was English.

His name was William Mariner, and he had lived through a set of adventures more improbable than the wildest romantic fantasies of Lord Byron or Sir Walter Scott. He epitomized the early beachcomber at his best. As a fifteen-year-old cabin boy, he had become a castaway in 1806 after Tongan cannibals seized his ship and massacred his shipmates. But this young man was spared to become an adopted son of the most powerful chief in the Tongan Islands. Mariner had sloughed off his identity as a British subject, learned the language, customs, and manners of his captors, and lived among them for four extraordinary years. An enthusiastic public quickly bought out all copies of his book, and Mariner, now established as a stockbroker in the London financial community, found himself a celebrity.

William Mariner was born in London on September 10, 1791, to Magnus Mariner, a shipowner, who had commanded a naval vessel during the American Revolutionary War. His boyhood was spent beside the busy Thames River in an area of small docks, wharves, timber yards, breweries, and ships' chandlers serving the bustling shipping traffic plying between London and the sea. As a youth, he showed a keen interest in travel books and often remarked to his parents and friends "how much he would like to live among savages and meet with strange occurrences," a wish that was remarkably prophetic in light of his experiences a few years later. When he turned thirteen, both he and his father were eager for him to start a career at sea. However, his mother was opposed, preferring instead for her son the safety of a desk job in the office of a London solicitor.

But barely six weeks later, Captain Duck, who had formerly served his apprenticeship under Magnus Mariner, visited him at home to bid goodbye. He was about to sail on the *Port au Prince* with instructions from the owners to cruise the Atlantic plundering Spanish ships and then to enter the Pacific to hunt whales.

Young William listened eagerly to Duck's confident expectations of a speedy success and grand adventures and was smitten with a desire to join the ship. An agreement was quickly drawn up. He would go along as Duck's cabin boy, his chief responsibility being to keep the ship's log. On February 12, 1805, when the *Port au Prince* sailed from Gravesend Harbor, Mariner was on board.

Mariner's new home was a three-masted square-rigger of nearly 500 tons. She mounted twenty-four nine-pounders and twelve-pounders along with eight twelve-pound carronades on the quarter deck. She was a formidable vessel. She carried eighty-five men, far more than needed so as to have extra men on hand to crew captured enemy vessels.

The *Port au Prince* departed England under a double commission from her owner, first as a privateer sailing under a letter of marque and reprisal, and secondly as a whaler. Duck's instructions were absurdly rigid, permitting him no discretion. He was to raid Spanish shipping and coastal towns along the coast of South America but only up to a certain latitude—the Equator at the Galápagos Islands—and then he was to begin whaling and cease privateering.

The *Port au Prince* cruised along the Atlantic coast of South America but found no ships. Duck ordered the ship around Cape Horn and into the Pacific. There their luck changed. Numerous Spanish ships and vulnerable coastal towns were theirs for the taking. The richest prize was the small city of Ilo on the southern coast of Peru. The English quickly took possession of the town and looted the buildings of anything of value. The church yielded a rich booty of silver candlesticks, chalices, crucifixes, and statues. Afterwards they burned the city to the ground.

The *Port au Prince* sailed north to the Galápagos Islands, made an unsuccessful search for whales, and then returned to the more lucrative business of capturing Spanish ships and raiding undefended coastal towns. One victim was the small town of Tola at the mouth of the Rio Santiago on the coast of modern-day Ecuador. Duck and his men found few riches there. But the Spanish commander proved agreeable and bought off the English privateers with presents of food and

wine. He had a daughter, about sixteen, who had just completed her education at a nearby convent. She spoke decent
English. And soon she and Mariner became friendly. He
boasted to her of their sacking of Ilo and the loot they had
captured. She was horrified at his account of the church they
had pillaged. She told him that after such sacrilege, God
would take his revenge and the *Port au Prince* would never
return to England. Mariner laughed at her prediction and
brought her a large cheese, a rare item on the coast. The girl,
in return, presented him with gold buckles from her shoes,
but warned him he would not live long to enjoy them.

They were now on the Equator and embroiled in an impossible situation. Duck's orders were at this latitude to
cease raiding Spanish shipping which had proven so successful and to take up whaling. But the owner could never have
foreseen there would be so few whales at this time and so
many Spanish ships. Duck wanted to ignore the original orders and continue as privateers. But the owner's orders gave
James Brown, the whaling master, a veto over Duck's com-
mands when the ship was north of the Equator. Brown was
adamant and Duck finally had to give in to him. They sailed
north up the Mexican coast, searching for whales.

Eventually, the *Port au Prince* reached Cedros Island off
Baja California, drawn by its vast population of elephant
seals. On August 7 they rendezvoused with the American
ship, the *O'Caen*, from Boston and learned that three days'
sail up the coast lay a very rich prize, a Spanish sloop of war
laden with tributes for the viceroy of Peru. Duck and the
crew immediately voted to ignore the owner's orders and set
out to capture the vessel. They never reached their prize.
Duck died of malarial fever three days later and was buried
on a remote stretch of beach on Cedros Island.

The command of the *Port au Prince* passed to Brown, as
incompetent a captain ever to sail the Pacific. From this time
on everything seemed to go badly. The ship began leaking
profusely, and the men grew visibly more discontented each
day. Brown ordered them to the San Benitos Islands, a small
collection of barren, rocky islands to the northwest. The
rocky beaches there were home to thousands of sea lions.
The crew spent three weeks engaged in the bloody task of
clubbing the animals to death, skinning and salting their

skins. Soon they had some 8,338 skins stowed away in the ship's hold.

The leakage in the *Port au Prince* continued to worsen. Brown ordered the ship to the Hawaiian Islands for repairs. Ten days later they sighted the great mountains of the main island and soon afterwards sailed into the bay at Honolulu Bay, accompanied by scores of native outrigger canoes. Two months had passed since they had last filled their water casks and three weeks since they had last enjoyed fresh provisions. Now ahead lay a land of plenty, of fresh pork, green vegetables, delicious fruits, rushing streams, and beautiful women.

Hawaii at this time was under the rule of King Kamehameha I. Twenty-five years earlier when Captain James Cook had discovered the islands, there were three separate kingdoms. Kamehameha determined to unite all the islands under his command. He had seen the power the white men brought with them in the form of muskets and cannons and knew that with these weapons he could easily subdue his neighbors. Several beachcombers provided him with weapons and taught his warriors how to use them. Then Kamehameha set out on his conquest, attacking and defeating the other two kings whose warriors were armed only with spears, clubs, bows, and arrows. He was proclaimed king of all the Hawaiian islands in 1795.

Kamehameha refused the *Port au Prince* permission to land. Not long before, an American ship had called there with one crewmember sick with measles. The disease swept like a plague through the island population, killing hundreds of Hawaiians. The British ship dropped anchor in the outer harbor and traded with the Hawaiians for fresh provisions. Even though he refused to allow the English crew to go ashore, Kamehameha paid repeated visits to the *Port au Prince* and quickly made friends with her crew and officers. He met the young Mariner and quickly took a liking to him, asking him to come ashore, live with him in his palace, and be his secretary. It was a marvelous opportunity. But Mariner was eager to get back to his parents' home. He also knew that if he left the *Port au Prince* in Hawaii he would forfeit his share of the captured Spanish goods, the skins, and barrels of oil. And so he thanked the king for his generous offer but declined.

For two weeks the *Port au Prince* took on provisions. The water casks were filled, live hogs and chickens were brought on board, along with baskets of sweet potatoes, taro, plantains, coconuts, and other fruits. Brown's plan was to sail to Tahiti, reprovision there and do more extensive repairs on the hull, and then head on to Sydney. The ship's company was now short-handed, so Brown hired eight Hawaiian natives who had worked on British or American ships before and knew some English.

On October 26 the *Port au Prince* sailed from the beautiful bay at Honolulu and pointed her bow south toward the Society Islands. Soon afterwards she sprang another serious leak. On the way to Hawaii the leakage had been at the rate of seventeen feet in the hold in twenty-four hours, and that was bad enough. Now the sea water poured in at the rate of nineteen feet a day, or nine and a half inches an hour. The crew had to work the pumps around the clock, a punishing ordeal. Furthermore, steps had to be taken to lessen the straining of the heavily-laden vessel, as she rolled dangerously through the swells before the winds. First, some of the cannons from the upper deck were moved below into the hold. Then all the heavy tryworks of brick and metal, the furnaces and cauldrons used to convert blubber into oil were tossed over the side, much to the relief of the crew.

Brown had none of the navigational skills of Captain Duck and missed Tahiti by a wide distance. He then ordered the ship toward the Tongan Islands, named the Friendly Islands by Captain Cook. Brown was not worried. The islands were reported to be lush and agreeable and the natives hospitable, hence their name. The *Port au Prince* dropped anchor in late November 1806, off the island of Lifuka in the very place where Cook had stopped some thirty years before.

The Tongan Islands are a collection of coral atolls, formed into three main groups stretching over 180 miles of the Pacific east of Fiji. These are the atolls of romance and fantasy, each one crowned with a forest of coconut palms, feathered tops tossing in the trade winds, and encircled by a coral reef like a loose-fitting necklace. The Tongans had evolved the most sophisticated and comprehensive agricultural system of all the Pacific islands. The people lived in houses scattered among the plantations rather than in villages. A network of spacious roads crisscrossed the larger islands. Reed fences separated the plantations. Inside the fenced enclosures crops were cultivated, of which yams and plantains, regularly spaced at intervals of two or three paces, formed the major part.

Captain James Cook was thoroughly impressed with the Tongan countryside. "I thought I was transported into one of the most fertile plains in Europe, here was not an inch of wasted ground," he wrote in his journal during his 1773 visit. "Nature, assisted by a little art, nowhere appears in a more flourishing state than at this isle."

Settlers from Fiji had arrived in the Tongan Islands some 3,000 years earlier. They brought with them many of the food crops as well as chickens, pigs, and dogs, the latter a favorite food source among the island people. The Tongans were great sailors, and regularly made long trading voyages to Fiji and Samoa in search of wooden bowls, fine mats, pottery, weapons, and decorative red feathers. Sperm whale teeth served as a medium of exchange. And like all other Pacific island societies, the Tongans lacked draft animals, wheels, propelling oars, metals, and any system of writing.

Captain James Cook had called there on three separate voyages. In 1777 he discovered Lifuka and named it the Friendly Island because of the warm reception his people had received from the natives. Later Europeans applied the name to the entire Tongan group, a fact that proved the undoing of many a trusting ship's captain and crew in later years. What Cook had not known was that as he and his men enjoyed a Tongan feast and dance celebration, a dozen chiefs conspired to murder them and seize their ship. The plot fell through at the last minute, and Cook departed Lifuka without ever suspecting how close he had come to death. Now thirty years later the same scene was to be replayed, but this time with catastrophically different results.

The *Port au Prince* dropped anchor off Lifuka Island in the late afternoon. The natives appeared to live up to their name. That evening Brown welcomed on board several chiefs and their warriors, bearing a large barbecued hog and many dressed yams as presents for the ship's company. Their interpreter was a Hawaiian named Kuikui, who had sailed to Manila on an American whaling ship and then to Tonga. He introduced the head chief, Finau, whom he described as a great man. He assured the English captain that he would find only hospitable people and an abundance of good food on Lifuka. He also advised him not to worry about the numerous heavily armed warriors crowding the deck because they had come aboard merely out of curiosity, having never seen such a large ship before.

Two Hawaiian sailors took Brown aside and advised utmost caution. The Tongans could not be trusted, they warned him, and probably intended to seize the ship. The Englishman, who had been charmed by the soft-spoken chiefs, shrugged off the warnings as silly nonsense. Later while Brown politely served several chiefs some brandy in his cabin, the Hawaiians were advised by the Tongans that they would be much safer if they spent the next several days ashore.

The next day a larger number of Tongan chiefs and warriors assembled on board the *Port au Prince*, armed with clubs and spears, and acted belligerently toward the ship's company. Again Brown was warned of the threatening nature of the natives. This time he asked the Tongans to get rid of their weapons, which they did. And then Brown in turn foolishly ordered all the ship's muskets and boarding-pikes stored below as a gesture of good will.

On the following morning, Monday, December 1, some 300 heavily armed warriors crowded on board the English ship for the third and last time. Brown went ashore at the invitation of the chiefs, still convinced of the friendly nature of his hosts. Now everything was in place to seize the ship and its valuable cargo of guns, gun powder, and metal. On strict orders from Brown, none of the sailors were armed. The Tongans struck. Dixon, the first mate, was the first to die. He tried to stop another group from coming on board when a stocky warrior quickly moved in behind him, raised a heavy war club, and shattered his skull with a single blow. Within a few seconds the other Tongans closed for the attack. The unarmed British sailors offered little resistance and were quickly slaughtered.

Hearing the sounds of the massacre, young Mariner

peeped out of a hatch and saw that the ship was lost. He ducked down and sought out the cooper, the only other Englishman still alive on the vessel. They consulted and quickly decided to explode the magazine and destroy the *Port au Prince* rather than be captured alive. They hurried to the powder room, only to discover the door blocked by a great mound of boarding-pikes and muskets.

As the sounds of the struggle on deck died away, Mariner decided to meet his fate without flinching. The two surrendered in the captain's cabin to several warriors, who escorted them on deck. The Englishmen were appalled by what they saw.

"Upon the companion a short squat naked figure, about fifty years of age, was seated, with a seaman's jacket soaked in blood, thrown over one shoulder; on the other rested his iron-wood club, splattered with blood and brains," Mariner recalled. "On another part of the deck there lay twenty-two bodies perfectly naked, and arranged side by side in regular order, but so dreadfully bruised and battered about the heads, that only two could be recognized."

Several warriors hurried Mariner ashore. On the beach he saw the bloody bodies of Brown and three other sailors. An old man, club in hand, approached the boy and through gestures made him understand that they intended to kill and roast him that afternoon. The youth was stripped naked and marched to a village at the far end of the island. An island woman, out of compassion, gave him an apron made from ti leaves to hide his nakedness.

In the late afternoon Mariner was taken before the high chief, Finau Ulukalala II, the man who had organized the seizure of the *Port au Prince* and the most powerful man in all the Tongan islands. Although he had no way of knowing it, Finau had taken an extraordinary liking to the cabin boy when he had first seen him earlier on the ship. He thought he must be a young chief of great importance in his own country.

Now at this first formal meeting in the chief's spacious hut, Finau greeted Mariner courteously as an equal. The island ruler towered above the English boy—six foot two inches tall, stout and muscular, with jet-black curly hair, a prominent lower jaw, and high cheek bones. "All his features were well developed and declared a strong and energetic mind," Mariner wrote much later. "His actions were, for the most part, steady and determined and directed to some well studied purpose. He appeared almost constantly in deep thought and did not often smile."

Finau observed that the boy was dirty and ordered one of his female attendants to take him to a nearby pool and bathe him. Then she anointed his body with sandalwood oil, and another woman brought him some roasted pork and cooked yams; soon afterward he fell into a deep sleep.

The next morning Mariner visited the beach and met with several other crewmembers who had also escaped the massacre. They had the good luck to have been ashore at the time. In all, half the crew, twenty-six in number, had survived along with the eight hands from the Hawaiian Islands. The bodies of the twenty-six sailors who had been slaughtered were buried, and a cache of Spanish silver coins found in the ship were scattered over their graves, as the Tongans, naturally, were ignorant of their value.

Finau took Mariner and several other sailors back on board the *Port au Prince* and ordered them to sail her through the reef and ground her on the beach. For the next several days the Tongans swarmed over the ship, pulling out the nails, stripping the iron from her upper parts, and knocking the hoops off the casks in the hold. More important for Finau's ambitions were the guns and cannons. He ordered several of the heavy cannons dragged ashore with the casks of gun powder from the magazine. He also allowed young Mariner to take ashore his sea chest with his belongings, including the ship's precious log, ashore. On December 9 the Tongans torched the *Port au Prince* in order to get at the rest of her iron work more easily.

Afterwards most of the whites were transported to nearby islands. Mariner and five companions remained on Lifuka. In the days that followed the young Englishman made his residence in the royal compound inside a reed fence. Finau's wives, attendants, and bodyguards lived in the smaller houses alongside the palace. Retainers came and went at regular intervals. Finau advised the boy not to go out of the compound unescorted until his status within the local community had been clarified. Otherwise, he warned, he ran the risk of death or injury at the hands of the lower class of Tongan society who took every opportunity to insult him.

Mariner created quite a sensation when he produced a watch from his sea chest. He wound it up and passed it around. The islanders listened intently to its ticking sound, murmuring in awe, "It is alive!" They then pinched and hit it, expecting it would squeak in protest. The Englishman through sign language and his rudimentary vocabulary of Tongan words explained its purpose. The islanders were astounded. "Is it an animal or a plant?" they wanted to know. When Mariner told them it was neither but rather a manufactured item, they exclaimed in a chorus, "What an ingenious people!"

But the Tongans found other things about the English culture beneath contempt. Finau and his associates were startled and amused when Mariner and his mates finally worked up the courage to ask how they were supposed to eat when not specifically invited. He recorded the response:

> Finau inquired how food was obtained in England. When he heard that every man purchased the necessary supplies for himself and his family, and that his friends only partook by invitation, he laughed at what he called the ill nature and selfishness of the white people. He advised [Mariner] that he had nothing to do when he felt himself hungry but to go into any house where eating was going forward, sit himself down without invitation, and partake with the company. After this, when any stranger came into their houses to eat with them, they would say jocosely, "No! We shall treat you after the manner of the papalagis. Go home and eat what you have got and we shall eat what we have got!"

Mariner had arrived in Tonga at a critical juncture in its history. When Cook had visited in 1777, the whole of the Tongan islands had been under the rule of the despotic chief Tuku-aho, who ruled from the island of Tongatapu. All the other chiefs paid tribute to him. The islands had been peaceful then. But young Tongan warriors traveled regularly to the

Fijian islands to the west where they eagerly embraced the vices of that society: blackened faces, war dress, cannibalism, ritual murder, and rebellion.

On April 21, 1799, Finau and several other chiefs assassinated Tuku-aho, plunging the surrounding islands into chaos. Each chief set up his own petty state, which he garrisoned with heavily fortified stockades, and warred upon his neighbors. The constant skirmishes made farming impossible. Human flesh became a necessary staple of the Tongan diet. Squads of young toughs went on hunting expeditions near enemy villages.

Finau bemoaned the devastating effects of civil strife upon his island. "I have seen with sorrow the wide destruction occasioned by the unceasing war carried on," he complained to the young Mariner. "We have indeed been doing a great deal, but what is the result? The land is depopulated. It is overgrown with weeds, and there is nobody to cultivate it. Had we remained peaceful, it would have been populous still. What madness!"

Out of this chaos Finau Ulukalala II emerged as one of the country's most powerful chiefs. Physically, he was imposing, even at fifty-five—tall, muscular, handsome with jet black curly hair. He rarely smiled and spoke only after careful deliberation. In his youth he had acquired a reputation as one of his society's greatest warriors. Mariner quickly learned that Finau was a highly effective, if ruthless, leader with a quick intelligence and an insatiable curiosity.

Finau invited Mariner to accompany him on a hunting expedition for rats on a nearby island. The Tongans used bows and arrows, weapons that had recently been introduced from Fiji. Through hand gestures and helped by the rudimentary understanding of the Tongan language that Mariner had begun to acquire, Finau confided his ambitions to the young boy. He wanted to attack and subdue the nearby islands and thereby become the king of all the Tongan islands. But he needed the whites and their knowledge of muskets and cannons to make his plans work. This would be Mariner's job, he explained. Together, as equals, they would go into battle and subdue the enemies of the mighty Finau.

Mariner was not the first European to enter into service with Finau. A few years earlier George Vason, a missionary turned beachcomber, had decided to go native. He adopted Tongan dress and took three high-class women as his wives. Purchasing a fifteen-acre plot, he worked hard to establish a model plantation of plantains, taro, and sugarcane. When civil war broke out after the assassination of Tuku-aho, he swore allegiance to Finau, allowed his body to be tattooed in the Tongan style, and rose to a high rank at his court. But the instability of Tongan politics worried him. When a missionary ship called at Vava'u in August 1801, Vason decided to quit the islands. He returned to England and became the warden of the Nottingham City jail.

Politics, Mariner quickly learned, would keep him and his fellow sailors in Tonga for a long, long time. Soon afterward Finau appointed one of his own wives, Mafi Habe, to be the boy's Tongan mother. This remarkable woman took care of Mariner as though he were one of her own children and became his tutor in all aspects of Tongan society and culture. Within a few months he was fluent in the islanders' language, customs, and manners.

Mariner had come to Mafi Habe a desperate European castaway. She turned him into a confident young Tongan chief, ready to play a pivotal role in the area's history. The English youth assumed the dress of Tongan men, the *vala* or skirt made from beaten tapa cloth that hung from the waist to the calf, fastened about the midriff with a brightly colored girdle.

Mariner, in turn, undertook to educate his Tongan friends in the British notion of morality. But it was the white man's magic of reading and writing that stunned Finau. He demanded a demonstration. He ordered the English boy to write on a piece of paper from the *Port au Prince* his name. Mariner accordingly wrote "FINAU." He then sent for another Englishman. When the man arrived, Finau told Mariner to turn his back. He handed the paper to the sailor and asked him what it meant. The man glanced at it and spoke the word "Finau." The chief was astonished. He snatched the paper back, turned it in around and over, examining it at length, and then exclaimed: "This is neither like myself nor anybody else! Where are my legs? How do you know it to be me?" In time the king came to understand. Writing, he decided, was a noble invention for whites but it would never do for the Tongan Islands. "There would be nothing but disturbances and conspiracies, and I could not be sure of my life another month."

Soon afterwards Finau formally adopted Mariner into his own household, appointing him a chief and giving him the Tongan name of Toki Ukamea, meaning the Iron Axe, after one of his favorite sons who was about the same age as Mariner when he died.

Mariner quickly came to learn the dark side of Tongan society—its brutality. He had his first exposure to it a few days after the *Port au Prince*'s seizure. Finau was outraged to discover a lower class man atop the ship cutting some iron away from a mast. He turned to a nearby Hawaiian shooting a musket off the deck and demanded he bring the man down. Without any hesitation, the Hawaiian raised his musket and fired. As the man crashed to the deck, breaking his thighs and fracturing his skull, Finau laughed heartily. Mariner never forgot the incident. Months later after he had become fluent in the local language, he asked the chief how he could have been so cruel to order the death of one of his subjects over such a trifling matter. He replied curtly that the man was a mere cook, a low and vulgar fellow whose death was of no consequence to any one.

On another occasion Finau demanded that Mariner bring a musket and shoot a demented old woman wandering about. She had become insane years before from excessive grief caused after her child was strangled as an offering to the gods. Finau wanted her killed because she had become a pest, but also to observe close up the effects of a musket ball. Mariner refused. But a few days later Finau ordered one of the Hawaiian crewmembers from the *Port au Prince* to shoot the old woman as she walked along a beach. This was quickly done. The ball struck her just as she bent over to pick up a shell. She screamed and fell dead into the surf. Mariner witnessed the killing from a distance.

Horror stories abounded about the chieftain on the nearby island of Tongatapu, an absolute monster of cruelty. He ordered that all twelve of his cooks must have their left arms severed above the elbows, not as punishment but rather as a sign for all to see that these men were his servants. Mariner later met one of the unfortunates who explained how his arm had been amputated. One warrior had pressed the edge of a stone axe against his upper arm, while another swung a heavy stone hammer. He reported that two of the cooks had died after the operation.

And, of course, there was the matter of cannibalism. When Cook had visited the islands thirty years before, the practice was unknown. The Tongans learned the practice from their neighbors on Fiji where man-meat was a highly prized gourmet dish. The Tongans ate their vanquished enemies only, except in times of great scarcity. A famine brought on by the civil wars at the end of the century had spread the practice throughout the islands. Mariner's island friends advised him that the hands were the choicest parts and generally reserved for the chiefs. Sometimes a chief would wear a necklace of smoked and dried human fingers to snack on, much as a modern man stuffs a couple of granola bars into his pocket before leaving home. And when a Tongan man cursed, he generally ordered the object of his anger to perform a variety of taboo acts connected to the eating of relatives: "Dig up your grandfather by moonlight and make soup of his bones; devour your mother; swallow the eyes of your uncle; suck the brains of your grandmother, etc."

He also learned that they considered the flesh of white men unhealthy. Some years before a group of Tongans from another island slew three Englishmen from a visiting boat, roasted them whole in great ovens as they did their pigs, and ate heartily of them. The next day all the participants in the feast fell ill with severe nausea and vomiting, and three actually died.

(As a footnote to the above, Ann Butcher, the tagalong mistress of a whaling ship captain, made history of a sort in 1814 when she became the only white woman who was ever eaten by Polynesians. Her ship called at Rarotonga in the Cook Islands a few hundred miles to the east of Tonga. The crew carelessly allowed themselves to get caught up in a local feud between rival chiefs. Several were killed, including Butcher, and the bodies were roasted in ovens. History does not record whether those islanders suffered any gastronomical upsets.)

Mariner also heard stories about the recent famine when

Tongans ambushed and murdered one another in order to get food. One story in particular horrified him:

> They still tell an anecdote of four brothers, who, in this time of scarcity, invited their aunt to come and partake of a large yam, which they said they had secretly procured. The poor woman, glad of the idea of getting something to eat and pleased with the kindness of her nephews, went to their house, where soon they dispatched her, and she herself formed the materials of a repast.

Finau began his preparations for a great war. He ordered vast quantities of weapons—clubs, spears, slings and stones, bows and arrows—stockpiled. All the great war canoes, some capable of carrying up to 100 warriors and their weapons, were repaired and new sails made. Mariner and his band of British sailors swore formal allegiance to Finau and promised they would fight to the death in support of his cause. Mariner ordered the ship's heavy cannons mounted on carriages. Scores of heavy shot were rounded up.

In the summer of 1807 Finau ordered his army to move against Tongatapu, seventy miles away. Mariner found himself with Finau at the head of a vast Tongan fleet of 170 war canoes and over 5,000 warriors. Most had discarded the traditional Tongan *vala* skirts, and wore instead the Fijian *mahi*—scanty loincloths. Their bodies had been elaborately tattooed from the navel line to the tops of their knees. Their faces and chests were painted in the fierce Fijian style to frighten their enemies. And their heads had been shaved, leaving a long tuft of hair tied upright on the crowns.

When the flotilla reached Tongatapu, Finau and his warriors began a siege of the great fortress at Nuku'alofa. Sitting atop a hill overlooking the sea, the fort was made of reinforced bamboo lattice and surrounded on the outside by deep ditches. The defensive perimeter was composed of two concentric circles of ten-foot-high vertical fencing separated by a dry moat. Nine-foot-square platforms stood every fifty feet around the fort's wall where defending warriors could stand and shoot arrows or throw stones down on their attackers.

The structure was virtually impregnable to the traditional Tongan siege methods and had resisted all assaults for eleven years.

The first wave of warriors landed on the shore. On a nearby reef Finau sat in a chair from the *Port au Prince* and directed the entire operation. A warrior blew a conch-shell horn to signal the start of hostilities. Several hundred defenders rushed from the fort to repel the invaders. Mariner quickly ordered his men into action. They formed a square, British fashion, and fired several musket volleys into the crowd of Tongatapu warriors, routing the attackers. Then he had the cannons, shot, and powder brought ashore.

Finau ordered his British sailors to bring their cannons into action. The four guns began a constant bombardment. The shot made only neat round holes in the wicker lattice. But Mariner explained to a disappointed Finau that the balls would wreak havoc inside. The chief then ordered his warriors to attack the fort. The outer defenses were easily taken. The warriors flung lighted torches inside the compound. The flames spread quickly from building to building. Within a few hours the warriors, clubs in hand, broke through the inner defenses and slaughtered every one in the fort. Escape was impossible. The warriors shouted their war cries as they murdered the wounded and looted the buildings. Defenseless women and children were dragged from hiding and gleefully clubbed to death.

Within a few hours the most formidable fortress in all the Tongan islands had fallen. When Finau entered the battle site, he was stunned at the dreadful carnage that Mariner's people had effected with their heavy cannons. The bodies of over 350 warriors lay scattered about, the victims of ricocheting cannon balls. Severed arms and legs littered the ground.

That evening a great victory celebration was held. Fifteen captives were clubbed to death. Several were roasted whole in earthen ovens, as though they had been pigs. The other bodies were cut into small pieces. The flesh was then washed in salt water, wrapped in banana leaves, and roasted under hot stones. Mariner refused to eat the human flesh offered him. Instead he fasted for three days until supply canoes brought fresh provisions from Lifuka.

Mariner urged Finau to follow up quickly on his victory and destroy all the forts on the island while the people were still fearful of the new guns. But such European tactics were contrary to the Tongan way. Finau consulted his priests on the most propitious action to take. They ordered him to re-build the Nuku'alofa fort, which was done after just two days' labor. Finau then withdrew his forces to Lifuka to await a time when his priests could tell him that the gods fa-vored a second campaign against his enemies.

About this time Finau's twenty-two-year-old son and heir, Moenga, returned from Samoa where his father had sent him five years earlier to advance his education. A brave war-rior, Moenga, nonetheless, lacked his father's ruthless ambi-tion. Mariner described him later as "well proportioned, athletic, and graceful. His whole exterior was calculated to win the esteem of the wise and the good." The two young men quickly became fast friends.

Finau had earlier chosen two young ladies, daughters of chiefs, for his son and immediately ordered a double wedding ceremony. The preparations for the wedding, and the feasting and dancing afterward, delayed Finau's war plans for another month.

As soon as the wedding ceremonies were finished, Finau assembled an army of 4,000 warriors. He then made a speech in which he declared that the Tongan mode of warfare was wrong and they would fight English-style. Henceforth, in-stead of running forward and retreating as soon as they en-countered opposition, they would stay together as a body and press forward, regardless of the opposition, until they had prevailed.

"And if any man sees the point of a spear advancing upon his breast," Finau told his troops, "he is not to run back like a coward but push forward upon it and, at the risk of his life, deal destruction on his foe."

Soon afterwards Finau moved against the island of Vava'u, accompanied by Mariner's small band of sailors and their four cannons. They arrived off the coast towards evening. Vava'u is quite different from all the other Tongan islands, an enormous plateau of coral limestone that has been lifted high out of the sea. The northern coast consists of several immense cliffs 600 feet high, while the cliffs on the southern coast are half the height but penetrated by numerous deep fjords.

Finau dispatched four canoes, manned by some of his finest warriors, with orders to get as close as they could to the fortress and kill whomever they could. Soon afterwards they returned with the bodies of three men they had slain. Finau and his priests were extremely pleased because it signalled they had the protection of the gods and could expect great success.

The fortress proved to be a formidable structure set atop a hill with sheer sides. Its extent seemed enormous to Mariner on the plain below. It was surrounded by broad earthworks dug from the red soil of this part of the island. Along the top of the fortifications numerous warriors, their bodies hideously painted, waved their spears and clubs and threatened Finau's warriors below.

Finau assembled his army and gave his orders—his men should keep themselves perfectly steady and not attack the enemies until they were quite close to them. As they approached the fortress, a shower of arrows rained down upon them. The four English cannons were finally brought up and began pounding the fort but with little success because of the height of the hilltop.

However, this time the two sides were more evenly matched, and Mariner's cannons failed to prove decisive. The war bogged down into inconclusive skirmishing and dragged on for several months. At last Finau resolved to gain his victory through diplomacy rather than warfare. He opened negotiations with the chief of Vava'u, who agreed to recognize Finau as his superior chief, thus allowing him to withdraw back to Lifuka without any loss of face.

But young Mariner found other uses for his time. Moenga had become not only his friend but his tutor, carefully instructing the young Englishman in such Tongan arts as the use of the club and spear, boxing, wrestling, swimming, diving, handling a canoe, and such social graces as dancing and singing. By the fall of 1809 after almost three years on Lifuka, Mariner had become in all respects a polished courtier in the Tongan court. He was *faka eiki*, or "chieflike," and was loved and respected by all who knew him.

Finau made his adopted son a landowner, granting him large holdings on the island of Vava'u and the powers of life and death over the thirteen men and eight women who lived there. And thus an eighteen-year-old English youth, who only a few years earlier had been a common cabin boy, found himself living out a romantic idyll on his own little island kingdom as one of the most highly regarded chiefs in all the Tongan islands.

Mariner was now at leisure to do as he wished. He decided to visit the nearby island of Tofua to investigate the stories he had heard regarding the grave of an English sailor who had been with Lieutenant William Bligh on the *Bounty*. The ship was on its way to the West Indies with a cargo of breadfruit plants collected in Tahiti. Vast columns of smoke and flame belched from Tofua's volcano as the *Bounty* sailed past on that fateful day of April 28, 1789. The crew, under the leadership of Fletcher Christian, mutinied and put Bligh and eighteen loyal crew members into a twenty-one foot long open boat and set them adrift, while they sailed the *Bounty* back to Tahiti. The dauntless Bligh made immediately for Tofua to get food and water and landed in a small cove. He began to trade with the islanders. More gathered. And soon the entire beach was filled with warriors ominously knocking stones together. Bligh was convinced they meant to attack. He ordered his men to return quickly to their boat, taking the provisions with them. John Norton, the quartermaster, paused on the beach to cast off the stern rope. Suddenly, the natives attacked, throwing their stones "like a shower of shot." Norton was knocked down by a Tongan carpenter who wanted his axe and beaten to death. Bligh cut the stern rope and so prevented the Tongans from hauling the boat back upon the shore. Because of that encounter he determined to proceed straight to the nearest European settlement at Timor and not risk a landing again on a populated shore.

Mariner had heard some of the details regarding the killing of Norton. But what intrigued him was what had happened to Norton's body after the rest of Bligh's group had escaped. Several islanders dragged it to a temple enclosure where it lay in the sun for three days before being buried. What awed the natives was that no grass ever grew again along the track where the body was dragged nor on the spot of ground where it lay before burial. Several islanders on Tofua guided Mariner to that place and showed him a bare track leading from the beach and at its end a patch of bare ground about the length and width of a man.

In his travels Mariner met a chief who with his wife had the distinction of being the first Tongans to visit Botany Bay, Australia. Their experiences were traumatic and shattered their illusions about the superiority of European life. They were guests at the governor's house. But he demanded they earn their keep by cleaning the house and grounds. In vain, they explained he was a chief back in Tonga and accustomed to having servants do all his menial labor. Unlike in Tonga, they found all the houses closed to them and no one would share their food with them. Nothing could be had without money, which could only be obtained in very small amounts for very long labor. When he complained that he was a chief, the whites told him that only money made a man a chief. Later he expressed his astonishment to Mariner that white men would work from morning to night just to get money.

Mariner relayed the man's experiences to Finau, who was curious to understand exactly what money represented in the white man's culture. When it was finally explained to him, he was flabbergasted. He told Mariner: "Certainly money is much handier and more convenient, but then, as it will not spoil by being kept, people will store it up, instead of sharing it out, as a chief ought to do, and thus become selfish. Whereas, if provisions were the principal property of a man, and it ought to be, as being the most useful and the most necessary, he could not store it up, for it would spoil, and so he would be obliged either to exchange it away for something useful or share it out with his neighbors and inferior chiefs and dependents for nothing." And he concluded by saying, "I understand now what it is that makes the papalangis so selfish—it is this money!"

Finau was now at the height of his powers. He finally secured control over Vava'u, not by open warfare but treachery. He called a truce and invited the opposing chiefs to a conference. While they all sat in a circle, drinking kava, Finau sprang a trap. Warriors jumped from the shadows. A dozen chiefs were quickly clubbed to death on a nearby beach. The others were tightly bound and set adrift in leaky canoes to await a more lingering death by drowning. Soon afterward the high chief of Tongatapu, weary of years of warfare, sent word to Finau acknowledging him as the supreme chief of all the Tongan islands. After ten years Finau had achieved his goal. The islands were now united. And he was their undisputed king.

But Finau's happiness lasted only a short time. He had long been known for his irreverent attitude toward the Tongan religion, its priests, and laws. When his beloved six-year-old daughter took deathly ill, the priests told the people that the gods would punish Finau for his arrogance and sacrilege by taking his daughter. She died shortly afterwards.

In a rage at the priests, Finau hurled insults at the gods and changed many of the traditional religious ceremonies at his daughter's funeral, even ordering mass fights, one of them a grim combat involving 1,500 women. Then he sent four of his most trusted warriors to seize and murder the high priest. But before this could be done, Finau himself was gravely stricken. Moenga in desperation ordered the sacrifice of one of his own children to appease the angry gods. But it did no good. Within twenty-four hours Finau was dead.

Moenga succeeded his father without any disturbance, initiating a sharp break with his father's warlike policies. He visited the various islands in his kingdom, pointing out to his people the enormous damage that a decade of constant warfare had cost them. He ordered them to take up farming once again and to return their lands to the former prosperity. Throughout this time Mariner was the new chief's constant companion.

All this drama came to an end quite suddenly later that same year. Mariner was returning to Vava'u from a nearby island when he saw in the sunset the sails of a ship. He ordered his three paddlers to change direction and promised them gifts of beads, axes, and spyglasses. The three paddlers refused, saying the chiefs had warned them they would be killed if they ever helped their beloved Mariner escape from the island. Teu, the head boatman, swore that although they held their lord in high respect they could not disobey their tribal chiefs. He picked up his paddle and began steering the canoe toward the shore.

Mariner was furious. "Are you not my servants?" he demanded. "Do I not have the power of life or death over you?" He also knew that during the recent famine Teu had killed and eaten his wife. He seized his musket, which was worn about the muzzle almost to a point, and violently stabbed him in the stomach. Teu collapsed, bleeding profusely in the bottom of the canoe. Mariner then aimed his musket at the other two and demanded once again they paddle toward the ship or he would blow their brains out.

Several hours later they were alongside the ship. A sentry heard a disturbance, came to the rail, and saw below, trying to board the ship, a brown-skinned young warrior, his long hair tied in a knot, wearing a turban around his head and a skirt of leaves about his waist. He cocked his musket and ordered the man away.

"I'm an Englishman, formerly of the ship *Port au Prince*," Mariner called out. "Let me come on board."

The ship was the American brig, *Favorite*, bound for China with a cargo of pearl shell and sandalwood. Her captain welcomed Mariner and gave him a shirt and trousers, so that he would start feeling European again. The *Favorite* stayed off Vava'u for three days. Mariner refused to go ashore, fearful that once he was away from the ship his Tongan friends would not permit him to return. For he knew that as much as they loved him and wished him well he had made himself much too valuable to them as a cannon and musket instructor as well as an interpreter of all things European.

Mariner managed to send messengers to his other shipmates scattered about the islands. A half dozen successfully made it aboard the *Favorite*. Another messenger visited Mariner's adopted mother, Mafi Habe, to collect the ship's log that she had carefully preserved all these years along with sixty dollars from the treasure locker of the *Port au Prince*.

Moenga came on board to bid his friend a tearful farewell, bringing as gifts to the crew five large pigs and forty giant yams, some weighing upwards of sixty pounds. The ship's cook prepared a fine banquet for Moenga, his sister, and several female attendants. Mariner gave his Tongan friend a quick lesson in the use of the knife and fork and was pleased to see him handle both with considerable dexterity. The young king pronounced the roast pork with its sage and onion seasoning the best he had ever eaten.

After the meal the captain gave Moenga a tour of the ship. The islander's curiosity knew no bounds, and he asked questions about everything. But his manner was so truly polite no one was offended. Then he made one final request before leaving the ship. Would the captain permit him to lie upon his bed, so that he might boast to his subjects that he was the first Tongan to know the pleasures of a papalangi bed. "Permission being readily granted," Mariner reported later, "he lay down and was delighted with his situation; and said that being now in an English bed, he could fancy himself in England."

The next day Moenga returned to the *Favorite* and announced he now wished to accompany his friend to London. Mariner patiently explained that back in England he would have none of the high status he enjoyed on his island. But Moenga was insistent. He was even prepared to resign his kingship in order to start a new life in England. "He thought if he could but learn to read and write and think like a papalangi, a state of poverty with such high accomplishments was far superior to regal authority in a state of ignorance," Mariner recalled later.

Finally, in late November 1810, almost four years to the day after that dreadful slaughter on the *Port au Prince*, Mariner sailed away from Tonga, his great adventure at an end.

In Macao Mariner booked passage on another ship returning to England. In June 1811 he landed at Gravesend, the same port from which he had sailed six years and six months earlier as a boy of thirteen. He found a brutal welcome waiting for him. On his way to his father's home he ran into a press-gang, rounding up young men to serve in the Royal Navy. Within three hours of landing, he suddenly found himself impressed and carried a prisoner on board a press-tender anchored in the middle of the Thames. Mariner was able to get word out to his father. But a full week passed before Magnus Mariner was able to secure his son's release.

Mariner settled comfortably into the routine of a London business community, working as a commodity broker. One night while out dining, he met by chance a young doctor about his age. Dr. John Martin enjoyed a fine medical practice, but his first love was anthropology. He was fascinated by Mariner's account of his years in Tonga and urged a collaboration on a book about his experiences. Mariner consented. He had always been blessed with a strong memory. Soon Martin learned that for all his adventures, Mariner had total recall of the speeches of the chiefs, the chatter of everyday life, and the lullabies the women sang to their babies. From his notes and persistent interviews, Martin compiled the whole remarkable adventure and much more. The book instructs the reader in every aspect of Tongan society, from the sexual habits of teenagers to the proper way to roast a dead man. They also appended the first dictionary and grammar of the Tongan language. Mariner enjoyed a brief moment of fame in 1817 when his book appeared. It went through several editions and is even today considered a major source on the Pacific island culture before the impact of the missionaries.

The lust for adventure that had swelled so strongly in his youth seemed satiated by his adventures in Tonga. Now Mariner wished for the tranquility of a domestic routine. In 1818 he married Margaret Roberts, the daughter of a banker, and together they had eleven children. (Family tradition insists that all six of his sons died at sea.) In 1829 he went to work as a stockbroker and became a highly respectable member of the London Stock Exchange. He prospered throughout the 1830s.

Mariner proved to be a very private man. After his collaboration with Martin, he seemed to turned his back altogether on his years in Tonga. His children apparently grew up with only a vague knowledge of that period in their father's life. A governess, who lived with the family for several years, recalled much later: "I can't remember ever hearing any talk of his adventures in Tonga at all."

In 1841 Mariner was tainted in a scandal involving forged exchequer bills. A major financial crisis developed.

The Treasury was never actually defrauded of any money, for the bills were never cashed but used as collateral. A subsequent investigation found Mariner and his associates innocent of any fraud themselves but charged them with a lack of proper caution. His reputation had been severely compromised. "I cannot wipe away the stain the Commission has thrown on me," he wrote in his defense afterwards. "I shall be made to undergo pain and penalty unjustly." He fell into bouts of depression. And then on October 20, 1853, twelve years to the day after the scandal first broke, William Mariner, the boy-chief of Tonga, drowned himself in the Grand Surrey Canal south of London.

CHAPTER FIVE

Paradise Found:

Herman Melville in the Marquesas Islands

In 1842 the aspiring young American writer, Herman Melville, stood on the deck of his whaling ship, the *Acushnet*, as the vessel slowly entered the bay at Nuku Hiva in the Marquesas Islands. A small canoe drew alongside. Soon afterwards a "genuine South Seas vagabond" climbed aboard and offered the ship's captain his services as a pilot. The captain refused, but the beachcomber went through the motions anyway, shouting out orders and waving his hands in a comic fashion, much to the amusement of the crew.

Melville was fascinated by this piece of Pacific flotsam. "We afterwards learned that our eccentric friend had been a lieutenant in the English navy. But having disgraced his flag by some criminal conduct, he had deserted his ship, and spent many years wandering among the islands of the Pacific until, accidently being at Nuku Hiva when the French took possession of the place, he had been appointed pilot of the harbor by the newly constituted authorities."

Melville was thus initiated into the curious world of the

Pacific beachcomber. Within a few days he, too, jumped ship to begin a sojourn among cannibals in a verdant mountain valley on Nuku Hiva, a place that was to become his Garden of Eden. A chief extended his hospitality to the young whaler and gave him over to the care of his beautiful daughter. She became his guide, teacher, and lover.

The years from 1841 to 1845 were the most significant in Melville's life. They furnished him with the experiences that made up the great body of his published work. *Typee, Omoo, Mardi, White Jacket,* and *Moby Dick* were published within six years and "The Encantadas" a few years later. All of them involved, to varying degrees, his voyage on a whaling ship, his life in the South Pacific as a beachcomber, and his return on an American man-of-war, the *United States.* He was the first literary artist to write knowledgeably about the South Seas.

Born in New York City during America's first great depression on August 1, 1819, Melville's childhood was spent in comfortable affluence, as the second son of a well-to-do merchant. By 1830 his father's business had begun to fail, and he went heavily into debt. Bankruptcy followed and almost certainly contributed to his death in early 1832. The family was reduced to virtual poverty. The young Melville took a position as a clerk at a bank. A few years later he was appointed to a teaching position in a school near Pittsfield, New York. But the job proved temporary. Then the Panic of 1837 devastated the country. Melville was learning that in this world, as Ishmail observes in *Moby Dick,* "head winds are far more prevalent than winds from astern."

With his options severely limited by the depression gripping the country, Melville asked his older brother to secure him a position on a merchant ship. He was not the first in his family to seek his fortune at sea. His father had been an indefatigable traveler. Several of his family had enjoyed successful careers at sea, and the young Melville had avidly listened to their tales of adventures in distant seas. The most influential of these was Thomas Melville, his father's older brother, who had been a midshipman in the U.S. Navy. He had lived for twenty years in France before returning to his homeland in time to serve as a major in the War of 1812 against the British. Later he settled in Pittsfield, New York, where the boy listened avidly to his reminiscences. His travels had taken him to the Marquesas Islands, and he had even visited Typee Valley where Melville would later pass two months among the cannibals. This talk of adventures in distant lands had a strong impact on the young Melville and instilled in him "a vague prophetic thought that I was fated, one day or other, to be a great voyager."

In the spring of 1839 Melville faced the approach of his twentieth birthday with no resources and no prospects. In hard times, such as those following upon the Panic of 1837, the merchant marine was one segment of the economy with a seemingly bottomless capacity to absorb cheap transient labor. He signed on his first ship, the *St. Lawrence*, an ordinary merchantship bound for Liverpool, England. She carried a cargo of cotton and a crew of sixteen. At sea crossing the Atlantic in June, he felt free for the first time. Later in his novel *Redburn*, he recalled the exhilarating adventure of his passage, especially the furling of the sails during a hard blow:

> There was a wild delirium about it, a fine rushing of the blood about the heart; and a glad thrilling, and throbbing of the whole system, to find yourself tossed up at every pitch into the clouds of a stormy sky, and hovering like a judgment angel between heaven and earth; both hands free, with one foot in the rigging, and one somewhere behind you in the air. The sail would fill out like a balloon, with a report like a small cannon, and then collapse and sink away into a handful. And the feeling of mastering the rebellious canvas, and tying it down like a slave to a spar, and binding it over and over with the gasket, had a touch of pride and power in it.

The cruise aboard the *St. Lawrence* matured Melville. Back in New York in the lingering depression he found himself unable to secure other employment. He still had his deep, almost mystical longing for the sea. The image of the great whale loomed large in his imagination. He may well have read John Reynolds' article "Mocha-Dick or the White Whale of the Pacific" in *Knickerbocker Magazine* for May

1839, about a legendary "old bull whale of prodigious size and strength and white as wool." Mocha-Dick was the terror of the Pacific whaling industry, a sperm whale huge in size and instantly recognizable because he was a freak of nature, an albino. For decades he had been hunted and repeatedly harpooned, but had always emerged as the victor in a hundred fights with whaleboats, pulverizing them with his bulk and enormous jaws.

Melville almost certainly described himself some years later when he wrote in *Moby Dick* of Ishmael's urge to go to sea: "Chief among [my] motives was the overwhelming idea of the great whale himself. Such a portentous and mysterious monster roused all my curiosity. Then the wild and distant seas where he rolled his island bulk; the undeliverable, nameless perils of the whale; these, with all the attending marvels of a thousand Patagonian sights and sounds, helped to sway me to my wish. With other men, perhaps, such things would not have been inducements; but as for me, I am tormented with an everlasting itch for things remote. I love to sail forbidding seas and land on barbarous coasts."

And so it was that on the morning of January 3, 1841, Melville was on board the brand-new whaler *Acushnet*, when she sailed from Fairhaven, Massachusetts, on a maiden voyage from which he would not return for nearly four years. The crew's list, still preserved, recorded the basic information: "Herman Melville/ Place of Birth, New York/ Place of residence, Fairhaven / Citizen of U.S./ Age 21/ Height 5' 9 1/2"/ Complexion, dark/ Hair, brown." He received the sum of $84 as an advance against earnings. Most of this he would have spent on the purchase of a seaman's standard outfit consisting of a blanket, straw-filled mattress, pillow, sheath knife, razor, and some incidentals for his sea chest. The new year promised momentous changes for the young man.

Much later in *Moby Dick* Melville would confess, "A whale ship was my Yale College and my Harvard." The *Acushnet* was as good a vessel as any whaler could hope for. She was of a standard design with two decks, three masts, and a square stern. She had been designed for carrying capacity, not speed. And she had the characteristics that set whalers off from other merchantships—a crow's nest atop each mast where the lookouts were stationed and amidships on the top deck the try-works, the brick furnaces holding several great iron kettles, in which the blubber was boiled down to odorless oil. Whaling ships took a terrific abuse, and their lifespan was short. The *Acushnet* lasted just eleven years, sinking on August 31, 1851, within a month of Melville's completion of his novel *Moby Dick*.

In 1841 the American whaling fleet numbered 652 ships, while the combined fleet of the rest of world was only 230 vessels. This imbalance was due, in no small part, to the efforts of the American captain David Porter of the frigate *Essex*. He sailed into the Pacific during the War of 1812 and virtually destroyed the British whaling industry there, making room for an American dominance later. The Nantucket fleet was steadily shrinking because of the increasing size of the ships and an intractable sand bar across the harbor's entrance. New Bedford, Massachusetts, took over as the whaling capital of the world.

This was the golden age of whaling. Prices for whale oil and bone rose to unheard of figures—$1.77 a gallon for sperm oil and 97¢ a pound for the bone. By 1840 the United States exported half a million gallons of sperm whale oil, four and a half million gallons of oil from other whale species, and two million pounds of bone. The whaling industry was one of the country's largest. Shipowners made vast fortunes with profit margins that ran well over one hundred percent on many cruises. But change is the order of the world. In time the whale oil that had lighted and lubricated the nation gave way to petroleum from the oil fields discovered in Pennsylvania. Whalebone vanished from women's fashions. And sail retreated before the efficiency of steam on the ships of the world.

The average whaling voyage in 1841 lasted forty-five months. The crew endured appalling food, living quarters infested with rats and roaches, and constant brutality from their captains. Their job was cruel, exciting, and very dangerous. Long periods of dead calm were interrupted by a sudden intense activity that threatened their lives, even the ship itself.

Melville's contemporary J. Ross Browne, who sailed on a whaler from Fairhaven in mid-summer of 1842, concluded in his book, *Etchings of a Whaling Cruise* (1846): "There is no class of men in the world who are so unfairly dealt with, so oppressed, so degraded, as the seamen who man the vessels engaged in the American whale fishery."

Shipboard conditions were dreadful, and whalers among the most exploited workers in America. Their pay may have been the lowest in the country at the time. Each crewmember was paid, not a wage but a "lay," that is, a fractional share of the proceeds of the voyage. However, the owners almost universally undervalued the cargo of a returning ship, while grossly overcharging the crew for purchases en route from the ship's stores. The officers, boat-steerers, and harpooners could generally count upon a reasonable return for their time and efforts. But a green seaman shipping out on his first voyage might be put down for as little as a one-two hundredth share. Historian Samuel Eliot Morison calculated in *The Maritime History of Massachusetts* that the average green hand's gross compensation before deductions for four years' labor at sea was between $285.72 and $428.57. And most of the sailors shipping out on whalers were green. Few professional seamen would accept the wretched pay and harsh working conditions of the typical whaler.

Charles Olson described these appalling conditions in *Call Me Ishmael*: "During the 1840s and 1850s it cost the owners 15¢ to 30¢ a day to feed each crew member—combine inefficient workers and such costs by maintaining lowest wages and miserable working conditions—the result: by the 1840s the crews were the bottom dogs of all nations and all races. Of the 18,000 men in the Pacific whaling and sealing fleet one-half ranked as green hands and more than two-thirds deserted every voyage."

Captain Valentine Pease ordered the *Acushnet* to sail due east to the Cape Verde Islands and then south toward the coast of Latin America. The voyage began promisingly. By the time the ship had reached Rio de Janeiro on March 13, after seventy days at sea, they had enough oil on board to send 150 barrels north on the brig *Tweed* and could count themselves experienced hands. Captain Pease allowed a mere day at Rio before sailing on, not enough time for Melville or any of the crew to enjoy some shore leave. A month later the *Acushnet* rounded the Horn and fought her way into the Pacific Ocean. On May 7 they passed through the Juan

Fernández Islands and two days later were chasing after sperm whales in the hunting fields west of Valparaiso. Their luck held. Within the next two months, another 250 barrels of oil disappeared into the hold.

Ishmael's musing while in the crow's nest are probably those of Melville. There, through his watches, he would day-dream, he admits, "lost in the infinite series of the sea, with nothing ruffled but the waves. The tranced ship indolent rolls; the drowsy trade winds blow; everything resolves you into languor."

Then would come moments of sheer excitement and intense activity when a whale was spotted and the boats launched. Melville made clear in *Moby Dick* that there was no grander adventure than the pursuit of a great whale. "It was a sight full of wonder and awe! The vast swells of the omnipotent sea; the surging, hollow roar they made, as they rolled along the eight gunwales, like gigantic bowls in a boundless bowling-green; the brief suspended agony of the boat, as it would tip for an instant on the knife-like edge of the sharper waves, that almost seemed threatening to cut it in two; the sudden profound dip into the watery glens and hollows; the keen spurrings and goadings to gain the top of the opposite hill; the headlong, sled-like slide down its other side;—all these, with the cries of the herdsmen and harpoon-ers, and the shuddering gasps of the oarsmen, and with the wondrous sight of the ivory *Pequod* bearing down upon her boats with outstretched sails, like a wild hen after her screaming brood."

Captain Pease proved to be a violent, tyrannical officer, brutal in the extreme. "We had left both law and equity on the other side of the Cape," Melville complained later in *Typee*. The captain's reply to all complaints was "the butt-end of a handspike, so convincingly administered as effectu-ally to silence the aggrieved party."

Melville had other complaints, too. The provisions were scanty and often rotten on the *Acushnet* and consisted chiefly of "delicate morsels of beef and pork, cut on scien-tific principles from every part of the animal, and of all con-ceivable shapes and sizes, carefully packed in salt and stored away in barrels; affording a never-ending variety in their dif-ferent degrees of toughness, and in the peculiarities of their saline properties. Choice old water, too, two pints of which are allowed every day to every soul on board; together with ample store of sea-bread, previously reduced to a state of petrification, with a view to preserve it either from decay or consumption in the ordinary mode, are likewise provided for the nourishment and gastronomic enjoyment of the crew."

Desertions began to take place. By the end of her voyage the *Acushnet* would lose both the first and third mates, as well as thirteen members of a crew of twenty-three, either by actual desertions or by having to be put ashore in some port half-dead from a disease.

Captain Pease ordered the *Acushnet* to the Galápagos Islands, a popular killing ground with whalers, where they cruised extensively in the fall and winter of 1841-1842. But Pease's luck had run out. They saw no whales.

The barren islands of the Galápagos were Melville's introduction to the Pacific islands and far different from the island paradise of his fantasies. "A separate center of creation," Charles Darwin called them, the inspiration for much of his thesis on evolution when he visited there just a few years earlier. An archipelago of active volcanoes and arid, rocky terrain, the islands are home to some of the strangest and most wonderful wildlife imaginable.

The *Acushnet* anchored for six days at Chatham's Isle, possibly to collect some of the giant tortoises which could provide a ship with fresh meat for months afterwards. Melville slept at least one night ashore among the "heaps of cinders." He watched fascinated, as the ponderous tortoises slowly dragged themselves along in a search for pools of rain water. And he remembered a common superstition of mariners—the Galápagos Islands were a hell reserved exclusively for the torment of brutal ship officers, who after death were transformed into tortoises and damned to spend an eternity in that forsaken place.

The Galápagos tortoise provided Melville with one of his most powerful literary images and a symbol for the moral ambiguities of man's universe. In "The Encantadas, or Enchanted Isles" he reflected upon the two sides of a tortoise:

Even the tortoise, dark and melancholy as it is
upon the back, still possesses a bright side; its calipee

or breast-plate being sometimes of a faint yellowish or golden tinge. Moreover, every one knows that tortoises as well as turtles are of such a make, that if you put them on their backs you thereby expose their bright sides without the possibility of their recovering themselves and turning into view the other. But after you have done this, and because you have done this, you should not swear that the tortoise has no dark side. Enjoy the bright, keep it turned up perpetually if you can, but be honest, and don't deny the black . . . The tortoise is both black and bright.

Desperate after many weeks during which no whales had been taken, Captain Pease ordered the *Acushnet* westward toward the great hunting grounds of the sperm whale in the South Pacific. The intense equatorial sun made the pitch ooze and bubble from the seams of her deck. The maggots multiplied in the food, the cockroaches in the forecastle, and the ship seemed a floating hell all of her own. Six months had passed since the Galápagos Islands. The ship's supply of fresh food had been exhausted. Melville spent long hours in the crow's nest high above the deck, contemplating the "long, measured, dirgelike swell of the Pacific" rolling along. Neither he nor any of the other lookouts saw spouts of whales.

Sometime in the spring of 1842 the *Acushnet* rendezvoused with a Nantucket whaler. The captains decided to hold a "gam," an informal exchange of officers and crew-members, which always served as an excuse for a party. Melville chatted with a young man from the other ship who proved to be none other than the son of Owen Chase. He eagerly questioned the boy about his father's experiences on the *Essex* and was allowed to read the son's own copy of the published *Narrative.* Melville was deeply moved and noted later that he had read the book in the vicinity where the great sperm whale had sunk the *Essex.*

Melville had been at sea for eighteen months when the Marquesas Islands loomed ahead on the horizon in late June. His imagination had been fired years before by his uncle's stories about his visit to Nuku Hiva. "The Marquesas!" he exclaimed excitedly in *Typee*. "What strange visions of out-landish things does the very name spirit up! Naked houris—cannibal banquets—groves of coconut—coral reefs—tattooed chiefs—and bamboo temples; sunny valleys planted with breadfruit trees—carved canoes dancing on the flashing blue waters—savage woodlands guarded by horrible idols—*hea-thenish rites and human sacrifices.*"

The Marquesas Islands are among the most beautiful in the Pacific. Yet this beauty has little in common with the palm-fringed atolls of popular fantasy. With crumbling volca-noes forming a rough terrain of cloud-shrouded basalt rock peaks and abrupt cliffs interminably battered by the ocean waves, the Marquesas Islands seem to belong to a separate universe.

The *Acushnet* cruised along a rock-bound coast. Sea birds screeched and wheeled overhead. The scents of fruits and flowers wafted over the excited crew crowded against the gunwales. They caught sudden glimpses of lush valleys, deep glens, waterfalls, and waving grooves of coconuts. As they passed one particularly impressive valley, a sailor next to Melville suddenly urged, "There—there's Typee. Oh, the bloody cannibals, what a meal they'd make of us if we were to take it into our heads to land! But they say they don't like sailor's flesh. It's too salty. I say, matey, how should you like to be shoved ashore there, eh?" Melville shuddered at the thought, little knowing that within a few weeks time he would find himself a captive in that same valley.

The *Acushnet* sailed slowly into Taiohae Bay and dropped anchor. The ship rolled gently in the swells. Silvery waterfalls slipped out of niches high up the jungle-covered walls of lofty peaks, dividing the green, clear to the sea. The sweet smells of tropical blossoms scented the air.

To the astonishment of the men aboard the *Acushnet*, several French naval vessels, led by the sixty-gun frigate *La Reine Blanche*, were already anchored there. Unknown to the Americans or British, the French had laid claim to all the Marquesas Islands as a colony, and they had already put two hundred soldiers ashore at Taiohae Bay.

Foreign ships were still a novelty at Nuku Hiva. It had become customary for the island men to paddle out in ca-noes, while the women stripped naked and swam out to meet the approaching ships. And this was precisely the welcome experienced by the dumbfounded whalers. Melville described it later in *Typee* :

> As they drew nearer, and I watched the rising and sinking of their forms and beheld the uplifted right arm bearing above the water the girdle of tapa and their long dark hair trailing beside them as they swam, I almost fancied they could be nothing else than so many mermaids—and very like mermaids they behaved, too.
>
> We were still some distance from the beach, and under slow headway, when we sailed right into the midst of these swimming nymphs. They boarded us at every quarter; many seizing hold of the chain plates and springing into the chains; others, at the peril of being run over by the vessel in her course, catching at the bobstays, and wreathing their slender forms above the ropes, hung suspended in the air. All of them at length succeeded in getting up the ship's side, where they clung dripping with the brine and glowing from the bath, their jet-black tresses streaming over their shoulders and half enveloping their otherwise naked forms. There they hung, sparkling with savage vivacity, laughing gaily at one another, and chattering away with infinite glee. . . . Their adornments were completed by passing a few loose folds of white tapa around the waist. Thus arrayed, they no longer hesitated but flung themselves lightly over the bulwarks and were quickly frolicking about the decks. . . . The [*Acushnet*] was fairly captured. And never I will say was vessel carried before by such a dashing and irresistible party of boarders!

As dusk fell, the sailors hung up lanterns. The Marquesans then put on a display of dancing. Few dances are more sensual and provocative than those of the South Seas in which the arms and hips move in a manner suggestive of physical love. The slow, graceful movements of the hula soon gave way to the crisp, precise undulations of the drum dance chorus, as the dancers fluttered their bodies at impossible rhythmic speeds to the beat of a corps of drummers. The sexual excitement built quickly into a frenzy. Encouraged by their men, the women offered themselves to the sailors. Within a short time a sexual orgy was underway, which the ship's officers made little or no effort to stop.

"Our ship was now wholly given up to every species of riot and debauchery," Melville confessed later. "Not the feeblest barrier was interposed between the unholy passions of the crew and their unlimited gratification. The grossest licentiousness and the most shameful inebriety prevailed, with occasional and but short-lived interruptions, through the whole period of her stay."

By the late eighteenth century the South Seas loomed large in the popular imaginations of Europeans, less as a specific geographical place and more as a state of mind—what historian Gavin Daws called "a dream of islands." There one could still find, it was commonly believed, people living in a state of primal innocence, an Eden before the Fall, a paradise inhabited by Noble Savages. They were perceived to be both happy and good because they had not yet been corrupted by the unnatural bonds of civilized European society. The islands' natural beauty and fecundity and the inhabitants' striking lack of envy, greed, or hatred seemed to confirm the speculations of Jean-Jacques Rousseau and other philosophers about man's natural goodness.

"We have discovered a large, fertile, and extremely populous island in the South Seas," Captain Samuel Wallis of the H.M.S. *Dolphin* wrote shortly after his discovery of Tahiti on June 18, 1767. " 'Tis impossible to describe the beautiful prospects we beheld in this charming spot. The verdure is as fine as that of England, there is plenty of live stock, and it abounds with all the choicest productions of the Earth."

To the European explorers, more accustomed to the Mongoloid Indians of America and the Negroid primitives of Melanesia, the discovery of the Polynesians came as an exciting surprise. For there living on scattered islands of great beauty were a people with light skin colors who conformed closely to accepted European standards of beauty.

The islands of Polynesia, and especially Tahiti, became closely associated in the popular imagination with an unbridled, joyous sexual freedom totally foreign to the experience of Western civilization. The appeal was simply overwhelming, and few men were strong enough to resist the temptation. The Englishman John Turnbull, who circled the globe between 1800 and 1804 confessed after his visit to Tahiti and Hawaii: "Nothing can withstand the seduction and artifices of the southern islanders. Women and a life of indolence are too powerful for the sense of duty in the minds of our seamen. Had we relaxed our efforts for a single moment, our ship would have been deserted."

In 1768, the year after Wallis' discovery, Tahiti was visited by a second European expedition, two French ships, the frigate *Boudeuse* and the store ship *Etoile*, under the command of Captain Louis-Antoine de Bougainville. The welcome received by the Frenchmen was such that Bougainville named the island La Nouvelle-Cythère, the New Cythera, after the Greek island where Aphrodite, the goddess of love, had been born out of the sea.

The *Boudeuse* and the *Etoile* anchored off the northeastern coast of Tahiti. Bougainville was fascinated by the welcome the Tahitians extended to him and his men. He wrote later:

> As we came nearer the shore, the number of islanders surrounding our ships increased. The canoes were so numerous that we had much to do to warp in amidst the crowd of boats and the noise. All these people came crying out *tayo*, which means friend, and gave a thousand signs of friendship; they all asked for nails and ear-rings of us. The canoes were full of females; who, for agreeable features, are not inferior to most European women; and who, in point of beauty of the body, might, with much reason, vie with them all. Most of these fair females were naked; for the men and the old women that accompanied them had stripped them of the garments which they generally dressed themselves in. The glances which

they gave us from their canoes seemed to discover
some degree of uneasiness, not withstanding the
innocent manner in which they were given; perhaps
because nature has everywhere embellished their sex
with a natural timidity; or because even in those
countries where the ease of the golden age is still in
use, women seem least to desire what they most wish
for. The men, who were more plain, or rather, more
free, soon explained their meaning very clearly. They
pressed us to choose a woman and to come ashore
with her; and their gestures, which were nothing less
equivocal, denoted in what manner we should form
an acquaintance with her. It was very difficult, amidst
such a sight, to keep at their work four hundred
young French soldiers, who had seen no women for
six months. In spite of all our precautions, a young
girl came on board and placed herself upon the
quarter deck near one of the hatchways, which was
open to give air to those heaving the capstan below it.
The girl carelessly dropped the cloth which covered
her and appeared to the eyes of all beholders much as
Venus showed herself to the Phrygian shepherd—
having, indeed, the celestial form of that goddess.
Both sailors and soldiers endeavored to come to the
hatchway, and the capstan was never hove with more
alacrity than on this occasion.

The next day the chief of the district came on board the
Boudeuse with many gifts of fowls, pigs, and fresh fruit.
Because the welcome had been so cordial, Bougainville ordered a camp built on shore near a stream where the sick
might recover their health and the ships might replenish
their water casks. The French offered nails in exchange for
services, and the islanders were eager to help their visitors
gather wood, water, and fruits. Bougainville wandered about
the countryside and decided that he had been "transported
into the garden of Eden. Everywhere we found hospitality,
ease, innocent joy, and every appearance of happiness."

The officers in their cocked hats and powdered wigs,
breeches, stockings, and buckled shoes presented an out-

landish sight to the dumbfounded Tahitians. The amazed natives gathered around them excitedly. "The boldest among them came to touch us," Bougainville noted. "They even pushed aside our clothes with their hands, in order to see whether we were made exactly like them."

As the sailors wandered about the valley, young girls constantly invited them into their houses and offered them food and sex. When the Frenchmen accepted, as they almost always did, and the love-making undertaken, the rooms quickly filled with curious islanders eager to observe what sexual techniques and skills their white-skinned visitors had brought with them.

"Here Venus is the goddess of hospitality," Bougainville concluded approvingly. "Her worship does not admit of any mysteries, and every tribute paid to her is a feast to the whole nation."

But the most sensational discovery made during Bougainville's stay at Tahiti occurred not on the island but rather aboard his very own ship, the *Boudeuse*. Ahutoru, a young Tahitian warrior who had befriended some of the officers, was on board. His new friends had taught him some European manners, given him Western food to sample, and even dressed him in Western clothes. Suddenly, he caught sight of the servant to the expedition's naturalist, Philibert Commerson. "A woman," he shouted in his own language, "you have a woman with you." And so she proved to be. She had successfully kept her sex a secret throughout the voyage, masquerading as a man among several hundred soldiers and sailors until unmasked by an islander who saw through her disguise at a glance. Under questioning by Commerson and others, she confessed to the deception and explained she had been an orphan with no prospects who had gone to sea seeking adventure. And thus Jeanne Bare became the first woman to circumnavigate the world. Commerson never revealed in his writings his feelings about his assistant. But he did name a plant after her, *Baretia*, for its "uncertain sexual characteristics."

Ahutoru, the handsome young Tahitian who had made the discovery, was completely enthralled with European culture and pleaded with Bougainville to take him back to France. The commander was skeptical about the wisdom of separating the Tahitian from his culture but soon relented. He had proven himself quite useful to the officers in procuring them island women and made them promise that when they arrived in Paris, they would do the same for him. Once in France he apparently had no difficulty fulfilling his own sexual fantasies. His appearance in Paris created a sensation in 1769. Ahutoru was presented to the king. He learned to speak French and developed a passion for the opera. He was reputed to have had numerous liaisons with actresses. After eleven months, Bougainville put him on a ship bound for the South Pacific.

Bougainville had one doubt after his ships departed Tahiti. Some of his men developed gonorrhea. He assumed correctly that the disease had come to the island with the arrival of Wallis' ship the year before. This was the first warning that the paradise they had just enjoyed was, in actual fact, quite vulnerable.

The reception such as the Tahitians gave Bougainville became the norm for subsequent ships to call at the island. Unlike the French before him, Captain James Cook was shocked at what he saw on Tahiti and complained: "There is a scale of dissolute sensuality which these people have ascended, wholly unknown to every other nation whose manners have been recorded from the beginning of the world to the present hour, and which no imagination could possibly conceive." Then, as an example of this debauchery, he offered up a performance staged for himself and several of his officers by eager islanders.

> A young man, near six feet high, performed the rites of Venus with a little girl about eleven or twelve years of age before several of our people and a great number of the natives without the least sense of its being improper or indecent, but as appeared, in perfect conformity with the custom of the place. Among the spectators were several women of superior rank, who may be said to have assisted at the ceremony, for they gave instructions to the girl how to perform her part which, young as she was, she did not seem to stand much in need of.

Cook's men obviously did not share their commander's disgust at the open sexuality of their Tahitian hosts. Two of his Marines deserted shortly before the *Endeavour* was supposed to set sail. The islanders advised him that both had run away to the mountains with their girlfriends. Cook was furious. He imprisoned several Tahitian chiefs and threatened to execute them unless his men were returned. They were. He sailed away with his crew intact, but the Tahitians deeply resented his heavyhandedness, which appeared to them to be outrageously misplaced.

As more and more ships called at Tahiti, the islanders evolved an ingenious theory to explain the sexual frenzy of their visitors. Because they never saw any women on the visiting ships, they concluded that the white race consisted entirely of men who had to travel all the way to Tahiti to enjoy the pleasures of heterosexual sex. In their minds there was no other explanation for the eagerness with which the Europeans embraced the island women and the persistence with which they kept returning.

Of course, the European stays at the Polynesian islands were limited to just a few days, a couple of weeks at the longest. Thus, they could not in such a short time learn much of consequence about the island culture. They could not know, for example, that the Polynesians were among history's greatest navigators, able to cross thousands of miles of the Pacific and arrive at a predetermined island. Or that they had highly sophisticated skills at stone carving and masonry that allowed them to create vast temple complexes and enormous statues. They were also excellent farmers. Their neatly cultivated fields, abundance of food, and neatly constructed houses impressed all their early visitors.

Yet for the Europeans, and later the Americans, sex became the only thing that really mattered about Polynesian society. The sailors and whalers sought escape in sexual indulgences, while the later missionaries struggled to abolish such sexual activities. What the visitors failed to understand was that among the islanders promiscuity was largely a teenage privilege. After a certain age they were expected to marry. And in Polynesian society marriage always represented the union of two large families and so had political, as well as emotional, dimensions.

"Tahiti was a small civilization perfectly in balance," British historian David Howarth has observed. "But the balance was pathetically easily upset by intrusion. In spite of their good intentions, Europeans fatally upset it merely by their presence, and especially by the introduction of their diseases and two of their ineradicable concepts: the concept of private property and the concept of sin."

Within fifty years of Wallis' discovery of Tahiti, the local culture had gone into a fatal decline under the impact of a corrosive foreign influence. The islanders enjoyed none of the immunities to Western diseases. A people whose isolation had sheltered them from all serious infections suddenly found themselves grappling with such diseases as tuberculosis, smallpox, diphtheria, measles, and pneumonia. Venereal diseases became almost universal within a fairly short time. Entire populations in some valleys perished within the space of just a few months. When Melville arrived in Tahiti after his Marquesan adventure, he cast a disbelieving eye on the cultural blight caused by a corrupt and unsought civilization and concluded sadly: "But amidst . . . tokens of improvement, painful proofs are everywhere making themselves manifest that the natives are doomed to extinction, from the operation of causes more or less connected with the arrival of the white men."

Hand-in-hand, the imperialist and the missionary together shaped the nineteenth century, as they took charge of much of the world. The most destructive of these foreign influences in Polynesia were the missionaries, most of whom came from London to found an empire of God on earth. In their view the state of paradise proclaimed by such early explorers as Bougainville did not exist. The Tahitians lived in a state of sin, and the missionaries had a divine obligation to journey to the Pacific to redeem them.

The missionaries introduced the concept of laws into a society which had never had any legal system in its history. Along with the laws came the entire complicated bureaucracy of judges, lawyers, and clerks. Having created crime, they then quickly established a police force and a jail. Virtually, all the traditional entertainments of Tahitian society were declared sinful, hence criminal. Dancing, wrestling, play-acting, singing (except hymns), tattooing, and nudity were prohibited. And, of course, sex outside marriage was strongly condemned and discouraged. Henceforth, the island women were required to go out in the cumbersome dresses and bonnets favored by the missionary wives, cut off their long tresses, and stop wearing garlands of flowers. The goal was to make them as unattractive as possible to the men. The Tahitian love of sex continued, but was now carried on in secret, away from the prying eyes of the missionaries.

So when Melville visited Tahiti in late 1842 the two-fold impact of diseases and the missionaries had already destroyed much of the idyllic society that had prevailed until so recently. The Noble Savages of Polynesia were no more. Instead he found aged Tahitians sadly chanting a song of impending doom:

The palm tree shall grow,
The coral shall spread,
But man shall cease.

The Marquesas Islands lie 850 miles to the north of Tahiti along an area of ancient volcanic activity that developed upon deep fissures in the Pacific floor. There are no springs of fresh water in the Marquesas, so that all fresh water arrives from the southeast on the trade winds. Archaeologists believe the islands were originally settled about the second century B. C. by voyagers from Samoa, 2,000 miles to the west. By the time the Europeans arrived in significant numbers in the early nineteenth century, the Marquesans had lived for almost 2,000 years without any outside interference.

The Polynesians called this archipelago *Te Henua, Te Enata*, the Land of Men. Fierce warriors and great builders, they erected vast fortresses and temples in the high central plateaus of their islands. They were brave mariners, too. Before the ninth century voyagers from the Marquesas Islands settled remote Easter Island some 2,500 miles to the southwest. Other voyages of exploration took them to the Hawaiian Islands and New Zealand.

The Marquesas Islands have no continuous coastal plain, such as Tahiti does. All thrust straight out of the sea without the benefit of encircling coral reefs. Except for Ua Huka and Ua Pou, each island is dominated by a giant crater rim that has been blown away to leave sheer cliffs and jagged ridges. The divided land meant a divided society. Small clans lived independent existences in the deep, high-walled valleys, each isolated from its neighbors by the precipitous peaks and formidable ridges. A single chief ruled over each self-sufficient, politically independent group.

The Spanish explorer Don Alvaro de Mendana discovered the islands in 1595. He named them *Las Marquesas de Mendoza* for his patron, the viceroy of Peru. The next morning he led a party ashore to celebrate a Catholic mass on the beach. Drawn by curiosity, a crowd of natives pressed in too closely. The Spaniards opened fire, killing 200. Later the sailors slept with the island women and infected them with syphilis. The Marquesas Islands were left alone with their newly introduced diseases for 179 years, until Captain Cook rediscovered them in 1774.

Western civilization came to the Marquesas Islands fifty years or so later than to Tahiti. The inaccessibility of many of the more remote valleys kept both the missionaries and the politicians away. Even as late as 1842, a foreign visitor, such as Melville, could easily find an unspoiled pocket of Polynesia where he might go to indulge his fantasies.

But that cultural purity would not be sustained for much longer. In August of 1833 an American party of missionaries with wives and children landed at Nuku Hiva for the express purpose of establishing a beachhead of civilization among the heathens of the South Seas. "Two weeks ago the *Dhaulle* weighed anchor and left us on these heathen shores, whose inhabitants for ages have sat in darkness living without God, devoted to the most bestial sensuality and perpetuating deeds of horrible cruelty," William Alexander, the group's leader, wrote in his journal. The Americans lasted less than a year, defeated finally by the indifference and contempt of the Marquesans and their own fear of death when tribal warfare erupted.

Alexander was not the first American to cast covetous eyes on Nuku Hiva. Twenty years earlier in a bizarre footnote to the War of 1812 the American naval captain David Porter of the U.S. frigate *Essex* took it upon himself to wage war against the British in the Pacific by striking at their whaling fleet. He landed at Taiohae Bay in Nuku Hiva and impulsively annexed the island to the United States, constructed a fort on a small peninsula, and named it Madisonville, after James Madison, who was president. He even invaded Typee Valley where Melville would find himself and fought two battles against the inhabitants. But it was all for naught. Congress never ratified Porter's claim, and it was left for the French thirty years later to seize the islands.

Melville had arrived in Nuku Hiva at a critical time in its history. The French occupational forces had settled in just a few weeks before. Two hundred French soldiers were busy constructing Fort Collet. In early July of 1842 the two thousand years of independence enjoyed by the Marquesans was about to come to an end. But for the time being, at least, Melville was to find refuge in a healthy, smoothly functioning culture quite determined to go its own way.

The *Acushnet* spent two weeks at Nuku Hiva. Melville had ample opportunity in that time to gather information on the island society, learn some words of the local language, and make plans for an escape to one of the valleys beyond the French or American reach. Certainly, the reception and hospitality the islanders had already shown the crew of the ship convinced him that he would find a friendly reception among them ashore. He secretly put together a cache of several pounds of tobacco and a few yards of cotton cloth, which he planned to use as trade items to purchase the good will of the islanders, along with some hard tack biscuits.

Melville found a shipmate willing to accompany him in his adventure, Richard Tobias Greene, or Toby as he preferred to be called. "Toby was a young fellow about my own age," he wrote in *Typee* of his seventeen-year-old shipmate. "Arrayed in his blue frock and duck trousers, he was as smart a looking sailor as ever stepped upon a deck. He was singularly small and slightly made, with great flexibility of limb. His naturally dark complexion had been deepened by exposure to the tropical sun, and a mass of jetty locks clustered about his temples and threw a darker shade into his large black eyes."

The two young men deserted the *Acushnet* on July 9, while preparations were being made on board for a departure the following day. They went ashore in the morning, slipped away from the shipmates during a heavy tropical downpour, and struck out immediately for a high mountain at the back of the bay. In late afternoon they had reached the top of a rugged ridge and gazed down upon their ship, bobbing at anchor in the harbor over 2,000 feet below them. To their surprise and disappointment they found no coconuts or wild fruit at the higher altitudes. The pair spent several miserable days and nights with nothing to eat but their sweat-soaked, tobacco-flavored ship's biscuits. They became hopelessly lost, scrambling up and down the ridges and ravines with no sense of where they were or where they were going. At last, by sheer luck and perseverance they made their way down into Typee Valley. Fearful of falling into the hands of cannibals but unable to go farther, they had little choice. Melville was suffering from severe chills and a mysterious infection in his leg. They cautiously made their way to the bottom of the valley. Melville's later description of what they discovered echoed the rapture of Bougainville seventy-five years before:

> I chanced to push aside a branch, and by so doing suddenly disclosed to my view a scene which even now I can recall with all the vividness of the first impression. Had a glimpse of the gardens of paradise been revealed to me, I could scarcely have been more ravished with the sight.
>
> From the spot where I lay transfixed with surprise and delight, I looked straight down into the bosom of a valley, which swept away in long wavy undulations to the blue waters in the distance. Midway toward the sea, and peering here and there amidst the foliage, might be seen the palmetto-thatched houses of its inhabitants, glistening in the sun that had bleached them to a dazzling whiteness. The vale was more than [nine miles] in length and about a mile across at its greatest width.

On either side it appeared hemmed in by steep and green acclivities, which, uniting near the spot where I lay, formed an abrupt and semicircular termination of grassy cliffs and precipices hundreds of feet in height, over which flowed numberless small cascades. . . . There was nothing about the scenery I beheld more impressive than those silent cascades, whose slender threads of water, after leaping down the steep cliffs, were lost amidst the rich herbage of the valley.

Over all the landscape there reigned the most hushed repose, which I almost feared to break, lest like the enchanted gardens in the fairy tale, a single syllable might dissolve the spell.

The two young sailors contemplated their future. What would they find? A cruel death at the hands of fierce cannibals or a kindlier reception from a gentler people? They stepped out of the bush to begin their adventure in the Valley of the Man-Eaters.

Some minutes later Melville and Greene spotted two figures hidden in the dense foliage, standing close together and perfectly motionless. Melville hurried forward toward them, unrolling the calico cloth he had brought as a gift. They proved to be a young boy and girl, almost completely naked except for loin cloths made of tapa. The couple led them to their family's large bamboo house and motioned for them to enter. Several dozen chiefs and warriors, tattooed over most of their bodies, sprawled upon mats woven from coconut tree leaves, while young women served them refreshments. The arrival of the whites created a commotion. The islanders stripped them of their rain-soaked clothing and examined their bodies closely.

"They scanned the whiteness of our limbs," Melville wrote later, "and seemed utterly unable to account for the contrast they presented to the swarthy hue of our faces, enbrowned from a six months' exposure to the scorching sun of the Line. They felt our skin, much in the way that a silk mercer would handle a remarkably fine piece of satin." He concluded that they were the first whites these people had examined up close.

After Melville and his companion Greene had blundered into Typee Valley, they found themselves entirely dependent upon the inhabitants and completely at their mercy. As a consequence, they were forced by their situation to study the customs of their hosts with an eye toward assuring their own survival. That attitude prevailed the next morning when they met Mehevi, the most powerful chief of the valley. He was a splendid physical specimen—tall, well-proportioned, muscular, his body tattooed from shaven head to feet. Around his neck he wore several enormous necklaces of boars' tusks. Elaborately carved sperm whale teeth hung from his earlobes. A dark tapa cloth girded his waist. In his hand he carried a carved paddle spear, fifteen feet in length, one end sharply pointed, the other flattened like an oar blade.

"I forthwith determined to secure, if possible, the good will of this individual, as I easily perceived he was a man of great authority in his tribe, and one who might exert a powerful influence upon our subsequent fate," Melville wrote later in *Typee*. The young American whalers played their cards properly, for soon afterwards Mehevi took both under his protection. Melville's satisfaction was intense: "I could not avoid congratulating myself that Mehevi had from the first taken me as it were under his royal protection, and that he still continued to entertain for me the warmest regards, as far as I was able to judge from appearances. For the future I determined to pay the most assiduous court to him, hoping that eventually through his kindness I might obtain my liberty."

The Typees extended to their two American visitors that same uninhibited hospitality the Tahitians had shown toward the first Europeans to land there seventy-five years earlier. They were fed and clothed, slept on mats with the family, and bathed with them in nearby streams. The whole tribe came to visit them. And Melville, who had injured his leg, was carried everywhere like a chief.

The Typees were at this time the most powerful tribe on Nuku Hiva, inhabiting the most favorably situated of the valleys. The numerous kindnesses Melville received from his hosts for a time dispelled his doubts about sojourning among cannibals. The horror stories the missionaries had circulated about the ferocious savagery of the Typees proved largely untrue, much to his relief. Later in his book he would insist on the moral superiority of this culture to his own: "Entering their valley, as I did, under the most erroneous impressions of their character, I was soon led to exclaim in amazement, 'Are these the ferocious savages, the bloodthirsty cannibals of whom I have heard such frightful tales!' They deal more kindly with each other and are more humane than many who study essays on virtue and benevolence. I will frankly declare, that after passing a few weeks in this valley of the Marquesas, I formed a higher estimate of human nature than I had ever before entertained."

While the days slowly passed, Melville immersed himself in the life of the Typees, as he sought to understand every aspect of it, much as young William Mariner had done during his years with the Tongans. Several of Mehevi's older wives rubbed a soothing lotion on his injured leg, which soon began to heal under their supervision. He drifted into the languid routine of his hosts—bath shortly after daybreak, a morning meal, smoking locally grown tobacco, social visits to other houses, noon siesta, an afternoon meal, dances soon after sunset, and finally an evening meal. "Life here is little else than an often interrupted and luxurious nap," he concluded.

But his most constant companion was Mehevi's beautiful, soft-spoken daughter, Fayaway, who took Melville as her lover soon after his arrival in the valley, much to the pleasure of the chief. He passed many happy hours on a mat outside the door of Fayaway's hut. She became his mentor and taught him her language and explained the ways of her people. While they conversed, she wove fans of pandanus leaves or ground taro in a hardwood bowl with a masher made of dark volcanic stone. Her robe fashioned from tapa cloth stopped just below her round breasts. Brightly colored flower blossoms decorated her long, black hair. She was the eternal South Pacific fantasy, and her place in the story undoubtedly helped the success of Melville's book. (The gossip by later beachcombers in the Marquesas that he had a child by the original Fayaway seems plausible, and his experiences in

Typee Valley certainly did much to intensify the emotional perplexities of his later life.)

In Fayaway's company Melville explored Typee Valley. In the dense tropical vegetation of the valley slopes he discovered the vestiges of an earlier people, the lichen-covered stones of ancient house platforms and temples, some nearly intact, others tumbled down in chaos. Stone tikis—squat figures with goggle-rimmed eyes bulging over flaring nostrils, their hands clasped over protruding abdomens—kept silent watch at the sites. Sometimes he met the former inhabitants, their green-stained skulls and other bones, jumbled up among the ruins. He had clearly come to a ghost-ridden paradise.

Later Melville visited a more recent site, the mausoleum of a warrior chief. The dried body of the man himself sat in his war canoe inside a stone hut. The body was wrapped in brown tapa cloth. A headdress of long plumes sat upon his head, gently swaying in the light breeze. Glaring at him from the prow of his canoe was a polished human skull, turned backwards to stare at the chief as if to urge him along in his paddling.

In time Melville came to understand the enormous importance of the coconut palm, not only to the Marquesans but to all the peoples of the South Pacific. Most of the smaller islands would never have been permanently settled had it not been for an abundance of coconut palms on their shores. So critical were they to their survival that the early Polynesian voyagers carried many coconuts in their canoes and planted them on distant islands visited during far-flung expeditions through the Pacific.

The coconut palm lay at the heart of the Typee culture, permeating all aspects of the daily lives of the people. It would be hard to imagine a more versatile plant than the ubiquitous coconut palm. The sky-farm poised on its pedestal fifty feet or more above the ground provided almost everything an islander needed. The Marquesans had over twenty different words to express the many progressive stages in the growth of the nut. Later in *Omoo* Melville catalogued the many uses they had evolved for the plant and its products:

The blessings it confers are incalculable. Year after year, the islander reposes beneath its shade, both eating and drinking of its fruit. He thatches his hut with its boughs and weaves them into baskets to carry his food. He cools himself with a fan platted from the young leaflets and shields his head from the sun by a bonnet of the leaves. Sometimes he clothes himself with the cloth-like substance which wraps round the base of the stalks. The larger nuts, thinned and polished, furnish him with a beautiful goblet; the smaller ones, with bowls for his pipes. The dry husks kindle his fires. Their fibers are twisted into fishing lines and cords for his canoes. He heals his wounds with a balsam compounded from the juice of the nut and with the oil extracted from its meat embalms the bodies of the dead.

The noble trunk itself is far from being valueless. Sawed into posts, it upholds the islander's dwelling. Converted into charcoal, it cooks his food. Supported on blocks of stone, it [provides fences] on his lands. He impels his canoe through the water with a paddle of the wood and goes to battle with clubs and spears of the same hard material. . . .

Thus, the man who but drops one of these nuts into the ground may be said to confer a greater and more certain benefit upon himself and posterity than many a life's toil in less genial climes.

Melville found himself quite smitten by the beauty of both the Marquesan women and men. Most of the men were over six feet in height and proportioned, he thought, like Greek gods. The women were smaller than the men but also extremely well proportioned. He was particularly impressed by the whiteness of their teeth, "far more beautiful than ivory itself." And some of the women had skins as light as the women back in his native New York, the result of bleaching their skins with the juice from a papa vine and carefully avoiding direct sunlight. Melville was amazed at the considerable efforts both the men and women expended on their personal grooming, such as plucking out unsightly hairs using a small clam's shells as tweezers, dressing their hair with perfumed coconut oil, and ornamenting themselves with garlands and earrings of flowers. They held cleanliness in such high esteem that both men and women bathed twice a day.

Sexuality had such a conspicuous place in the society life of the Marquesans that Melville must have been stunned at much of what he observed. Ritual orgies played an important part in Marquesan society long before the first Europeans appeared. But in most instances they were an integral part of important religious ceremonies and served to promote social solidarity. For obvious reasons Melville could not include all such details in the books he wrote soon afterwards. However, historian Walter Herbert has documented the extent to which the island culture was suffused throughout with sexual energy:

> Specific physical qualities of the male and female genitals were regarded as having special degrees of sexual attractiveness, so that there was a vocabulary differentiating penises according to various sizes and shapes. An extensive program of beautification was applied to the vagina, which began in babyhood with massages and exercises intended to increase its muscle tone. There was, in addition, a mild astringent that was applied in an effort to decrease the production of vaginal fluid and to inhibit unpleasant odors. A ritual focusing upon these efforts marked the passage of females into adulthood. First, they were formally examined to determine whether their labia were pale, their pubic hair pliant and short, and to what extent other desirable characteristics had been achieved. Then they took part in *kioka toe haka*, the festival of the clitoris dance, at which they displayed their genitals to the tribe at large. . . . During this period they had apparently unlimited sexual access to each other and pursued their opportunities with alacrity.

Melville was impressed with the domestic life of the Marquesans and the good relations between the sexes.

Unlike many other primitive cultures, there in Typee the men did all the heavy work, while the women had only light housekeeping as their responsibility. He was particularly interested in their institution of marriage, which was defined loosely enough so as not to restrict either partner's sexual choice and could be terminated at either partner's discretion in the event of unhappiness.

The one feature about the marriages in Typee Valley that most stunned him was produced by an imbalance of the sexes. The men outnumbered the women. As a result, the wives were polygamous and took several husbands. "Infidelity on either side is very rare," he insisted in *Typee.* "No man has more than one wife, and no wife of mature years has less than two husbands—sometimes she has three. . . . As nothing stands in the way of a separation, the matrimonial yoke sits easily and lightly, and a Typee wife lives on very pleasant and sociable terms with her husbands."

Melville apparently did not exaggerate in his description of the contented marital life of Typee Valley. Certainly, the equality of status enjoyed by both men and women was a major factor contributing to the happiness and stability of the family. But, as Melville clearly saw, another major factor was the natural abundance in which they lived.

> A gentleman of Typee can bring up a numerous family of children and give them all a highly respectable cannibal education with infinitely less toil and anxiety than he expends in the simple process of striking a light. Whilst a poor European artisan, who through the instrumentality of a [match] performs the same operation in one second, is put to his wit's end to provide for his starving offspring that food which the children of a Polynesian father, without troubling their parent, pluck from the branches of every tree around them.

Melville looked around with an alert, if not always comprehending eye. He found little government in the conventional sense existing in Typee Valley. Each valley on Nuku Hiva harbored its independent, self-sufficient tribe. And at

the head of each tribe was the chief, the first-born male of
the direct male descendant of the tribal ancestor or god. He
rarely was the cruel, arbitrary despot common in the Tonga
Islands but rather a patriarch to whom respect and devotion
were willingly given. In fact, there was often little in
Mehevi's appearance to distinguish him from his subjects.
Equality, not hierarchy, Melville decided, was the most important condition of Typee society:

> No one appeared to assume any arrogant
> pretensions. There was little more than a slight
> difference in costume to distinguish the chiefs from
> the other natives. All appeared to mix together freely
> and without any reserve. . . . What may be the extent
> of the authority of the chiefs over the rest of the tribe,
> I will not venture to assert. But from all I saw during
> my stay in the valley, I was induced to believe that in
> matters concerning the general welfare it was very
> limited.

Religion, like government, sat lightly on the inhabitants
of Typee Valley, much to Melville's satisfaction. Temples and
sacred sites were everywhere, and the people often left offer-
ings of food and flowers. But he could not detect any coercive
effects of the priests upon the people. He finally concluded
that the Typees practiced their religion according to individual whim rather than any fervent belief and that their religious enthusiasm was at a low ebb.

With government and religion at a minimum, the natives were able to live together in almost perfect harmony in
a spirit of communal cooperation. "During my whole stay on
the island I never witnessed a single quarrel nor anything
that in the slightest degree approached even to a dispute,"
Melville related in *Typee*. "The natives appeared to form one
household, whose members were bound together by the ties
of strong affection." The reasons, he decided, lay in the fact
that their society had neither laws nor money to breed discontent.

Melville discovered in Typee Valley what Mariner had
found in Tonga—a society ruled by a prevailing custom of

mutual giving. If a person was in need of food, shelter, clothes, sex, whatsoever, all he had to do was simply request it of his neighbors and they would provide without any obligation. If his house collapsed in a strong wind, the people in the valley simply came together and rebuilt it, usually in a matter of a day or two. If his canoe was pounded into pieces on the rocks, then his neighbors quickly made him a new one. No one thought of himself as the permanent owner of anything. The result was a safety net more secure and complete than any Western society had ever envisioned.

Melville even considered making Typee Valley his permanent residence, of never returning to civilization. "When I looked around the verdant recess in which I was buried and gazed up to the summits of the lofty eminence that hemmed me in," he admitted later, "I was well disposed to think that I was in the 'Happy Valley' and that beyond these heights there was nought but a world of care and anxiety."

Typee Valley was, in Melville's eyes, an unspoiled Eden, fresh as at the moment of creation. This, he decided, must have been the way Man existed before the Fall. As a result, his concept of civilization quickly disintegrated, leaving him with no alternate philosophical concept to put in its place. At one point in *Typee*, he even toys with the idea that perhaps the Marquesas Islanders should send missionaries to the United States and England. But then he realizes that the harmonious society of Typee Valley will face an inevitable extinction at the oppressive hands of European and American political and religious interests. They will turn this Valley of Life into a Valley of Death.

> Among the islands of Polynesia, no sooner are the images overturned, the temples demolished, and the idolaters converted into *nominal* Christians, then disease, vice, and premature death make their appearance. The depopulated land is then recruited from the rapacious hordes of enlightened individuals who settle themselves within its borders and clamorously announce the progress of the Truth. The spontaneous fruits of the earth, which God in his wisdom had ordained for the support of the indolent natives, remorselessly seized upon and appropriated by

the stranger, are devoured before the eyes of the starving inhabitants or sent on board the numerous vessels which now touch their shores. When the famished wretches are cut off in this manner from their natural supplies, they are told by their benefactors to work and earn their support by the sweat of their brows!

"Enjoy the bright, keep it turned up perpetually if you can, but be honest and don't deny the black," Melville had written about the enormous tortoises on the Galápagos Islands. Now he had to apply that lesson to his lush paradise in Typee Valley. There were two sides, he was learning, to both civilization and savagery. And the dark side of the Marquesans was their cannibalism, their obvious relish of human flesh or "long pig," as they called it. This was more than ritual cannibalism. The islanders really enjoyed human flesh as a food.

From the time of their arrival, Melville and Greene had feared the possibility they might end up in one of the great ovens. And this possibility had driven Greene to escape after two weeks. Nothing happened to confirm Melville's dread. And so he put it aside, rationalizing to himself that his hosts might eat others but never him. Then he made two discoveries which completely unsettled him. One day he returned unexpectedly to Mehevi's house and found the inmates clustered around three tapa packages he had often observed hanging from the ridgepole. He forced his way inside the circle and saw three dried human heads, one apparently of a white man, which he assumed to be war trophies. (Most likely, these were all probably revered skulls of departed kinsmen.) Then soon afterwards a war party returned from a nearby valley carrying bloody packages, which Melville knew had to be the flesh and heads of the three enemy warriors slain in battle. Mehevi sternly warned him away from the ceremonies that followed. For three days he listened apprehensively to the steady, thunderous sound of beating drums coming from a house in the taboo area. He knew in his heart that a cannibal feast was in progress. Finally, on the third day he was allowed into the area. He saw a wooden box, lifted the lid, and found inside to his horror the jumbled and bloody bones of a human skeleton.

A frightened Melville lay awake all that night, his imagination run wild, caught up in unmanageable terrors. "Was the same doom reserved for me?" he asked himself. "Was I destined to perish, to be devoured and my head to be preserved as a fearful memento of the event?"

Melville's dread deepened after he realized that Mehevi had no intention of allowing him to return to his civilization. He saw his fate was that of "indulgent captivity" in Typee Valley. One or more warriors escorted him wherever he went. All of his requests to walk out of the valley to the sea were refused. Typee Valley ceased to be his "Happy Valley" and became rather a hellish cage in which his captors were indulgently fattening him for a cannibal feast.

Melville's fears may have been understandable, but they were largely unfounded. His hosts had no intention of eating him. He had become much too valuable to them as a beachcomber to let him depart freely from their sheltered valley. He was a curiosity, to be shown off to visitors from other valleys, in a sense the reverse of the "Wild Man from Borneo" on exhibit in American freak shows. But he also provided them with valuable information on the French forces of occupation and Western ways in general. He had taught them how to use a needle and thread, showed them how his straight razor could make that daily chore much easier than the shark teeth they had been using, and even entertained the children with pop guns he assembled. Only once did Mehevi show disappointment in his American guest. One day he brought him an old musket, badly rusted, and asked him to restore it to its original condition. Melville insisted he lacked both the skills and tools to do the job, much to the distress of the chief, "who regarded me for a moment as if he half suspected I was some inferior sort of white man, who after all did not know much more than a Typee."

Melville's escape came in the form of an Australian whaler, the *Lucy Ann*. Desperately short of crew, the captain, having learned of Melville's presence, offered to buy him out of Typee Valley. He sent an interpreter ashore with various trade goods to secure the American's release. Mehevi and Fayaway, accompanied by several warriors, brought him

down to the beach. But the chief indignantly rejected the calico cloth and gun powder the Australian captain had offered.
Melville suddenly broke loose from his captors, ran along the
shore, and leaped into the whaler's boat, as it headed out to
sea. The startled warriors dashed into the surf and began
swimming after the boat. Melville grabbed a boat hook from
the bottom, just as one warrior reached the boat and seized
him. He swung the hook with all his strength and buried it
into the man's throat.

A few minutes later he was safely aboard the *Lucy Ann*.
A sailor brought him some fresh water. Melville stared at the
man dumbfounded. Four years before in Liverpool, England,
they had met at a boarding house for sailors and become
friendly. "And here we were together again . . . under circumstances which almost made me doubt my own experience,"
he wrote later.

For all her problems the *Acushnet* had been newly constructed and was fundamentally sound. The *Lucy Ann*, on
the other hand, was in such disrepair that she was little more
than a floating coffin. She had seen her first service during
the War of 1812 on the American side before being captured
by the British, who many years later sold her to an Australian firm. The authorities at Sydney had condemned her
two years before, but her owners continued to send her to
sea. The crew's quarters swarmed with cockroaches and rats.
Parts of her bulwarks were rotten and ready to collapse. The
lower masts were dangerously weak, and both her standing
and running rigging were sorely worn.

Her crew was equally sordid. "A wild company,"
Melville called them, "men of many climes—not at all precise in their toilet arrangements but picturesque in their very
tatters." Only one of them could even write his name, a disgraced doctor named John Troy whom the crew had called
Dr. Long Ghost because of his appearance. He stood six feet
tall—"a tower of bones," Melville described him. But he was
well educated, sprinkling his speech with quotations from
writers as diverse as Virgil and Hobbes. And he had seen the

world. The two quickly became fast friends. Troy suggested the two of them jump ship in Tahiti. Melville agreed.

But first the *Lucy Ann* called at the nearby Marquesan island of Hiva Oa, where sixty years later the French artist Paul Gauguin would end his days in a syphilitic torment. They anchored in the bay. Soon afterwards a canoe came alongside with eight or ten island youths and a beachcomber, an Englishman who said his name was Lem Hardy. Melville stared at him in horror. The young man was tattooed from head to foot and sported a blue shark across his forehead.

The two beachcombers talked at length. Melville was both fascinated and repelled by a man who had obviously gone far more native than he would have ever done. Hardy explained that he had jumped ship ten years earlier and was the only white man on Hiva Oa. He was a perfect example of how easily one white man could suddenly alter a local balance of power among neighboring tribes. He had gone ashore armed with a musket and a bag of powder and balls. The island was divided among several tribes, each in the possession of its own valley. The Englishman immediately formed an alliance with one chief and waged war on his behalf against his enemies. In a bold night attack, armed with his musket and backed by a small army of determined warriors, he vanquished two tribes, and the next morning forced the others to surrender. The grateful chief awarded him the tattooed hand of his daughter along with four hundred pigs, ten houses, and fifty double-braided mats of split grass. Back in England he had been an orphan boy without any prospects, scorned by everyone. There on Hiva Oa he was the powerful war-god of the entire island.

"And for the most part, it is just this sort of men—so many of whom are found among sailors—uncared for by a single soul, without ties, reckless, and impatient of the restraints of civilization, who are occasionally found quite at home upon the savage islands of the Pacific," Melville observed later in *Omoo*. "And, glancing at their hard lot in their own country, who can marvel at their choice?"

After Hiva Oa the *Lucy Ann* set on a westward course, and for several weeks cruised about the Pacific in a fruitless search for whales. Discontent ran high among the crew. Food supplies were scanty and consisted entirely of condemned

Royal Navy stores bought at auction in Sydney. Half the crew was sick and unfit for duty.

On September 20, 1842, the high peaks of Tahiti loomed over the horizon. A few hours later the ship anchored just off the small town of Papeete. Once again Melville had arrived at a moment of crisis. Ten days before Rear Admiral Dupetit-Thouars in his flagship *La Reine Blanche* had forced Queen Pomare to yield up her island's independence for a future as a French colony. Her preference had been for the English, but Dupetit-Thouars' threat of a naval bombardment proved persuasive. A few hours later she fled to the nearby island of Moorea.

Melville, Troy, and eight other seamen appealed to the British consul to condemn the *Lucy Ann* as unseaworthy. Her captain retaliated by charging them all with mutiny, and they were put in the Broom Road jail, famous throughout the South Pacific as the Calabooza Beretanee. It consisted of a thatched roof above several sets of stocks and an easy-going Tahitian jailer who let his prisoners roam freely about the town during the day. There they stayed until the *Lucy Ann* unfurled her sails and limped out to sea again.

Melville used his time on Tahiti to educate himself about the impact of Western civilization on the native Polynesian culture. He observed the actions of the "kannakippers," a native police force set up by the missionaries to monitor the behavior of the islanders for any signs of sinful activities. He visited the makeshift Catholic mission that had recently been installed where he knew he could hit upon the priests for food and brandy. The three priests were wizened men with pinched faces who went about Papeete in black gowns and black three-cornered hats so big that they almost disappeared beneath them, peeking out from under the brims like a trio of snails.

Melville found in Tahiti an island world whose native culture had been shamelessly debased under the onslaught of Western civilization. The Protestant missionaries had been particularly effective at snuffing out the vital customs and heritages that had once formed the backbone of Tahitian culture. They outlawed the native religion, dismantled the temples, and forbade the beautiful crafts, dances, games, and festivals. Within just a few decades the once vibrant islanders had been reduced to an idle, restless, bewildered, and disease-ridden people adrift in a world they no longer recognized.

"Their prospects are hopeless," an angry Melville lashed out in *Omoo.* "Years ago brought to a stand, where all that is corrupt in barbarism and civilization unite, to the exclusion of the virtues of either state; like other uncivilized beings brought into contact with Europeans, they must here remain stationary until utterly extinct."

After six weeks on Tahiti, Melville and his companion Troy took jobs on Moorea at the big State of Maine mission farm, digging potatoes for twelve hours a day under the cruel equatorial sun. Both men tired of the drudgery after a few weeks and decided to hit the open road. Their clothes in tatters, barefooted, and garbed like comic opera brigands, the pair started out on a tour of discovery of the island of Moorea. Their destination was the remote village of Tamai on the opposite side, where, they had heard, prevailed a Tahitian culture little changed since the arrival of Captain Cook. That was not quite true. The natives in that part of the island were nominal Christians, but many of their traditional customs were still very much alive. European articles were rarely seen, and the people there still wore their tapa cloth garments. An old chief received the two white youths with the customary Polynesian hospitality. They even persuaded him to arrange for a group of local girls to put on an exhibit of some of the erotic dances for which the islands were so famous. The performance took place late one night in the moonlight in a fern-carpeted clearing away from town. The two beachcombers found Tamai so enchanting they might have lingered there indefinitely. But the sudden appearance of several missionaries quickly put them to rout.

Troy then suggested they walk to Tareu on the western side of Moorea where Queen Pomare had set up a temporary court after the French seizure of Tahiti. He was convinced that she would be in such desperate need for foreign advisers she would appoint them both ministers in her government. In a flagrant act of poor taste and crude manners the pair bluffed their way in the palace—actually, a cluster of thatched huts. Queen Pomare sat on the floor eating poi, breadfruit, coconuts, and roast pig amidst a jumble of possessions—a folio volume of Hogarth's prints, gilded candelabras, laced hats, even a crown sent by England's Queen Victoria, all heaped up with rolls of tapa, paddles, fish spears, and coconut shells. Her bare feet stuck out from under a loose gown of blue silk while she had fastened two rich shawls about her neck. Troy boldly strolled forward and accosted the large, matronly queen. She looked up, surprised and offended. Her attendants quickly hurried the two beachcombers outside and ordered them never to return. (Within a few years the once proud queen had fallen on such hard times that she took in laundry from visiting ships to insure her survival.)

Melville and Troy parted company soon afterwards. An American whaler from Martha's Vineyard, the *Charles and Henry*, was anchored in the little harbor of Tareu to provision. Melville went on board, met with the captain, and signed on as an ordinary seaman for the next leg of her whaling cruise to the Hawaiian Islands, or the Sandwich Islands, as they were then known.

Melville found the Hawaiian Islands utterly unlike the Marquesas. Honolulu and Lahaina were the two busiest ports among all the Pacific islands. Hundreds of American whaling vessels and merchant ships called there each year, disgorging thousands of sailors upon the two towns. Once again Melville found himself treading in the wake of European imperialists. A few years earlier the commander of a British man-of-war had seized the islands from King Kamehameha III. But the British Foreign Office repudiated the action a few months later and dispatched another warship to return the islands to their lawful king. Melville arrived in May of 1843 at the end of the period of British sovereignty over the islands.

After a brief stay in Lahaina, Melville took up residence in Honolulu, working first in a bowling alley as a pin setter and later as a clerk for a British storekeeper. Once again he saw everywhere the evidence of a native people debauched and demoralized by the agents of a civilization that presumed its superiority. As in Tahiti there was the same contrast between the handsome dwellings of prosperous foreign merchants and the wretched hovels of the islanders who lived in misery and squalor. He particularly deplored the "Kanaka cab-horses," four-wheeled carts drawn by native Hawaiians in which the wives of missionaries rode. Later he drew the wrath of the American missionary societies when he bitterly complained that the islanders in Honolulu "had been civilized into draft horses and evangelized into beasts of burden."

Melville's adventures in the Pacific were now nearly at an end. Shortly after his twenty-fourth birthday, he enlisted as an ordinary seaman on the American naval frigate *United States*, heading toward her home port of Boston. She set sail shortly after noon on August 17, 1843. Impatient to get home, Melville traded the relaxed freedom of a South Seas beachcomber's life for the stern discipline of a man-of-war.

Fourteen months later on October 14, 1844, the *United States* finally pulled into Boston Harbor and discharged her crew. Melville was just twenty-five years old. He had been away for four years. But the experiences of those voyages would yield the novels and stories that would make him famous. He began writing soon after he had settled ashore. The next year an English publisher brought out his first book, *Typee: A Peep at Polynesian Life*. It was a sensational success and generated enormous discussion and controversy. But the reviewer for the English magazine *John Bull* perhaps summed up the feeling of a majority of the readers when he wrote: "Since the joyous moment when we first read *Robinson Crusoe* and believed it, we have not met so bewitching a book as this narrative of Herman Melville's." An American edition soon followed and was equally successful. In time the popularity of *Typee* eventually reached back to Nuku Hiva. A naval officer reported after a visit there that the name of Fayaway had become all the rage among the island girls.

"Ill-fated people!" Melville warned in *Typee*. "I shudder when I think of the change a few years will produce in their paradisiacal abode."

Melville's pronouncement of doom for the idyllic society in Typee Valley proved prophetic and came to pass all too quickly. When Captain Cook visited the Marquesas in 1774, he estimated their population at 100,000. But the Europeans and Americans who followed brought disease and disaster. Plagues of smallpox and measles wiped out entire valleys. By the time the French artist Paul Gauguin arrived in 1901, the 492 square miles of the Marquesas Islands supported just 3,500 confused, hostile, and apathetic people.

Perhaps even more important to the destruction of the cohesive tribal society of Typee Valley that Melville had experienced was the ascendancy of the missionaries on the Marquesas. The French military forces that had landed at Nuku Hiva shortly before *Acushnet's* arrival soon gave a later generation of zealous missionaries both the security and muscle they needed to undertake the systematic destruction of the native culture. On Tahiti and the other South Sea islands, as in the Marquesas, the European and American missionaries were completely uncompromising toward all aspects of native life. They prohibited music, dances, songs, festivals, nudity and tattooing, and enforced their edicts with the bayonets and muskets of the armies of occupation.

Melville had lived among the Typees when they were in their glory as a strong, vigorous, and self-confident people. When the American traveler Frederick O'Brien visited Typee Valley seventy years later, he found only a remnant of people, too listless and demoralized to care for themselves. They no longer cultivated the coconut palms, breadfruit trees, and other plants that once flourished, but preferred to sit sadly near their fires and recollect their past. "I found myself in a loneliness indescribable and terrible," he wrote in his book, *White Shadows in the South Seas.* "No sound but that of a waterfall at a distance parted the somber silence. Humanity was not so much absent as gone, and a feeling of doom and death was in the motionless air, which lay like a weight upon leaf and flower."

In 1956 Robert C. Suggs, an anthropologist from Columbia University, arrived in Nuku Hiva to begin the first serious archaeological and anthropological study of the island's people and their past ever undertaken. He returned as head of several other expeditions over the next half-dozen years. Suggs spent many months on extensive excavations in Typee Valley. One of his workers was a woman named Heiku'a, whose grandfather had died at a very old age in 1943. He had been the chief depository of the valley's oral history and had passed along the legends and anecdotes to his granddaughter. A favorite story had concerned an

American whaler they called Merivi who had come to Typee Valley at the time of the arrival of the French fleet at Taiohae Bay. He had lived among the people and taken as his lover the beautiful Pe'ue.

Thus, it was that Suggs had his encounter with the ghost of Herman Melville. He had read closely *Typee*, a work he considered the most authoritative description of the Marquesan culture as it existed before the arrival of the missionaries. At his urging, Heiku'a recounted at length the Typee version of the story of Melville and Fayaway. The anthropologist was stunned to learn that in their oral history, so carefully preserved through all those generations and the near-genocidal death of the people, Melville (or Merivi, as they knew him) still existed. But he existed for them, not as a young sailor in Polynesia for the adventure, but as a semi-god. As Suggs recorded the history later:

> The [Typee] inhabitants were struck by Melville's fair skin, his eye color, and his reddish hair, according to the story, and treated him as a minor supernatural being. . . . Wherever he went, according to Heiku'a, he was carried in a litter and treated with utmost respect. He was given a wife, Pe'ue by name (Fayaway according to Melville's quaint orthography), who was supposedly an ancestress of Heiku'a on her father's side. He was not given the chance to escape, however, for the [Typees] believed his presence to be a good omen. Finally, after much pleading, he was carried to the beach to see an American ship that had stopped there and managed to reach the visitors' longboat while his native guards were occupied picking up trinkets that the American seamen had scattered in the water to attract their attention. Once in the longboat, he was borne safely to the waiting whaler under a shower of spears and slingstones hurled by his former captors, who were furious at losing their half-god. The story interested me, for it was rather unusual to hear the entire episode passed on by word of mouth in such a faithful fashion, with all the details so well tied in to the local geography.

CHAPTER SIX

Islands of Despair:

The Castaways of the Torres Strait

The Torres Strait lies north of the Cape York Peninsula in Australia, across from the large island of New Guinea, and separates the Coral Sea to the east and the Arafura Sea to the west. Scores of small islands and submerged coral reefs choke this shallow sea, making navigation, even in this modern age, hazardous. Numerous vessels and their crews have perished in these waters.

The Torres Strait has been a principal waterway for over three hundred years for ships entering and leaving the Pacific. The first Westerner to visit the area was the Spaniard Luis Vaez de Torres, who discovered it in 1606. Stories abound in the region of the discovery of ancient relics from the Spanish ships that once regularly plied the area. In a cave on Prince Wales Island a crumbling skeleton of a man was reputedly found, alongside a sword of Spanish design. Nearby rested a valuable gold goblet. On another island in the late nineteenth century a white official saw a group of native children using antique Spanish gold coins as counters in a game in which flat beans usually serve as the medium.

Captain James Cook in the *Endeavour* rediscovered the Torres Strait for England in 1770. Lieutenant Bligh passed through there in his small boat after the mutineers had set him adrift in the Tongan Islands in 1789. He set his course for the Australian coast, sailed north, and then headed west through the Torres Strait to the Dutch colony of Timor. He named two of the islands Sunday and Wednesday because he had passed them on those days.

In 1791 Captain Edward Edwards on the frigate *Pandora* sailed through the strait with fifteen mutineers from the *Bounty* he had captured earlier on Tahiti. The ship ran aground on a reef off Murray Island on August 28. Thirty-five people drowned, including four of the mutineers. The survivors took to four open boats and followed Bligh's route to Timor.

In the latter part of the nineteenth century a pearl rush to tiny Warrior Island and its nearby reefs developed after an Australian captain found that all the islanders there wore necklaces and ornaments made of pearls. They were so common that the children used them for marbles. By 1900 treasure seekers had scoured the reefs clear and hardly an oyster was to be found any longer in the area. Other than those pearls, the outside world has had little interest in the region.

In recent years the Torres Strait has been known only to a handful of anthropologists studying the island cultures and hardy travelers with a love for the exotic and remote who visited the region on small sailing vessels or an occasional expeditionary cruise ship. The region came briefly into the limelight in 1983 with the publication of Lucy Irvine's book, *Castaway*, an account of a year she had spent on a small, uninhabited island in the Torres Strait with an Englishman. Her intelligent, well written memoir captured the imagination of tens of thousands of readers and was later made into a major feature movie.

Irvine and her companion, G.W. Kingsland (whom she refers to simply as G throughout her memoir), were never castaways in the proper sense but beachcombers. Both had fallen in love with the fantasy of a Robinson Crusoe existence on a deserted tropical island. They had met by chance.

Irvine came across a brief classified advertisement that Kingsland had run in a London tabloid. It stated simply: "Writer seeks 'wife' for year on tropical island." They discovered they shared a passion for the same fantasy and decided to become partners in the adventure.

Born in 1956 in Middlesex, England, Irvine had run away from school at thirteen. For the next ten years or so she worked at a variety of jobs as a cleaning lady, clerk, waitress, pastry cook, and concierge. She briefly was married to a stone mason.

Kingsland was twenty-six years older than Irvine. He was a farm boy who had become a publisher and had then gone into bankruptcy. He had married twice, fathered two families, fought in one war, and traveled widely. And he had been on a personal quest for his Isle of Desire for many years. He had actually set up as Robinson Crusoe twice before, once appropriately on the same Juan Fernández island where Selkirk had spent his four years. But each time the experiment had proven a disappointment, largely because the two islands were already inhabited and in regular communication with the outside. He now sought a deserted tropical island without safety nets of any sort.

This time Kingsland had decided upon the Torres Strait where his research had suggested he would stand a better chance of finding an isolated, uninhabited island. His fantasy had expanded to include a female companion, hence his classified advertisement in a London paper. The project was enormously impractical from the first. Between the two of them they had only enough money for one-way air tickets to Australia with little left over for supplies. Even more disconcerting, neither of them had any real survival skills, only boundless hope and enthusiasm to get them through a year on a deserted island. The Australian government proved prudish about allowing an unmarried couple to settle one of their islands and demanded they have a marriage of convenience for appearance's sake before granting them permission. The fact that Irvine had lost her sexual interest in the older Kingsland after a few nights together in London suggested that emotional problems would be every bit as challenging as the physical demands of survival.

The couple eventually secured permission to settle on

uninhabited Tuin Island, a small piece of flat land located near the much larger Moa and Badu islands in the western island group of the Torres Strait. Two Torres Strait islanders took them over in an aluminum dinghy, along with their meager supplies. Their food for the next year consisted entirely of one box of tea, a couple of pounds of oat flakes, two bags of dried fruit, one box of noodles, six packets of brown rice, three pounds of dried beans, a box of spaghetti noodles, a large bottle of cooking oil, a couple of pounds of salt, and some black pepper. They also had a selection of seeds with which they hoped to grow a garden, but that never succeeded because the Torres Strait was experiencing its driest year in decades. Their other supplies included some water bottles, a machete, fishing line and hooks, a two-person tent, a few kitchen utensils, some knives, and not much more. They had no boat. They could not have been more poorly prepared for their adventure. Yet neither was particularly worried. Irvine wrote in her diary:

> We are here simply as 20th century castaways and our main aim is simply to survive, not to achieve. People do things in different ways. We have not come to Tuin to write a book on expert bush living or how to tame the jungle. We claim no great knowledge in any of the fields that could serve us most usefully here: raising crops in tropical and drought conditions; locating and securing a permanent supply of fresh water; being able to forecast weather and tidal conditions—but we are managing. We are alive, and all things considered, very much kicking.

They pitched their small tent on the edge of the beach. A few large flat stones arranged in a circle with a refrigerator grill laid on top became their cooking fire. The branches of a nearby tree held their mugs, oven gloves, and cooking utensils. A couple of conch shells stuck in the sand on either side provided a decorative flourish.

They quickly learned some of the dangers facing them on Tuin. Sharks abounded in their lagoon. But saltwater crocodiles, up to twenty feet in length and boasting voracious appetites, were a greater potential danger although they never saw one. The island supported a limited variety of wildlife, mostly monitor lizards, geckos, flying foxes, and lovely white Torres Strait pigeons.

The couple discovered a small fresh water spring and limited supplies of wild fruits which were available on a seasonal basis. Much of each day was spent in securing sufficient food for the evening meal. Even getting coconuts proved a taunting challenge, as neither had the islanders' skill of scrambling barefooted up a fifty-foot trunk to the cluster of nuts in the canopy.

In fact, the limited food supplies, mostly fresh fish and coconuts, soon caused them to become malnourished. Small infections on their legs quickly became nasty ulcers in the tropical heat and humidity. They soon exhausted their supply of medicine. They had no way of communicating with the world beyond and had foolishly neglected to make arrangements with local islanders to check on them regularly. As it happened, a life-threatening emergency, an infection caused by Irvine's IUD, forced her evacuation to nearby Badu Island where she was airlifted to the hospital on Thursday Island.

Complicated problems developed from Irvine's early decision to be a Mrs. Robinson Crusoe without sexual duties. She soon found herself in a *No Exit* situation, in which hell was a rude, obnoxious, boorish man she could not escape, who continued to press her to do her sexual "duty" as his wife in their nights together in their small tent.

"It was clear from the start that I was not going to get away lightly with having committed the sin of falling in love with the idea of an island, and not with G. Playing the conjugal role in the tent was not one of the duties I felt to be imperative for survival, and if my values were being revised in other areas, this was the one sensitive spot I could not allow to be violated. Sex was something too valuable to be misused. But the pain and resentment my coldness caused had a wretched effect on the quality of our daily life."

In spite of the hardships, Irvine found compensations in other areas. Tuin did not disappoint her. As the weeks passed, she spent countless hours on solitary explorations of its varied terrain, the groves of coconut palms and mango trees, its fields of purple grasses, the isolated white sand beaches where marine turtles came ashore at night to lay their eggs in the warm sand above the high tide mark, and the surrounding reefs where she fished for their evening meals.

"The island had me like a lover," she confessed in her book. "I was totally captivated by the very indifference of its charm, aware always that my soft body was the alien, but as it toughened and moved more naturally to the rhythm of Tuintime I felt that I was beginning to blend. It was almost as though the less I consciously observed, the less frequently I recalled the fact that being on Tuin was something to do with a plan, a project, and the more I simply existed, obeying the few rules that made existence possible, the more 'at home' I became. Feeling at home meant no longer gushing effectively about the beauties of the island or shrinking from the harshnesses. It meant fewer and fewer comparisons, voiced or in thought, between conditions on Tuin and those in 'civilization.' "

After several months they had their first visitors, several pidgin-speaking natives from the nearby island of Badu, who were shy but helpful, and in time became a lifeline from another world. The islanders built them a permanent shelter before the start of the rainy season, taught them how to weave mats and wall coverings from palm leaves, kept them supplied with food and water, and became their friends. Worried about their deteriorating health, they ferried over two white nurses from the clinic on their island to attend to their medical needs. Their support allowed them to stay on their island. Any semblance of self-sufficiency was long since gone.

The islanders' arrival brought about a remarkable transformation in Kingsland. Their only industry was lobster fishing. That provided enough money to buy outboard motors for their dinghies. While this modernization greatly increased their range and thus their income, it also put them at the mercy of their engines. If an engine failed to work, the whole system fell apart. The nearest mechanic was on Thursday Island to the south. Having a motor sent there for repairs could take several months.

One day the islanders discovered that Kingsland knew

how to repair engines. Soon afterwards one of them showed up with a red Honda generator in his boat. The Englishman took it apart, cleaned it thoroughly inside and out, and soon had it working again. In due time he made himself indispensable to the islanders. A steady stream of broken engines and motors ended up in their camp. One day a message came about an engine on Badu too large to transport to Tuin. It belonged to the chairman of the Badu Island Council, who wanted Kingsland to come to his island for as long as it took to repair his tractor. The islanders provided their honored guest with both lodging and food. They lined up at his door to tell him their engine problems. He soon became an important economic asset to the community. "G was rediscovering himself as a man," a pleased Irvine recalled later, "a lively, resourceful, confident man, well respected by others."

Kingsland had finally found his piece of paradise on Badu Island. Like the beachcombers and castaways of an earlier era, he began a process of gradual absorption into the local community. When Irvine left after a year to return to England, he remained there on Badu among his new friends.

The experiences of Irvine and Kingsland on Tuin Island contrast sharply with those of earlier castaways unfortunate enough to come ashore in this region. Perhaps no place in the world was more inhospitable for castaways than this pocket of Melanesia. Beachcombers rarely figured in the culture of these islands. The ship-jumping sailor, the escaped convict from Australia, and the dreamy romantic always avoided this area. The islanders there were ferocious warriors, eager headhunters, and ravenous cannibals. They callously dispatched the aged and infirm. Birth control was practiced after birth. A woman who had one baby too many might simply bury alive her extra child. If some mongrel puppy caught her fancy, she might take it in and nurse it like her own child. And when it had grown to be a dog, she would gladly offer it up for the cooking pot without the slightest show of emotion.

Disasters at sea were a normal and prominent feature of the Victorian world. The press, popular literature, theater, and arts in general thrived on tales of shipwrecks. The eastern coast of Australia, especially the region of the Torres Strait, provided a greater abundance of sensational castaway stories than any region in the world. Among the large number of female castaways was Mrs. Fraser, a survivor of the *Stirling Castle*, wrecked off the Australian coast in 1837, who subsequently was exhibited in a London peep show.

The worst disaster to befall castaways in these waters occurred in 1858. The ship *St. Paul*, bound from Hong Kong to Sydney with 327 Chinese coolies destined for the Australian goldfields, ran aground on a nameless reef in the northern waters off the coast. The captain with eight of his crew abandoned the unfortunate Chinese to their fate. A nearby tribe of islanders hurried to the wreck. They quickly stripped the ship of everything of value, including all the metal objects. Next they rounded up the Chinese and hustled them to a nearby island. There they put the unfortunate castaways in pens, fattened them, and then butchered small groups for special feasts. When rescue finally came many months later, only sixteen of the Chinese were alive to tell their gruesome story.

So dangerous were the waters of the Torres Strait that in the early 1800s captains on ships that regularly cruised the area set up a post office in a cave on tiny Booby Island. This bleak spot of land had been discovered independently by Cook and Bligh, both of whom named it after the tens of thousands of nesting gannets there. Inside the cave they placed a large box with the words *Post Office* painted on its sides. Letters left there were picked up by captains heading in the appropriate direction. They also maintained a log in which they wrote navigational advice for novice captains attempting the strait for the first time. In 1847 the New South Wales Legislative Council voted funds for a cache of supplies to be kept in the cave on Booby Island for shipwrecked sailors. Other ships added clothing and spare stores. Australian historian Bill Beatty reported that as recently as 1964 the old *Post Office* box was still there, while the names of nineteenth century sailing ships and crewmembers who had visited the island were scratched on the walls of the cave.

The natives who inhabited the islands and coastal areas of the Torres Strait and northern Queensland evolved a curious theory to explain the mysterious white visitors who occasionally sailed pass in great ships or came ashore on their beaches. They were the Lamars, spirits of Aboriginal people who had been misdirected after death. Instead of leading a happy existence on their island paradise they called Boigu far up in the heavens, they had gone astray to another place they referred to as Shadowland. They were pale because they were dead. And they were often malevolent because only discontented spirits up to mischief would return to the land of the living. They were also restless, sailing about endlessly in their ghost ships. The natives knew from experience that such ships were invincible because they were armed with the big "thunder sticks" and protected by the Thunder God. But they also brought valuable objects, such as iron tools, from the Shadowland.

The natives believed that by killing the Lamars who washed mysteriously up on their beaches, often after a storm, or who foolishly came ashore in their little boats, these would return to their proper place and never trouble the living again. And Lamar heads, properly preserved, were valuable trade items with the tribes in New Guinea to the north which believed them to be powerful charms.

On occasion castaways were spared because of a perceived resemblance to deceased natives. When this happened, they were promptly adopted by their "former" family. This was never an easy task. The Lamars had always forgotten everything they had known before and would need to know again to survive in the harsh world of the Torres Strait. Even their language had to be learned anew.

The first of these remarkable survivals involved two young boys, John Ireland and William D'Oyley, from the English barque *Charles Eaton*, which wrecked in August 1834. They lived for two years with a group of headhunters and cannibals notorious throughout the Torres Strait for their savagery.

The *Charles Eaton*, a 313-ton barque, sailed from Sydney bound for India with a crew of twenty-six under the command of Captain Frederick Moore. The passengers were

George Armstrong, a London lawyer, Dr. J. Grant, a surgeon, and Captain D'Oyley of the East India Company's Artillery, who was accompanied by his wife, two young sons, and an Indian servant woman. Captain D'Oyley was returning to his regiment in India.

The ship arrived at the Torres Strait on August 14. Sailing conditions worsened, as a storm swept in from the Coral Sea. Captain Moore decided to seek calmer waters and took the *Charles Eaton* through a narrow channel in the Great Barrier Reef. But he soon found himself caught up in a maze of deadly reefs. An enormous wave lifted the ship up and brought it down with a sickening crash on a reef. Both the keel and rudder snapped off. The ship stuck fast. The crew and passengers huddled together, while giant waves crashed over the deck. They felt the ship grinding, crunching down on to the reef until only the poop remained above water.

Frantically, the crew lowered the boats. The first longboat was quickly smashed by the enormous waves pounding against the coral. A second boat was also lost, its two crewmembers disappearing beneath the waves. Then George Pigott, the bosun, Laurance Constantine, a carpenter, and three seamen hurriedly launched the dinghy. The waves caught them and immediately swept them away.

The storm abated in the night, and the next day dawned clear and sunny. The survivors saw three miles away another ship stranded on a reef, masts still standing and sails set, a victim of an earlier storm. Captain Moore and his men gathered loose timbers from the wreck, and soon they were busily at work constructing two rafts. The captain ordered the D'Oyley family and their Indian servant to take to the first raft along with several of his own crew.

Two days later the crew completed the construction of a second raft and launched it with the remaining seventeen people on board, including the two cabin boys, John Ireland and John Sexton. They had been unable to salvage any firearms. Their daily ration consisted of two swallows of water and half a biscuit per man. Over the next week the raft slowly drifted northward with the current some forty miles and finally ground to a halt on remote Boydong Island, a barren mound of sand with a handful of wind-blown trees and patches of drab green bushes.

The mariners' luck had run out. Also on Boydong Island were a group of fierce headhunters from Aureed Island in the Torres Strait. Soon the castaways found themselves surrounded by dozens of club-carrying warriors. Several wore polished bones in their ears and noses, necklaces of shark teeth, and shell armlets. Others sported headdresses of beautiful birds-of-paradise feathers and curious leggings of split bamboo. Some were bearded, others clean-shaven.

Shouting "Toree! Toree!" the savages rushed the raft and crowded the castaways aside, eagerly looking for scraps of iron, the "toree" which was to them far more valuable than gold. All they found were a few knives. Then they turned their attention to the Lamars, those spirits returned to earth life from the dead. The two cabin boys fascinated them. The islanders examined them closely, arguing among themselves. "Wak! Wak!" they said repeatedly about Ireland. Sexton they called Kabi.

The adults slowly walked around Boydong Island looking for food and water, the warriors dogging their footsteps. Hunger, thirst, and fatigue had so exhausted them they could scarcely make it back to their raft.

The savages grew increasingly agitated and began shouting and waving their war clubs. The crew of the *Charles Eaton* believed they would die shortly. Robert Clare, the first mate, read some prayers aloud from a book he had salvaged from the ship. But the blacks tried to reassure them, urging them through hand gestures to sleep. The whites lay down on the sand in a shaded area and immediately fell into a heavy sleep. Ireland suspected the worse. He only pretended to sleep and instead watched the blacks. He recalled later: "I saw one of the natives advance from a canoe in a strange manner; stealing cautiously along with a club in his hand, hid as he thought from our sight behind his back, and which he dropped on the beach."

Ireland tried to waken an older sailor nearby, but the man slept too soundly. Then the boy himself collapsed into an exhausted sleep. Less than an hour later shouts awoke him abruptly. He looked up and saw the blacks moving among the sleeping whites, swinging their clubs. Within a few minutes only he and Sexton were left alive. As the horrified boys watched, the natives stooped over the bodies, bamboo knives in hand, and swiftly severed the heads.

Then a warrior approached young Ireland. "A black came to me with a carving knife in his hand, which I could see belonged to the cabin and recollected its being put in the raft. He seized me and tried to cut my throat. But I grasped the blade of the knife in my right hand and held it fast. I struggled hard for my life. He at last threw me down and placing his knee upon my breast, tried to wrest the knife out of my hand. But I still kept it, though one of my fingers was cut to the bone."

Ireland broke away, ran into the surf, and swam a short distance offshore. Sexton soon joined him. The natives paid them no attention. Instead they collected up the heads and danced around a flickering fire. "From these heads, I saw the savages every now and then cut pieces of flesh from the cheeks and pluck out the eyes and eat them, shouting most hideously."

The two cabin boys returned to the beach, expecting the worst. But the islanders' blood lust was dissipated. The two boys were spared only because the warriors believed they were the dead sons of islanders they knew and could probably be ransomed.

Early the next morning the savages broke their camp on Boydong Island, piled the two cabin boys and the fresh heads of their shipmates into their long war canoes, and sailed northward to the top of the Cape York Peninsula and then out into the Torres Strait to Pullan Island. Flourishing their heads and weapons, they marched into a small collection of huts, where an excited group of natives greeted them as conquering heroes.

Ireland and Sexton were stunned to discover alive in the village the D'Oyley brothers, George who was eight and little William, barely three years old along with Portland, the ship's Newfoundland dog. From poles stuck in the sand near the huts hung the heads of the others on that first raft. Ireland recognized those of Mrs. D'Oyley and Captain Moore, but the others had been so badly mutilated he could make no positive identification. He also saw the gown worn by Mrs. D'Oyley when she left the *Charles Eaton*, the steward's white hat and watch, and several other articles belonging to those on the first raft.

For the next three months the four English boys lived with the headhunters. They were treated cruelly, but little William bore the brunt of the headhunters' anger. He cried constantly for his mother. This infuriated their captors, who tied him a tree trunk and beat him with long bamboo poles.

Much of the time was spent in the war canoes with sails made from woven palm fronds, traveling from island to island, from reef to reef. They quickly learned both the language and the important survival skills—where to find fresh water, how to make a fire by rubbing sticks together, how to handle the weapons, where to find edible fruits, and how to spear fish. Finally, they arrived at Aureed Island, a popular congregation point for all the tribes in the Torres Strait. There the four white boys were separated. One group took George D'Oyley and John Sexton. They were never seen again.

A second group sailed with John Ireland and William D'Oyley to Mer Island (now known as Murray), located at the extreme northern tip of the Great Barrier Reef. There they were brought before Duppah, a chief whose two sons had been blown to sea in their fishing canoe and drowned the year before. He examined the boys closely. Yes, he decided, these were his two sons miraculously returned from the dead. He ordered his warriors to pay the ransom and joyously welcomed the two Lamars back into his household.

Home for the two English boys was now a sprawling village of some 700 people living in beehive shaped huts beneath towering palm trees, protected by a tall stockade. A fleet of swift war canoes was drawn up on the sandy beach in front. Ireland soon learned that the villagers lived in a state of constant alert, fearful of an attack by raiders from one of the distant islands. The men and boys never left the security of their village without their bows and arrows, spears, or clubs. Sentries stood guard at the high points of the island. And each house was guarded by an ancestral mummy, its shrivelled figure stretched out upon bamboo poles.

The two white boys were soon absorbed into the island community. The three-year-old D'Oyley forgot his birth language and became for all purposes, except his blond hair, an island child. As Wak, Ireland slipped easily into the daily routine of the village. His adopting family pierced his ears and hung tassels of braided grass through them. By now, he was quite fluent in their language. He spent many happy hours, exploring the oval-shaped island. He calculated its circumference at five miles. Gelam, an extinct volcano, dominated the western shore. The elders carefully explained to him that he must never enter the desolate valley leading down from the 750-foot summit. This was a taboo area, the abode of the dead before they departed to the blessed island of Boigu.

Like the other peoples of the Torres Strait, those on Mer Island were avid headhunters. Ireland sometimes saw the returning warriors brandishing their trophy heads from rattan slings inserted under the jaw bones. These they hung over a low fire to singe the hair off. While this went on, the girls of the village danced and sang in a circle nearby. Next the head was stripped of its remaining flesh, and hung on the main post of the house belonging to the warrior who had taken it in battle.

With the other boys his age, Ireland was trained as a warrior and in the course of time became proficient with both the hunting and fishing spears, the bow and arrow, and the various types of war clubs. He even took part in skirmishes when they encountered enemy warriors on their voyages to other islands. Eventually, he gave up all thought of rescue. The possibility seemed too remote.

And yet, unknown to Ireland, events were slowly unfolding thousands of miles away that would eventually lead to his rescue. The dinghy with the bosun, George Pigott, and four other crewmembers from the *Charles Eaton*, reached the island of Timor in the Dutch East Indies. They were captured by Malays, who used them as slaves, and were eventually rescued by Dutch authorities. Only then was the fate of the *Charles Eaton* made known. The Dutch forwarded details of the disaster to the British authorities in India. Another year passed before word finally reached Sydney. British officials briefly considered sending a ship to search for additional survivors, but then decided so much time had lapsed that all efforts would be futile.

Sometime after that, the trading vessel *Mangles*, under

the command of Captain William Carr, anchored off Mer Island. The appearance of the graceful three-masted brig in full sail threw the islanders into a frenzy. The Lamars had come again! Here was another chance to acquire precious iron. Mindful of the deadly power of the "thunder sticks," the warriors left behind their weapons. Instead they filled their war canoes with trade items—coconuts, pearl shell, and tortoise shell. With them was Ireland. From his canoe, speaking English only with the greatest of difficulty, he told the captain the story of the wreck of the *Charles Eaton* and the subsequent fate of all its crew and passengers. Captain Carr asked the boy to return to Sydney with him, but the natives refused to allow him to go on board. He was devastated emotionally when the *Mangles* finally departed. "This vessel's sailing without me made such an impression upon my mind," he recalled later, " that for three or four days I could eat no food and at length became extremely ill."

The *Mangles* eventually returned to Sydney with news of the two castaways. The governor immediately dispatched the schooner *Isabella* under the command of Captain C. Lewis to rescue the boys. She left Sydney for the Torres Strait in June of 1836, almost two years after the wreck of the *Charles Eaton*. This time Ireland persuaded Duppah to let him go by promising to get axes and other precious metal objects. Once he was on board, Captain Lewis hurried him below to his cabin and gave him a shirt, a pair of trousers, and a straw hat. He then ordered some bread, cheese, and beer brought in.

The captain made clear to Duppah that the chief must give up the two boys and offered him brand new hatchets for them. He argued to keep the young D'Oyley, who had become a favorite in the village, but soon relented. The young boy was crushed. His parents were long dead. He no longer remembered them or his native English. He knew no other life except that on Mer. And he loved his adopted parents.

"Duppah seemed to feel pain," Ireland observed later. "He cried, hugged me, and then cried again. At last he told me to come back soon and bring him plenty of things and not to forget the 'toree.'"

The *Isabella* departed Mer Island on June 28, 1836. They cruised for several weeks among the islands of the Torres

Strait, offering iron hatchets to any islanders who could produce information on the whereabouts of the other two survivors. Eventually, they learned that both were dead. George D'Oyley had taken sick and died. John Sexton had quarrelled with his captors and been speared to death.

On Aureed Island, now deserted, they found gruesome evidence of the slaughter of the crew and passengers of the *Charles Eaton*. There was a huge turtle shell painted to resemble a mask; around its edges hung seventeen human skulls, with their hair still in place. Captain Lewis examined one skull with long tresses and found a comb still clinging to the hair. This was undoubtedly all that remained of Mrs. D'Oyley.

The skulls were brought back to Sydney. On November 12, 1836, they were buried in a mass grave at Bunnerong Cemetery. Young William D'Oyley was sent to England and raised by his father's family there. He followed in his father's footsteps and made a career with the East India Company.

John Ireland arrived back in England in August 1837, four years after he had left. We know nothing about his later life except that six years later he wrote a simple, moving account of his experiences. His narrative concluded with a final hope: "All I wish the kind reader to do is to avoid the savages of Boydong Island, but lend a helping hand to civilize the kind natives of Mer Island."

There are a handful of other stories of white castaways receiving kind treatment from the savage natives of this pocket of Melanesia. The most unusual concerns a young Scotswoman, Barbara Thompson. That a young white girl should be the only survivor of a wreck, be taken captive by savages, her life spared solely because the chief claimed her as his dead daughter returned to earth life in spirit form, that she should marry a minor chief, that she should survive years of primitive life among savages and at last be rescued by a British warship—all this sounds like some implausible plot from a bad melodrama about the South Pacific. But it is true. The story of Barbara Thompson actually happened.

Barbara was born in Aberdeen, Scotland. Her father was a tinsmith, who emigrated to Sydney in 1835 when his daughter was eight years old. He prospered at first, but then his business fell off, as he developed a reputation for unsteadiness and unreliability. At the age of fifteen, Barbara eloped with her lover, Jack Thompson, the owner of a small cutter, *America*. They married and moved to Brisbane.

There temptation came in the form of an old sailor. He told Thompson he had served on a whaling vessel that had wrecked on a reef in the Torres Strait. He insisted the ship was not badly damaged and her hold was filled with barrels of high quality sperm whale oil. He urged a partnership to salvage the ship, constantly reminding Thompson of the fortune to be made by anyone bold enough to visit the wreck and walk off with the "jetsam and flotsam." Finally, the young man gave in. In 1843 Thompson with his wife, the old man as a guide, and two crewmembers set forth for the Torres Strait from Brisbane in his cutter *America*.

For several days the *America* cruised among the islands and shoals of the Cape York Peninsula without finding the wrecked vessel. Finally, Thompson understood that the old man's entire story had been invented. There had been no wreck. In anger he marooned him on a deserted sandbank.

Soon afterwards a storm swept through the area and drove the *America* on to a reef at Possession Island. The gale lasted two days. Two of the crewmen were swept overboard and drowned. Thompson drowned when he attempted to swim through the heavy waves to a nearby shore. On the third day the storm passed, but not before it had pushed the wrecked boat to tiny Entrance Island, just off the much larger Murralug (now Prince of Wales) Island.

A few hours later Barbara saw to her horror a dozen dark figures crowding the nearby shore, pointing in the direction of the wreck and shouting, "Lamar, Lamar." They pushed a large canoe into the surf and with quick strokes soon came alongside the remains of the *America*. The terrified Barbara watched as the warriors clamored on board and began a furious search of the ship for metal objects.

One young man, obviously their leader, wore a short skirt of black cassowary plumes around his waist, mother-of-pearl gleamed upon his chest, and armlets of boar's tusks encircled his powerful arms. He carried a broad wooden sword double-edged with rows of shark's teeth. His polished skin was a rich, dark brown. This was Boroto, the chief of Entrance Island. He stared hard at Barbara, the first Lamar he had ever seen.

"Gi'Om," he finally said.

The other natives crowded around, examining Barbara. "Gi'Om," they kept repeating. The white woman had no way then of understanding that she had been recognized as the reincarnated daughter of an important chief from nearby Murralug Island. The girl had drowned two years before. Her name had been Gi'Om.

Boroto took Barbara ashore to his tiny village, little more than a cluster of crude huts set on a rocky ledge near some mangrove trees. Barbara might not have known, but it was there on Possession Island that in 1770 Captain Cook landed upon a narrow beach and claimed the whole of the eastern seaboard of Australia in the name of His Majesty, King George III.

A few days later Boroto set off to nearby Murralug Island. Dull gray-green mangrove trees, densely entangled one with another, surround virtually the entire shoreline. In the village he presented Barbara to Piaquai. Yes, the old chief said, this white-skinned woman was Gi'Om, his daughter miraculously returned from the Spirit Land after her death many months before. Other members of Piaquai's tribe crowded around the bewildered white girl, carefully assessing her features. They all agreed. This was most certainly Gi'Om, his reincarnated daughter returned to live on earth again in the form of a Lamar, a spirit girl. In a formal ceremony Piaquai adopted Barbara as his daughter.

The cluster of islands off the northern shore of the Cape York Peninsula were home to the powerful Kowraregas people. The island of Murralug was the center. Old Piaquai was the chief of all chiefs. Boroto, who had rescued Barbara from the wreck, was a minor chief on little Entrance Island, so close to Murralug's shores that his people spent much of their time among relatives and friends at Piaquai's village. They were not cannibals, although on rare occasions after battles the warriors ritualistically ate portions of important enemy warriors slain in the fighting. They were, however, headhunters.

Barbara spent her first few weeks among the family of Piaquai in a state of numb panic, crouched on a mat inside a hut, understanding little of what was happening around her. Her hosts treated her with patience and tolerance. They pressed dainties upon her, urged her to eat, and watched out carefully for her welfare. They all understood that Lamars needed considerable time to adjust after their return from the Spirit Land. Gi'Om had died and forgotten everything about her previous existence. Now that she had been miraculously reborn to earth life, she must relearn everything. She would remember nothing, not even her language or such simple tasks as to how to dig for yams or where to search for edible mussels on the shore rocks. All such skills must be re-learned. And so the family and their friends undertook the second education of Barbara "Gi'Om" Thompson.

For the next five years Barbara's universe would shrink to these two remote islands of Murralug and Entrance. She would live among savages and in time become a savage herself.

Barbara dressed as the other women in the tribe dressed—in short grass skirts and nothing else. The coral rocks cut her feet, the insects tormented her, and the sun blistered her skin. The other women taught her the important survival skills. How to use the sharply pointed digging stick to unearth yams, how to spear fish in the shallow tidal pools, where to go to catch succulent crabs and mussels, which plants to harvest to make soothing poultices of healing herbs, how to make a fire with two sticks, what taboo areas needed to be avoided, and, of course, how to speak the Kowraregas language. She ate what her hosts ate—snake, rat, porcupine, opossum, kangaroo, grubs, ant eggs, moths, almost anything that moved.

As a Lamar, Barbara enjoyed a special position in the tribe. The natives treated her like a pet, and she became a great favorite. She rarely had to share in the heavy duties of the other women. Rather she stayed in camp and looked after the children while the women went out to do their chores. In little ways she hardly noticed, she was being absorbed into the tribe. That absorption was complete when she married Boroto, the minor chief who had rescued her after the shipwreck.

For the first year Barbara managed to keep some sense of the passing time. But then she gave up. She ceased to know anything of the days or months. She even found herself forgetting her own language. She fought this by singing to herself at night all the fragments of songs and ballads she could remember, but in time she thought and dreamed only in her adopted language. When the ordeal finally came to an end, she would communicate to her English rescuers only by translating her thoughts from the Kowraregas language into simple English, sometimes with great difficulty.

Despite her privileged position, Barbara suffered many hardships. She contracted ophthalmia, a common disorder among these people, and went blind in one eye. But her worst threat came from elsewhere, from a white man who lived among the natives on Badu Island to the north. He was a huge Frenchman, probably an escaped convict, who had managed through ruthlessness to make himself the chief over the natives there. He introduced some innovations in gardening and housing. He possessed several wives, a large canoe, and some property which several natives cultivated under his supervision. He adopted the native name of Wini. He ruled Badu with the absolute power of life and death. The natives there were terrified and looked upon him as a kind of living devil.

Barbara met this man just once, after a year on Murralug Island. Wini (she never knew his French name) had heard of her existence and journeyed down to see her for himself. A necklace of shark teeth hung around his neck. His loin cloth was made from shark skin. He wore a magnificent headdress of brilliantly colored bird-of-paradise feathers.

Wini told Barbara about his arrival on Badu Island in a small boat with four other men. He boasted how he had murdered his companions shortly after his arrival. Then he killed or intimidated the most important people in the tribe. Now, he boasted, he was the king of Badu Island and needed a white queen to found a dynasty. He demanded she return with him. She refused, unwilling to yield up the security she had there on Murralug Island under the protection of Piaquai for the dangers of a life with a man she perceived clearly must be mad.

The years passed. Occasionally, a ship's sails appeared in the distance. Sometimes smaller boats laden with castaways sailed past on their way to Timor. To the Aborigines they were all ghost ships peopled with the spirits of dead gone astray and doomed to endless voyaging. One of these was the British warship, the H. M. S. *Fly*, accompanied by the revenue cutter *Prince George*. Both were engaged in an exploratory expedition of the coasts of northern Australia and New Guinea. One day a party from the *Fly* went ashore at Murralug Island. The only thing of interest they found was a fresh burial mound for one of Piaquai's chiefs. A stout post stood at each corner; rows of bleached dugong ribs decorated the sides of the mound. On top of the grave were several dugong skulls. The bones and posts had been smeared with red ochre.

The sailors guessed correctly that unseen eyes watched them from the dense foliage beyond. Piaquai's warriors did indeed observe the visitors, weapons in hand. Much later Barbara advised the naturalist John MacGillivray, who had been a part of that shore party, of the dangers just beyond and what would have been their fate had they desecrated the chieftain's grave:

> While visiting the grave in question, Gi'Om told me, we were closely watched by a party of the natives, who were greatly pleased that we did not attempt to deface the tomb. Had we done so—and the temptation was great to some of us for several fine nautilus shells were hanging up, and good dugong skulls were lying on top—one or more of the party would probably have been speared.

Barbara lived with the natives for almost six years until October 16, 1848, when she finally made contact with a shore party from the British survey ship, H. M. S. *Rattlesnake*. She carried twenty-eight guns and one-hundred-and-fifty-four officers and men. They were in the Torres Strait to chart the waters, gather information on the flora and fauna, and observe the native cultures. On board the *Rattlesnake* was the naturalist MacGillivray, whose writings later would make him a major figure in that field, and a young biologist, Thomas Huxley, destined to become one of the influential scientists of his age. The *Rattlesnake* anchored off the western side of Cape York, some twenty miles from Murralug Island.

The Cape York natives announced by smoke signals to their friends on the nearby islands that Lamars had come. Barbara pleaded to Boroto and her friends to take her across to the mainland. She reassured them that she considered herself now a Kowraregas who only wanted to see the Lamars one last time and shake hands with them. She promised the natives that she would tell the whites how well she had been treated and they in turn would reward them with axes, knives, tobacco, and other prized trade articles. This argument decided the question at once. Boroto and the others eagerly escorted her to the mainland. They waited in the bushes near the beach for the whites to come ashore.

The shore party under the command of Able Seaman Scott landed on a desolate stretch of beach along the Cape York Peninsula. Their orders were to search for sources of fresh water and to collect birds and plants for scientific purposes. The sailors were all heavily armed. Suddenly, they found themselves surrounded by numerous natives, friendly and eager to trade for iron products. The well-armed party was cautious and kept the muskets at the ready. Scott ordered the natives away and led his men across the sand. A woman blocked their path. Scott ignored her and walked quickly past. Suddenly, she cried out in a pitiful voice.

"I am a white woman! Why do you leave me?"

The stunned Scott turned and examined the woman closely. She wore only a narrow fringe of leaves in front. Her skin was deeply tanned and blistered by the sun. He could see the scars from several nasty burns she had suffered while sleeping too close to the fire at night. She appeared to him to be just one more native woman. He thought he had misheard. But the woman persisted. She advanced and tried to speak again. She mouthed her words with difficulty, as though the language were unfamiliar.

"I am a Christian," she stammered. "I am ashamed."

And then she collapsed weeping on the sand.

The men were amazed. Clearly, here was a woman who had once been white and British. She pointed to the *Rattlesnake* riding peacefully at anchor just beyond the reef and signalled through gestures that she wanted to go on board. The natives surged forward, clearly intent on recovering the woman. Scott ordered his men to keep their muskets at the ready. Cautiously they retreated to their boat. Within a few minutes Barbara Thompson was back among her own kind for the first time in six years. Captain Owen Stanley welcomed Barbara on board and ordered she be given some clothing.

"The most remarkable occurrence that has yet befallen us happened yesterday," a dumbfounded Huxley wrote the next day in his journal, as he recorded the rescue of Barbara. "Not withstanding the hard life she must have led, she looks young. I have no doubt when she is appropriately dressed, she will not be bad-looking."

The *Rattlesnake* remained at anchor offshore for nine weeks. The change in Barbara's life, the medical attention, and the good food began to work wonders. Before the eyes of Captain Stanley and his crew, Gi'Om slowly was born again as Barbara Thompson. Boroto and several of her closest friends came repeatedly to the ship to persuade her to return with them. They were amazed that, having been among them for so many years and having been treated so well, she would exchange all that for another life among the Lamars.

Captain Stanley was fascinated by the constant exchanges. She had obviously become so much of a native during her years on Murralug Island and felt so strongly toward her husband and friends that he seriously questioned the wisdom of removing her. He took her aside one day and gently asked her if she had thought through her feelings. MacGillivray recorded her reply in his journal:

> Upon being asked by Captain Stanley whether she preferred remaining with us to accompanying the natives back to their island, as she would be allowed free choice in the matter, she was so much agitated as to find difficulty in expressing her thankfulness, making use of scraps of English alternately with the

Kowraregas language. And then, suddenly awaking to the recollection that she was not quite understood, the poor creature blushed all over and with downcast eyes beat her forehead with her hand, as if to assist in collecting her scattered thoughts. At length, after a pause, she found words to say, "Sir, I am a Christian and would rather go back to my own friends." At the same time it was remarked by every one that she had not lost the feelings of womanly modesty—even after having lived so long among naked blacks. She seemed acutely to feel the singularity of her position—dressed only in a couple of shirts, in the midst of a crowd of her own countrymen.

Boroto came on board one more time in a last desperate effort to convince his wife to return. Captain Stanley had already given him an iron axe but that did not compensate for his loss. He loved Gi'Om and wanted her back. Once again MacGillivray described the scene at length:

Gi'Om was evidently a great favorite with the blacks. Hardly a day passed on which she was not obliged to hold a levee in her cabin for the reception of friends from the shore, while other visitors, less favored, were content to talk with her through the port. They occasionally brought presents of fish and turtle, but always expected an equivalent of some kind. Her friend Boroto, the nature of the intimacy with whom was not at first understood, after in vain attempting by smooth words and fair promises to induce her to go back to live with him, left the ship in a rage. We were not sorry to get rid of so imprudent and troublesome a visitor as he had become. Previous to leaving, he had threatened that, should he or any of his friends ever catch his faithless spouse on shore, they would take off her head to carry back with them to Murralug. And so likely to be fulfilled did she consider this threat, being in perfect accordance with their customs, that she never afterwards ventured on shore at Cape York.

The crew of the *Rattlesnake* showed great compassion for Barbara. Captain Stanley provided her with her own cabin. Soon afterwards she had needles, thread, and as much calico and flannel as she needed to make new clothes.

Both Huxley and MacGillivray spent long hours with Barbara interviewing her about her experiences. They were fascinated by her knowledge of local plants and animals. She also provided a wealth of information about the Kowraregas people, their customs, legends, myths, and language.

"She has already given us a great deal of curious information about the habits of these people with an air of the most perfect truth and sincerity and no little intelligence," an admiring Huxley wrote later.

For the next eighteen months the *Rattlesnake* was Barbara's home, as it methodically charted the coastal areas of northern Australia and New Guinea. Finally, on February 5, 1850, she found herself at long last back in Sydney. An account of her experiences in a local newspaper generated considerable excitement. Soon afterwards she married a merchant (she was only twenty-three) and perhaps lived happily ever after. Nothing about her later life is known.

On January 16, 1882, a party landed on a deserted beach on tiny Howick Island on the Great Barrier Reef off the northern coast of Queensland and made a fearful discovery. They found in a four-foot-square iron tank the fully clothed skeleton of a young woman. A loaded revolver, fully cocked, lay at her side near a camphorwood box. The tattered remains of an opened parasol fluttered in the sand beside the body. On closer inspection they saw that the woman clutched at her breast the skeleton of a baby. A few yards away was another skeleton, obviously that of a Chinaman. A sun-bleached quilt covered the lower portion of his body. His skull rested on a small Chinese pillow. An unloaded rifle, some cartridges, and a sheath knife lay beside him. When the sailors opened the camphorwood box, they discovered a diary recounting in vivid detail the final events that led to the tragic deaths of Mary Watson, her infant son Ferrier, and their Chinese servant Ah Sam.

Mary Watson's story began across two oceans in the small village of Newlyn East in Cornwall, England, on January 17, 1860. She was born out of wedlock to the twenty-one-year-old Mary Phillips. Thomas Oxnam, the father, finally agreed to the marriage when his daughter was eight weeks old. She was the eldest. After Mary, eight brothers and two daughters were born, although five died.

The depressed agriculture of the 1870s devastated the Oxnam family finances and put her father into bankruptcy. Cornwall was particularly hard hit. In one six-month period over 10,000 emigrants left Cornwall for Australia. The Oxnams decided to join the exodus and selected Queensland as their destination. On July 27, 1877, the family arrived at Maryborough, still a frontier town in the northern Australian outback. Her father soon secured a job with a slaughterhouse buying cattle from the outlying ranches. Shortly afterwards gold was discovered on the Endeavour River seventy-five miles away. A stampede quickly developed. Within weeks a new town, Cooktown, had sprung up in what had been empty outback. Within the first year 30,000 Europeans and Chinese flooded into the area. They included Oxnam and his family.

Mary managed to find a position as a teacher. Not long afterwards she met and fell in love with Captain Robert Watson, a man the same age as her father. He proposed. She accepted. They were married on May 30, 1880.

A quiet, strong seafaring man, Watson was an acceptably safe father-figure. Like Mary, he was an enterprising, hard-working, "no nonsense" person and had little time for the froth of Cooktown. He came to port, though, from time to time to sell catches of *bêche-de-mer*—the brown sea-slug or sea cucumber—highly prized as a culinary delicacy by the Chinese in soups or braised with vegetables. They valued it as a stimulant and an aphrodisiac. Watson and his partner, Percy Fuller, ran two boats crewed by Chinese and Aborigines and were prospering.

Four days after the marriage ceremony Robert and Mary Watson boarded his little boat for Lizard Island seventy miles to the north on the Great Barrier Reef. Watson had not prepared his wife for the inhospitable terrain of this isolated island. Severely eroded peaks jutting abruptly out of the sea with only sparse shrubs to break the monotony—this was Lizard Island. Enormous prehistoric monitor lizards, some reaching lengths of four and five feet, roamed the island.

Watson had constructed a small fishing station a year earlier, which consisted of a stone two-room house, several huts, and a smoke house. He and his partner had six employees, including two pig-tailed Chinese servants. None of them realized that Lizard Island was a sacred island for the Aborigines on the nearby coast. The monitor lizards figured in their mythology as reincarnations of ancient gods, who had come to earth from the sky, made men and women, and then assumed the form of the large reptiles. There on the island every grain of sand, every rock, every hill, every shrub was sacred.

A nomadic people, the Aborigines of Queensland still clung to a primitive Stone Age culture. They had never seen a wheel. They had no knowledge of pottery and used shells as plates and skulls as bowls. They knew nothing about agriculture. They made crude weapons from sharpened stones and sticks. They slept in caves or out in the open desert at night, using pieces of beaten bark for blankets.

Captain Cook had discovered the island in August 1770. When he went ashore, he saw great mounds of empty shells and presumed that the mainland Aborigines visited this forbidding rocky thumb only for ceremonial purposes. The land, he concluded, must have special significance for them to risk the fifteen-mile journey from the mainland through hazardous seas. Because he saw no animals except lizards of every variety, the English explorer named the place Lizard Island.

On Saturday, January 1, 1881, Mary began a diary. The first entry read: "One Muscovy duck dead. Made a pair of pyjamas. Had a game of whist after tea. Heavy rain. Good tide. Wind changeable. Bob wanted to move the table farther into the middle of the room. I objected. Consequence a slight disturbance."

Daytime temperatures frequently reached 100° and beyond. Although typical of the Victorian era, Mary's voluminous skirts were hardly suited to the heat and humidity of the tropics. The darkness brought little relief since at night-time the mosquitoes came out in dreadful numbers. Heavy netting over the beds gave them some protection. But little of the discomfort of life on Lizard Island ended up in Mary's journal:

"Made bread and cakes. Gingerbread success. Wedding ring slipped off my finger. Found it later in the knife box when laying table. Made a flannel shirt for Bob, also two tablecloths. We had an early tea and spent a long evening outside humming a few songs and enjoying the moonlight."

Watson was generally away during the day fishing. Mary's companions were Ah Sam and Ah Leong, Chinese coolies from the Kwangtung province. They went around in blue pyjamas with baggy pants, their heads shaved except for enough hair in the back to make a long pigtail which they hid beneath their hats. Their job was to prepare the sea slugs Watson and his partner brought back at the end of each day. They lit a fire under a large four-foot-square water tank filled with sea water. They took the sacks of sea slugs from the small boat, emptied them into the water, and boiled them for thirty minutes. The sea slugs were gutted and dried in the sun on a rack for several days. Afterwards they were laid across wire racks in the small smoke house for two days. At that point they looked like charred and blackened sausages. Finally, they were bagged, sent to Cooktown, and shipped on to China.

Mary was now pregnant. After six months, Watson took her back to Cooktown to await her labor. A son was born on June 3. She named him Ferrier. On June 29 they returned to Lizard Island. "Ferrier very good," she noted approvingly in her diary. "The sea did not affect him. Self sick."

Mary and her young son arrived home at a critical time. Watson had decided to move the camp farther north to Night Island. The sea around Lizard Island was fished out for *bêche-de-mer*. He wanted to go north on an exploratory expedition with his partner Fuller. They decided it was best to leave his family on Lizard Island with the two Chinese servants rather than put the two of them at risk on the sea journey. On September 1 the two men set off on a scouting expedition expected to take six to eight weeks. Mary had no boat and no way of sending for help in the event of an emergency. She was a pioneer wife on a true frontier.

Mary settled back into her routine. Several weeks passed uneventfully. Then on September 26 canoes filled with Aborigines landed on a nearby beach and disappeared into the interior of the island. At night she heard the sounds of strange chanting and singing. During the day she saw occasional groups of heavily armed blacks moving around the outskirts of the little settlement. They became more aggressive. Then matters took a sudden turn for the worse on September 29. Mary wrote in her diary: "Blowing strong breeze SE, although not so hard as yesterday. No eggs. Ah Leong killed by the blacks over at the farm. Ah Sam found his hat which is the only proof."

Mary retreated to her house and prepared to withstand a siege. Watson had cut firing slots into each wall for just such emergencies. She had a rifle and a pistol and plenty of ammunition. One of Watson's first tasks upon bringing his wife to Lizard Island had been to teach her how to shoot and shoot accurately.

Mary's diary entry for Friday, September 30, read simply: "Natives down on the beach at 7 p.m. Fired off the rifle and revolver and they went away."

Mary barricaded herself in the house. Heavy shutters protected the windows, but the sun turned the inside rooms into an oven. The next day they ran out of fresh water. Ah Sam left the house and cautiously approached the spring, buckets in hand. Suddenly, he found himself ambushed by Aborigines. He staggered back to Mary, bleeding profusely from seven spears stuck in his arms and shoulders. Each spear was three feet long and decorated on the end with tufts of birds' feathers. She cut away the spears and bandaged his wounds. Then she helped him light his opium pipe to soothe the pain.

At the end of the day she wrote in her diary: "Natives (4) speared Ah Sam; four places in the right side and three in the shoulder. Got three spears from the natives. Saw 10 men altogether."

The next morning Mary ventured out. She saw to her horror that the Aborigines had been busy throughout the night. The walls of her house and the nearby smokehouse had been painted with figures of fish, animals, spirits, and warriors. She could not have known it at the time, but they were incantations to their gods to kill her and the two others. She saw three blacks, sitting cross-legged in a nearby shade, grasping their spears and patiently waiting.

Mary evolved a plan of survival. She had no boat. But she did have the *bêche-de-mer* cauldron, a four-foot-square tank. They could launch it from the beach and paddle it out to sea in the hope that a passing ship would spot them. It was their only hope.

She gathered some supplies—clothes, jewelry, a little money (two one pound notes and some silver coins), an umbrella, bonnet, pillow, a freshly sharpened pencil, a notebook, the guns, and some food, including cans of condensed milk for Ferrier. She also took several bags of water. She left her precious diary in the house. She strapped her baby to her back, picked up the supplies and the rifle, and walked out of the house, accompanied by Ah Sam. They cautiously dragged the heavy metal tank across the sand to the water's edge. The natives watched intently from the outskirts. They made no attempt to interfere, as Mary, Ah Sam, and little Ferrier slowly drifted out to sea.

The three of them were now at the mercy of the wind and currents. Mary rigged a large wooden spoon to serve as a steering rudder. That plus two wooden paddles gave her some small control over the unsteady craft. She raised her umbrella and fastened it to her back to provide a little shade for herself and her baby. Ah Sam was too weak to do anything except bail.

Writing in her journal had always given Mary a sense of comfort. So she resumed the habit, using the pencil and notebook she had brought along.

> **October 5.** Made for a sand bank off the Lizards but could not reach it. Got on a reef all day on the look-out for a boat, but saw none.
> **October 6.** Very calm morning. Able to pull the tank up to an island with three small mountains on it. Ah Sam went ashore to try and get water as ours was done. There were natives camped there so we were afraid to go far away. We had to wait return of

the tide. Anchored under the mangroves, got on the reef. Very calm.

On October 7 they watched a British ship pass in the distance, its red and white funnel so close yet so far. Mary tied Ferrier's white shawl to one of the paddles and waved it back and forth. But the ship steamed past and soon disappeared over the horizon.

October 7. Made for an island four or five miles from the one spoken of yesterday. Ashore, but could not find any water. Cooked some rice and clam-fish. Moderate S.E. breeze. Stayed here all night. Saw a steamer bound north. Hoisted Ferrier's white and pink wrap but did not answer us.

October 8. Changed the anchorage of the boat as the wind was freshening. Went down to a little kind of lake on the same island (this done last night). Remained here all day looking for a boat; did not see any. Very cold night; blowing very hard. No water.

Their situation was growing increasingly grim. They had exhausted their supply of fresh water and had no prospects for finding more. They were far from the usual shipping routes. And they were much too weak to build a shelter.

October 9. Brought the tank ashore as far as possible with this morning's tide. Made camp all day under the trees. Blowing very hard. No water. Gave Ferrier a dip in the sea; he is showing symptoms of thirst, and I took a dip myself. Ah Sam and self very parched with thirst. Ferrier showing symptoms.

October 10. Ferrier very bad with inflammation; very much alarmed. No fresh water, and no more milk, but condensed. Self very weak; really thought I would have died last night.

Finally, a weakened Mary picked up her pencil for the last time and wrote a final entry in her diary:

> **October 11.** Still all alive. Ferrier much better this morning. Self feeling very weak. I think it will rain today, clouds very heavy, wind not quite so hard. No rain. Morning fine weather. Ah Sam preparing to die. Have not seen him since 9. Ferrier more cheerful. Self not feeling at all well. Have not seen any boat of any description. No water. Near death with thirst.

Soon afterwards all three castaways died from thirst. The terrible irony is that Mary's forecast of rain was correct. But the storm arrived too late to help them. The bodies of Mary and Ferrier were found floating in the cast iron tank in fresh rain water.

Several weeks later the *Cooktown Courier* ran the following item:

> On Thursday, the 20th of October, 1881, the *Neptune*, cutter, in charge of some Chinamen, who returned from searching for their vessel in that locality, saw eight or ten native canoes up on the beach, and about forty blacks on Lizard Island, where a bush fire was raging. They reported the case to Mr. Fahey, Sub-Collector of Customs, Cooktown, who, with his usual promptitude, communicated at once with Inspector Fitzgerald, who consented to allow a police officer with five troopers to accompany him to Lizard Island. But Lieut. Izatt of H. M. S. *Conflict*, hearing of the affair, offered to convey the party, which left on the 21st of October. Mr. Fahey takes with him one of the Customs boatmen, as well as the police, and expects to return on Sunday, the 23rd October. In the meantime further intelligence is awaited in Cooktown with much anxiety.

The naval expedition made a thorough search of Lizard Island and found no bodies. However, they did discover

Mary's diary in the house and read her account of the attack. Another three months passed before the *Cooktown Courier* announced the sad conclusion:

> With the arrival yesterday of the schooner *Kate Kearney*, Captain Bremmer stepped ashore and hurried off to the Cooktown Police Station to report a melancholy discovery. Some days beforehand he had anchored off the Howick Islands.
>
> Members of the crew going ashore found a small half-tank resting partly on its side. Lying in it was the body of Mrs. Watson, the body of her child still held in her arms.
>
> The tank also contained a small pile of baby garments and food. Close by was a revolver, fully loaded and cocked, and a tattered parasol still open, used to protect the child from the sun, was also seen. There was a pair of roughly-shaped paddles that had helped to carry them a distance of nearly 50 miles from their home on Lizard Island.
>
> A further search resulted in the discovery of the Watsons' Chinese servant, Ah Sam.
>
> Captain Bremmer brought with him the diary of the late Mrs. Watson which tells the tragic story right up to the day of her death.

In 1886 the residents of Cooktown held a public subscription to raise money for a memorial in the town center to commemorate Mary Watson and her heroic efforts to survive. A baroque white marble column on a pedestal with two drinking taps was soon erected. The inscription reads: "In Memoriam, Mrs. Watson, the heroine of Lizard Island, Cooktown, North Queensland, A.D. 1881." Also chiselled into the marble is the final stanza of a poem by "A.F.," which had originally appeared in the Sydney *Bulletin* :

Five fearful days beneath the scorching glare,
Her babe she nursed,
God knows the pangs the woman had to bear,
Whose last sad entry showed a mother's care,
"Near death with thirst."

CHAPTER SEVEN

The Castaways of Minerva Reef

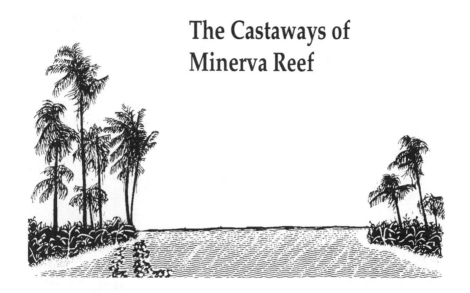

N o bleaker ordeal for a castaway can be imagined than that which befell an anonymous Englishman in 1615, who found himself forced to survive on a desolate rock off the coast of Scotland. For a year he made a desperate and ingenious struggle to combat madness and the elements in the dreadful solitude of the sea. He possessed none of those things critical to survival. He had no fresh water, no fire, and no material to make himself new clothes after his wore out. His refuge was not a tropical island with an abundance of fruits and vegetables. Instead he spent his ordeal in a hostile, cold climate and endured a bitter winter in the midst of one of the stormiest seas in Europe.

The Englishman was on a trip from England to Ireland when French pirates seized the ship. They set him and two other passengers adrift in a small boat without any provisions, except for a bag of sugar. One man died within a few days. The other two managed to reach a small sea mount, where the rough currents shattered their boat against a rock.

A cursory check revealed that their rock was without any vegetation whatsoever. Their only shelter at first was a long stone balanced upon two rocks. After a few days the pair concluded that they were, in the words of the chronicler, "in a more wretched condition than if, being swallowed up by the sea, they had been delivered from the extremities they were in for want of meat and drink."

Fortunately, the men had a single tool between them, a knife, with which they managed to kill a few seals and sea birds. They dried the flesh in the sun to make it palatable. Sea bird eggs, seaweed, and small mollusks rounded out their meager diet. For fresh water, they had only shallow pools of rainwater. But these were often contaminated by salt water during the frequent storms.

The two castaways salvaged some boards from their shattered boat and used them to construct a kind of shelter. After six weeks the Englishman awoke to find himself alone. His companion had disappeared during the night, probably slipping into the sea while relieving himself in the darkness.

His condition steadily deteriorated. He lost his knife through carelessness. He extracted a nail from one of the boards, sharpened the point by grinding it against a rock, and made this a poor substitute for his lost blade. His clothes disintegrated, and soon he was left with nothing to cover his nakedness. In winter the snows blanketed his little shelter. To get food, he spread seal fat on a stick and stuck it through a crack in his shelter's wall. When a bird landed to peck at the bait, he reached a hand under the wall and up through the snow to seize it.

For almost a year the man lived alone on his rock. Then one day a miracle happened. "The gracious Providence of God sent a ship thither, which delivered him out of as great a misery as perhaps any man was ever in," his chronicler, J. Albert de Mandelslo, noted. His rescuer was a Dutch trader becalmed in nearby waters who sent two of his crew to the rock to search for birds' eggs. The Englishman rose up and confronted them. In the words of the chronicler: "They saw something that was more like a ghost than a living person: a body stark naked, black, and hairy, a meagre and deformed countenance with hollow and distorted eyes, which raised such compassion in them that they endeavored to take him into the boat. "

The captain of the ship took pity upon the Englishman and transported him to the Irish mainland. The traveler eventually made his way to Dublin, where, like some Ancient Mariner, he stopped people on the streets to tell them his sorry tale and beg enough money to return to England.

Some 350 years later seventeen Tongan men found themselves stranded on Minerva Reef, 260 miles southwest of the Tonga Islands in the most remote part of the entire South Pacific, far from the usual shipping and air routes. At low tides a small expanse of coral reef becomes exposed. But most of the time waves sweep across the entire mass. To the east lies the Tonga Trench, an enormous marine canyon where depths over 35,000 feet have been measured.

Few travelers have visited Minerva Reef, and most of these have arrived on private yachts. In 1988 Tom and Jan Ginder stopped there in their yacht *Seark* and described it this way:

> After two days of fast sailing from Nuku'alofa, we came to Minerva Reef and entered through a narrow pass in the circle of coral. Here in the Pacific hundreds of miles from any terra firma we dropped anchor and looking around saw breaking waves during high tide and two feet of intriguing brown reef at low tide. Imagine standing in the middle of a vast ocean on a few feet of exposed coral and no land in sight. While exploring for shells, we found blocks of tarred pig-iron, a wonderful huge anchor, and many copper nails, all that remained of some long forgotten tragedy. For three days and nights we lay in quiet water, although the wind whipped up the seas outside our saucer. However, the combination of full moon, spring tides, and foul weather could make the Minerva Reef anchorage dangerous. It was just two days to full moon so with regret we left.

Minerva Reef is actually two reefs. South Minerva consists of two adjacent atolls, each seven and a half miles in circumference, positioned atop a submarine plateau. The highest portion of the reef lies on the southern side where the waves pound the hardest. A sand bar inside the reef has formed, suggesting that in one or two thousand years an island will be formed. Once that happens, an occasional coconut will arrive on the ocean currents and be deposited on the beach at the high tide mark to begin its growth. Eighteen miles to the northeast lies North Minerva, a single atoll with a circumference of eleven miles. It encompasses a sandy lagoon with a bottom free of coral heads. No sea bird ever comes to these waters because the reefs offer no shelter or nesting areas.

In 1854 Captain H. M. Denham of H.M.S. *Herald* charted these two reefs. He named them for the whaling ship *Minerva*, which departed Sydney on August 16, 1829, for the rich whaling grounds off the Tonga Islands. She carried a crew of twenty-three and a dog. The cruise began poorly, with the *Minerva* plagued by a constant leak, rough seas, and an absence of whales. Early on the morning of September 9 she sailed confidently across waters the charts showed as free of all obstacles. She suddenly rammed hard upon what today is called South Minerva Reef. Most of the crew quickly took to boats and made it clear of the coral heads to the open ocean beyond where they waited out the darkness. The next morning they returned to their ship which was quickly disintegrating under the impact of large waves sweeping across the deck. They gathered what supplies they could—some kegs of fresh water, provisions, and whatever equipment they could salvage. The twenty-three men were distributed among three boats, all dangerously overladden. One boat headed toward the Tonga Islands to the north and was never seen again, probably wrecked upon North Minerva Reef.

The other two boats stayed together and the crews survived. When they took inventory, they learned they had just two biscuits, two pounds of salt pork, and two pounds of cheese for each man, and all of it was soaked with seawater. They also had seven gallons of water. By September 14 they had exhausted their fresh water and began drinking seawater and their own urine. The next day, as they prepared to slaughter the ship's dog, they sighted an island. This later proved to be Vatoa, one of the Outer Lau group between Fiji and Tonga. One boat wrecked on the encircling reef, but all the crewmembers made it safely ashore. The next morning Tongans discovered the castaways and brought them to the chief who treated them kindly. The boat was rebuilt and half the men sailed on, eventually reaching Sydney from whence a rescue vessel was dispatched for the rest of the crew.

Over the years other ships occasionally ripped their bottoms out on Minerva Reef. Little is known of their history. Their anchors rusting in the shallow waters around the coral heads are all that is left to bear mute witness to these tragedies at sea. In 1960 a Japanese fishing vessel ran aground on the eastern end of South Minerva. Nothing is known about her. There was presumably no loss of life. She carried an efficient radio and her captain was, no doubt, in touch with the mother ship of the fleet soon after the grounding. Her crew was rescued, and the ship abandoned. In time, the huge waves of a passing storm pushed her farther on to the reef and rolled her over on her side. And there she lay, awaiting a slow disintegration.

On the morning of July 2, 1962, the small yacht *Tuaikaepau*, under the command of Captain David Fifita, set sail from Nuku'alofa in the Tonga Islands with a crew and passenger count of seventeen men, all Tongans. They were on their way to New Zealand, and for most of them this was their first trip away from their home. The yacht carried a cargo of vegetables, mostly yams and taro, sufficient to feed the group for the voyage and for a period of three months after their arrival. Fishing would augment their diet. Six of the passengers were boxers, hopeful of finding new opportunities in New Zealand.

The *Tuaikaepau* was already an old ship in 1962. She had been launched from a shipyard in Auckland, New Zealand, in 1902. Her length was just fifty-one feet overall. For the next forty-five years her owners sailed her throughout the waters surrounding New Zealand's North Island. Then in 1946 she was sold to the Free Church of Tonga which used her to carry supplies to the missions on the outer islands and pick up sacks of copra for the return trip. In 1956 she was sold again. This owner installed a new diesel engine, rebuilt her decking and deckhousing, and added new sails and rigging.

For the cruise to New Zealand the owner hired David Fifita, highly regarded as one of the finest captains in Tonga. Accompanying him as deckhands were Sateki, his legitimate son and heir, and Talo, an illegitimate son. Like most Tongans, Fifita was a large man, weighing 290 pounds but surprisingly light on his feet. He was born on November 28, 1919, the eldest of eight children. His father operated a cargo schooner traveling among the nearby islands. By the time he was eighteen, he was fully qualified as a master. And by 1943 he had his first command. He showed his mettle early when a hurricane overtook his vessel carrying 106 school children to the island of Pangai. He ran to shelter behind the island of 'Ata and waited out the storm for eight days. He arrived safely in port on New Year's Eve. Thus began the legend of David Fifita as the captain able to handle any emergency fate might thrust upon him.

When Fifita assumed command of the *Tuaikaepau* in early 1962, he enjoyed a reputation as Tonga's most experienced captain. In March he sailed the ship down to New Zealand for repairs. His crew included two boxers eager to make extra money in fights in Auckland. Because the first voyage went so well, the ship's owner was besieged with applications after he announced a second passage to New Zealand for that summer. When the *Tuaikaepau* sailed from Nuku'alofa in July, she carried a crew of seven, including her captain, and ten passengers. Several were boxers, including Sipa Fine, a handsome twenty-year-old, who was the current heavyweight champion in Tonga. The fact that the ship sailed with so many distinguished Tongans meant that the island people took a great interest in her progress.

The *Tuaikaepau* set sail in moderately high seas. Fifita expected to catch a trade wind blowing in a southeastern direction. Instead he encountered his first bad luck of the voyage—a strong head wind accompanied by high overcast that made the taking of proper navigational bearings chancy. They paid a brief visit to the uninhabited island of 'Ata to give some of the seasick passengers an opportunity to rest their stomach on solid land. Five of the Tongans crowded into the ship's seven-foot dinghy and went ashore, carelessly smashing the boat against the rocks as they navigated the surf. A frustrated and angry Fifita recovered the broken boat but quickly realized that the repair would have to await until after their arrival in Auckland.

As the *Tuaikaepau* headed south, Fifita tacked to port in the hopes of picking up a southeastern wind, confident that the Minerva Reefs lay well behind. As night fell on July 6 he was holding to a westerly course at seven knots. At about nine o'clock the crew and passengers heard an unexpected "thump," as the ship suddenly ran aground on the outer edge of South Minerva Reef. The *Tuaikaepau* slowed and then came to rest, held fast by giant coral heads in the middle of a crashing surf. The Tongans crowded together at the bow in waist-deep water, taking the full force of the seas breaking over the ship's stern. Fifita knew that the next four hours of rising tides and wind would be the most dangerous and that no wooden ship could long withstand the battering from heavy waves of the sort they were now experiencing.

The crew and passengers were exhausted and terrified, although few among them realized how bleak their situation really was. The cold wind blowing upon them from the south came from the Tasman Sea. Hypothermia was a real danger. The huge breakers swept several men overboard, but miraculously brought them back to the ship. The heavy blows of the breakers shattered the stern and brought down the mast. The ship began to split apart from stern to bow. As the high tide peaked, Fifita ordered his crew and passengers into the water. Together they maneuvered the broken mast into place as a boom to capture the wreckage that spilled from the disintegrating ship. He ordered his men to seize any pieces of driftwood that came by. His plan was to build a raft out of the only material on hand, the shattered pieces of the *Tuaikaepau.*

The first large piece they salvaged was the hatch cover. This was grabbed and tied to the mast. A few minutes later the entire port side of the *Tuaikaepau* broke away, and this too was captured. And then another large piece broke away. All these were tied together to make the crudest of rafts.

Finally, the seventeen men climbed on board to wait and pray until daybreak brought calmer seas.

At dawn nothing much of the ship remained. Her breakup had been complete. The engine and anchors lay at the bottom of a deep wedge-shaped chasm on the edge of the reef. The men scoured the nearby reef for useful items. They were everywhere—water-sodden pieces of clothing, the yams and taro which had been stored below deck, a ten-gallon oil drum. Each item, in turn, was placed upon the flimsy raft.

Fifita was intrigued by a shipwreck he noticed at a distance. He guessed she must be a Japanese fishing boat of the kind that were a common sight in the South Pacific. He sent one of his passengers, Vaiangina 'Unga, a copra planter, to investigate. Slowly, without shoes, the Tongan made his way across the coral toward the ship. When he got closer, he discovered she was perhaps eighty feet long with a beam of twenty-four feet. Japanese characters were still visible on her stern. She was made of wood and largely intact, lying on her starboard beam at an eighty-five degree angle. The lower five feet, where the tide regularly washed, had rotted away. But the upper portions of the ship were secure and offered shelter from the elements. With the tide ready to turn, he hurried back to tell Fifita that the ship offered them a refuge of sorts. Within a few hours, they were safely established on the Japanese wreck.

The first thing the Tongans did was to bait a large hook with a clam and catch a shark lurking nearby. In the afternoon they ate their first meat since leaving Nuku'alofa. Fifita ordered the sails removed from the raft and spread across the wreck to catch any rain that might fall that night. But the sky was clear, and no one was really optimistic they would have fresh water soon.

On Saturday morning, July 7, Fifita and the men began a systematic exploration of the wreck. They had entered a very strange maritime wonderland. Olaf Ruhen, the historian of their disaster, reported:

> Compared to their own disintegrating ship, it was a palace that opened up to them, but a nightmare palace. Locker doors opened down from the ceiling, the glass domes that protected electric light bulbs

thrust upward from the floor, doors opened like trapdoors, top and bottom, and there were portholes above their heads, keeping out the sky.

The lower part of the vessel was useless. The castaways gained access to the upper by climbing the smooth and almost perpendicular deck, taking footholds in what had been bridge windows, scraping away the slime that had gathered over years in all exposed places. They found a name on the wreck— *Number 10, Noshemi Maru, K 30*—but they never referred to her that way.

Within the wreck the pervasive smell of sea wrack and iodine dominated everything. . . . It was not a bad smell, not a symptom of decay; but it was alien and concentrated. Inside the tilted compartments they were protected from the cold and bitter wind; they warmed within their wet clothes and felt better.

Fifita quickly realized that some of the equipment on board was of no use in their new world of the reef. The radio was well preserved and would have allowed them to send a message back to Tonga or over to Fiji, but, of course, they lacked any source of power to activate it.

Fishing gear of all sorts was still in place—miles of tarred line, rolls of nets, and thousands of hooks. And just as valuable, a cache of cut-down rubber boots that proved a godsend for the barefoot men. Inside the storage lockers they found mountains of foul-smelling fish skeletons, the meat long since eaten off by the crabs of the reef.

The Japanese crew apparently had had ample time to evacuate the ship. They had taken all their personal possessions along with the ship's tools, the cutlery from the galley (except for a solitary knife), and all the stores of food. The Tongans did find some large cans of paint, blocks and pulleys of various sizes, several charts in Japanese, a compass, some very outdated medicine, and over 400 gallons of oil. They also found a six-inch iron spike with a chisel-end, which looked as though it might become a useful tool.

The Tongans settled into their new quarters with a renewed sense of hope. After all, they now had secure shelter. And their captain David Fifita was a man of legendary abilities in the Tonga Islands. Their spirits were lifted even higher, when one of them discovered in a cabin a single match. They quickly made a space for a permanent fire in a protected companionway. One of them cut a small pile of fine shavings and piled them over an oil-soaked rag on a metal sheet. They struck their only match and soon had a fire. There was plenty of fuel lying about. They were on, after all, a wooden ship. That evening Fifita called a prayer meeting and appointed guards to keep the fire going throughout the night.

On July 8 Fifita led the men back to the wreck site at low tide for a final search. They were lucky. Their efforts turned up a sextant, more clothing, and wedged in a hole in the coral a real treasure—a hammer.

Their major problem continued to be the lack of fresh water. Fifita asked every man to eat the mussels and fish raw to conserve as much of the water as possible. Then he constructed a small still to make fresh water from the sea water. The total amount it yielded was about thirty ounces a day, or one and a half ounces per man.

International politics suddenly intruded upon the faraway world of Minerva Reef during the night of July 9. American scientists 2,500 miles to the north on Johnston Island detonated a hydrogen bomb 200 miles above the Pacific to test the effects of such an explosion on American communications. The explosion was the equivalent of a million tons of TNT. It rolled back the night and generated a pink and red glow that painted the clouds like a sunset. People from New Zealand to Hawaii saw the colorful effects of the blast. The Tongans sitting on the top deck of their wrecked ship enjoyed one of the best views of the fireball and its after-effects of any people in the Pacific.

Fifita's major worry was the continued shortage of fresh water. His small still was hardly adequate to their daily needs. He knew they desperately needed more, but they lacked the materials to built a larger still. A fishing party discovered a forty-five gallon drum bobbing in the waves near the edge of the reef. Fifita turned it over to the ship's carpenter, David Uaisele. With the hammer and spike, he slowly modified the drum and within four days had constructed a larger still. This proved a great success, and soon each man had almost a pint of fresh water each day.

Fifita understood the importance to morale of keeping the men busy. They began making distress signals to tell the world of their location. The Japanese had left plenty of white paint. Using strips of canvas and dipping their fingers in paint, they painstakingly painted SOS in letters eight feet high across the upper hull of their ship where they would be seen by any airplanes flying overhead. Then they went to work creating message boards. They spelled out on each side of the boards: SOS 17 MEN ON MINERVA REEF APP 196M SW OF ATA. Each day at high tide several of these boards were cast adrift in the current in the hope that one would eventually wash ashore on an inhabited beach in Fiji or Tonga and alert the world to their crisis.

Food was plentiful on the reef, at least certain kinds. Fish abounded, especially in the small pools in the coral pockets at low tide—parrot fish, rock cod, snapper, and sharks. Octopus, lobsters, and eels also made their home in the reef. Clams, oysters, and sea urchins were everywhere for the taking. But there was no seaweed, which does not grow among coral. Without seaweed, Fifita knew, they could not get vitamin C. And over the long term that meant a lingering death from scurvy.

The most diligent of the fishermen was the mate, Ve'etutu Pahulu. He ate freely of every living thing he caught, cracking open the skulls of larger fish and sucking their blood and brains into his mouth. "The taste wasn't too pleasant," he admitted later to the writer Olaf Ruhen, "but it was like following an order. I didn't turn from any food—I ate shark raw. I ate crayfish. I even ate octopus raw—it was tough, but I could do it. I ate the first living thing that I came to. I tried to tell the rest to do the same, to follow suit."

The mate sometimes ventured as far as two miles away on the reef on his expeditions to gather food. He discovered the remains of three other ships that had smashed against the reefs. In most cases all that remained were the anchors. One such anchor was very large and very old, of a design that had not been used since the late nineteenth century. Another ship had carried a cargo of brassbound rifle stocks. He carried two back to the ship where they proved useful as sledgehammers.

Then on July 13 one of the men discovered at the site where the *Tuaikaepau* had wrecked the sodden remains of the ship's Bible. The covers and many pages were missing. The rest was stuck together in a soggy mass. Fifita painstakingly separated the pages one from another and dried them a few at a time in the open air. Later he used the Bible for readings at their evening prayer meetings.

Tension began to build among the castaways. Discipline slowly eroded. Fifita caught several men stealing food and fresh water from the common stores. Others refused to carry out his orders or shirked their tasks. Tempers flared. Everyone suffered from sleep deficiencies, the steep angle of the deck prevented them from getting more than an hour's sleep at a time.

On July 27 Fifita ordered the construction of more elaborate message floats than the simple boards they had been using. They devised a triangular shape of three boards nailed together, flying a piece of rotted canvas. Distress messages were painted on at least two of the boards. They proved more difficult to build but clearly were much more visible at sea. They made thirty of these and launched them into the currents off Minerva Reef.

On the night of July 29 they had their first rain since coming to Minerva Reef. The beating of the raindrops against the hull of the ship awoke them. Fifita ordered that no one was to drink from the canvas they had spread across the deck; that was communal water. Everybody sought a small spout or a depression where rainwater might pool to help themselves. "The smell of the rain was an intoxication, freshening the sea dank of the wreck and replacing it and creating new vapors," Ruhen wrote later. "The atmosphere held the fire smoke down; the night was warm and damp, and the circumstances exciting."

In early August the *Tuaikaepau* was officially listed as missing at sea. The authorities launched a sea search in the vicinity of the Kermadec Islands, far to the west of Minerva Reef. After several days they terminated the search, and the planes returned to their bases.

On August 10 a storm swept across the area. As the tide

rose, enormous breakers rolled in across the reef, rocking the stranded Japanese ship and grinding it down into the coral. At two o'clock the terrified men awoke their captain and asked him to lead a prayer service. Fifita did not believe their situation was dangerous, but he understood their fear. He called them together for a prayer meeting.

"It is you who rules the world, the waves, and the weather," he prayed. "And if it is thy divine wish that we should live to return to Tonga and our beloved homes, then we thank thee. But if it is thy wish that we should die upon this reef, then thy will be done."

A few days later the storm passed, and the skies cleared. The Tongans hurried out onto the reef at low tide and found an abundance of food. They returned with sixty lobsters. On that next Sunday for the afternoon prayer meeting Fifita read them the story of Job from the Old Testament, suggesting they should view their ordeal on the reef as a test of their faith in God.

Soon afterwards Fifita discovered a seventy pound bag of rice hidden away underneath a mass of rotting rope in a section of the stern. Although they had thought they had explored thoroughly every crevice in the ship, this had been overlooked. Its sudden appearance seemed a miracle. The captain decided to use the rice to reinforce his authority over the men, who were now becoming quarrelsome and difficult, and to reward those who did exceptional service. He called them together for a meeting, informed them about the rice, and explained they would eat it only on those days when everyone worked hard at the tasks he had assigned. He also found that the rice was so old that when he rubbed it between the palms of his hands it crumbled. But now they had flour they could use to thicken the broth of the fish stew they made on some evenings.

By late August Fifita realized that all chance of rescue from the outside had passed. Their survival depended upon their own efforts. He saw they had only one chance—to construct a sailboat to take three of them across the Pacific toward the Fiji Islands to the west. Construction began almost immediately with little more than their fingers for tools. Everyone was expected to share in the labor, except the half dozen men too sick to work.

Fifita wanted a boat eighteen feet long with a four-foot beam and a depth of eighteen inches—a formidable undertaking without a shipyard. Building it on the reef was impossible because of the twice daily high tides. Thus, space had to be cleared on the Japanese ship for the construction project. Fortunately, their group included two carpenters, who would provide the skilled labor. Their only tools were the large iron spike, a single knife with a serrated edge, and the hammer. Cutting the boards to the proper length and shape proved a formidable ordeal. Remembering the traditional shipbuilding techniques of their ancestors, the carpenters heated an iron bar with a quarter-inch edge and methodically burned a cut in the board along the path they wanted to cut. Then using the chisel and the improvised sledgehammers, they broke the boards at the desired places. Slowly, over the space of three weeks a boat began to take shape. Fifita searched the ship for something, anything, that could serve as a mast and found a twenty-foot bamboo pole that was perfect. For sails he intended to use the jib and the staysail from the *Tuaikaepau*. When the hull was finally finished, the two carpenters decked her over, leaving an opening five feet long and two feet wide where two men could find protection from the weather. At the end they painted her name on the bow— *Malolelei*, after Fifita's father's ship.

"That little boat I called *Malolelei*, so that my father would perhaps intercede for us," Fifita told Ruhen later. "He would know all that we were suffering, because he himself drowned in the sea."

Once the boat's construction was completed, the next challenge was to launch the one-ton vessel safely from the deck of the Japanese wreck. Fifita supervised the installation of two pulleys at nearby stanchions on the port rail. Slowly, inch by inch, she was lowered over the side until she finally settled safely on the sea below. Fifita tried her out and decided to add an outrigger to increase her stability.

On September 28 at the evening prayer service, the group sustained their first death, when Fatai Efiafi, a middle-aged widower, collapsed. "It almost seemed to some that the choice had fallen upon the man least necessary to his community," Ruhen wrote later. "Fatai Efiafi was a man without dependents, the oldest of such upon the reef. To the captain, the tragedy of the loss was complicated by this blow to his reputation. For in all his lifetime of authority, a lifetime in which he had been constantly responsible for the safety of others, this was the first man in his care to die."

After a night-long vigil, the other men scooped out a grave in a sandy area on the reef 300 yards from the wreck and buried Efiafi's body wrapped in a tarpaulin. Fifita conducted a burial service. They marked his final resting place with a wooden cross. Several of the survivors worried privately that later they might feed on crabs that had eaten of their companion and so become guilty of cannibalism once removed.

On September 30 the group suffered two more deaths just minutes apart. Johnny Lousi, a deckhand who had appeared in reasonably good health, suddenly fell over backwards and died. Then Johnny Sikimeti, one of the young boxers, slumped over dead. Efiafi's death they understood and accepted, for the older man had been ill for many days. But the loss of the two younger men had not been expected, and their sudden deaths devastated the survivors.

"It wasn't possible to tell how exposure and underfeeding were affecting the men," Fifita explained later. "For Fatai Efiafi was not sick, but died slowly wasting away, and he was forty-six years of age. On the other hand, Johnny Sikimeti was only eighteen, but died in exactly the same way. In the case of Johnny Lousi, he died while working, possibly through overexertion. He was only thirty years of age. So it wasn't possible to tell whether the older men or the younger showed the effects most. In my opinion, it was not a matter of age, but it was a matter of willpower, that is, the will to survive."

The survivors were too demoralized and weak to dig two additional graves on the reef. Instead they wrapped the bodies in canvas, lashed them to boards from the deck, and set them adrift at the edge of the reef. On the canvas shroud of each body they had painted their distress message—SOS MEN ON MINERVA REEF.

By October 2 the *Malolelei* was ready to sail. The survivors had successfully added an outrigger. Fifita now selected his two-man crew—David Uaisele, the ship's carpenter, and his son Sateki, who was the strongest swimmer of the group and stood the best chance of making it through a heavy surf if their small boat should capsize.

Fifita decided their best chance would be to head toward Fiji. In the privacy of his cabin he scratched the chart of the route he wanted to take on a board, knowing that no paper charts would survive in the wetness of the voyage. He drew two gallons of water and ten tentacles of octopus from the common stocks. On October 5 they loaded the little boat. There was precious little to take—the food and water, a daily log Fifita had kept since the wreck, the compass, a sextant, his chart scratched in wood, and a battered copy of the *Nautical Almanac*. He placed his first mate, Ve'etutu Pahulu, in charge of the group remaining on Minerva Reef.

In the early morning of October 7 Fifita and his two companions cast off in the *Malolelei*, hoisted their sails, and moved slowly off in a northern direction. Their destination was the island of Ono-i-Lau some 200 miles to the northwest, actually an archipelago of six small islands surrounded by a coral reef. High waves continually drenched the boat. This was not a problem during the day when the sun beat down intensely upon them. But night brought much cooler temperatures, and the three men sat cramped in their small boat, shivering uncontrollably. Fifita insisted on staying at the helm around the clock until Wednesday morning when he finally asked to be relieved. That day they exhausted their small supply of water and food. The weather improved.

On Thursday a sea bird circled overhead. The three men kept still. The bird came closer and finally landed on the gunwale next to Fifita's elbow. The carpenter slowly reached forward and grabbed the bird around its neck. They quickly cut its neck, drained its blood into a small cup, and drank it. Next they peeled off the skin and feathers, cut the flesh into small pieces, and chewed on them.

On Friday morning Fifita took a reading and discovered they had overshot Ono-i-Lau Island in the dark. He set a new course toward some of the high Fijian islands to the west. On Sunday morning the 2,700-foot-high mountain of the large island of Kandavu loomed above the horizon. A few hours later they were offshore. Between them and the beach was the Great Astrolabe Reef. They sailed along the reef for ten miles, desperately looking for a passage. A heavy surf broke along the entire length of reef.

Finally, the Tongans found an opening. But the heavy seas made it dangerous. Fifita decided to chance it and pointed the *Malolelei* into the channel. Almost immediately a sixteen-foot wave caught the little craft and tossed her in a somersault over her bow. The three Tongans struggled to reach quieter waters and then began to swim toward a distant beach almost two miles away. For a time they swam together. But they were too weak to maintain a sustained effort. Sateki, Fifita's favorite son and supposedly the strongest swimmer among them, began to flounder and swallow water. He held him in his arms, but the boy did not recover. Fifita felt himself growing weaker. He knew that if one of them did not make it safely ashore, then all the others back on Minerva Reef would perish. He said a short prayer, gently pushed his son aside, and resumed his swim toward the land. He looked back and saw Sateki swimming aimlessly in circles. Fifita continued on. An hour later the two men finally reached a sandy beach, crawled out of the surf, and collapsed beneath a canopy of coconut palms.

The two exhausted men lay on the beach, slowly recovering their strength. They husked some green coconuts and quenched their thirst. For as far as they could see in either direction there was no sign of any human habitation. Slowly, the pair began walking down the beach through heavy muck that made progress slow and painful. After several hours of hard work they had traveled less than two miles. They collapsed exhausted, wondering where to go to find help. Suddenly, in a distance they heard the booming sound of a wooden drum that Fijians use to announce the start of a church service. The two men lifted themselves up and headed inland along a path toward the sounds.

In time the men arrived at a small thatched-roof house sitting in the middle of a plantation. From inside they heard voices. Fifita called out a greeting in the Fijian language. A man appeared. They had made their first contact with the outside world. He hurried off to tell the local chief. It was 3:30 in the afternoon. The Tongans had taken eight hours to swim the two miles to shore and walk another four miles to the village.

The local chief welcomed the pair, brought them into the village, and gave them a guest cottage to use during their stay. Several local women brought them food, and then later washed them, rubbed their bodies with coconut oil, and kept watch while they slept. The next day a runner was dispatched to the nearest two-way radio with the news that eleven survivors remained on Minerva Reef.

On Monday night a Fijian seaplane lifted off from the Suva Airport and headed east toward Minerva Reef. There was no way they could manage a landing at night. The plane circled overhead and dropped several flares to illuminate the reef. As the exuberant Tongans watched from their wreck, the crew in the flying boat dropped a canister tied to a parachute. It drifted slowly down and landed nearby. The tide was at its lowest. And the moon was full. The big plane wagged its wings and then headed back to Suva.

Ve'etutu supervised the opening of the canister and took inventory. Inside he found ten cans of corned beef, five cans of vegetable and meat stew, five cans of sausages, ten cans of water, three cans of butter, four cans of milk, two cans of fish, six loaves of bread, two can openers, and a message that read simply, HELP COMING.

Ve'etutu first gave a prayer of thanks to God for granting Fifita a safe journey. Then he separated the food and water into ten equal shares; they had suffered another death the day before. The men sat cross-legged, making a midnight picnic of it. They drank their water first, and then started in on the bread and butter. Afterwards they ate the corned beef and fish.

"I was surprised when I counted them sitting around," Ve'etutu told Ruhen later. "Some of them had been bedridden for weeks, but here was a full count. I told them it was good to see them sitting in the circle."

Early the next morning another flying boat appeared overhead. The Tongans on the reef began jumping up and down, waving their arms excitedly, and crying. The plane circled overhead, the crew took some pictures, and then came to rest inside the reef in the lagoon a few hundred feet from the Japanese ship. The door of the plane opened and out came five men—the pilot, a doctor, a Tongan interpreter, and two crewmen. They launched a rubber dinghy with a motor on its stern and quickly covered the distance to the wreck. The rescuers approached the heavily bearded survivors, who clustered together on the coral. Ve'etutu greeted them. "We've been waiting for you to come," he said simply.

The Tongans gave their rescuers a tour of their living quarters. The Fijians marveled at the still and the ingenious ways the group had adapted to their situation. The survivors had precious little to take off Minerva Reef with them after their three months as castaways. Their most prized possession was the tattered Tongan Bible which stank of fish. That, of course, went back with them to be returned to Tonga. For all the Tongans the flight to Suva was their first trip in an airplane. They arrived in the late afternoon and checked into a nearby hospital.

The arrival of the castaways in Nukau'alofa a few days later was the cause of a major celebration. They had an audience at the royal palace. The king was out of the country. But Queen Salote, Prince Tu'ipelehake, and numerous attendants greeted the survivors. In a brief speech the queen told them proudly they had lived up to the Tongan motto, "The mountain of the Tongan is in his heart."

Later from his hospital bed Fifita spoke with members of the Pacific press about his experience. "When it happens again that I am lost on a reef, all I want is that it should be the same crowd with me. I don't mean that I want to be lost on another reef—no, no; never again—but if I am, I will be happy to have the same men with me. I had no trouble with them at all, they all worked together and did what they could."

Then a reporter from the *Fiji Times* asked him, "The sea has taken your father and your son. Do you think the sea is cruel?"

Fifita shook his head.

"I don't think the sea is cruel. I love the sea very much and I'll go back to it. There is no cruelty in the sea. It moves as God wants it to move."

CHAPTER EIGHT

Tom Neale:

The Hermit of
Suwarrow

"If there is a place where a man can grow old content-edly, it is on some quiet, drowsy atoll, where today is forever and tomorrow never comes; where men live and die, feast and sorrow, while the wind and the waves play over the wet sands and gleaming reefs," observed Julian Hillas, an Australian beachcomber who, during the 1940s, settled on Rakahanga in the northern Cook Islands atolls where some 250 people lived on 1,000 acres around a nearly landlocked lagoon.

Of the hundreds of beachcombers in this century, none pursued his quest with greater determination and success than Thomas Francis Neale, a drifter from New Zealand. He took as his life's motto Thoreau's words of wisdom, "A man is rich in proportion to the number of things which he can afford to let alone." For the better part of twenty-five years he lived a relatively idyllic life alone on his tiny atoll, 200 miles from the nearest inhabited land. He became a legend, a man known throughout the South Pacific simply as the Hermit of Suwarrow.

Born in New Zealand in 1902, Tom Neale was one of those rootless wanderers of the sort who captured the imaginations of Joseph Conrad and Somerset Maugham, a piece of human flotsam drifting with the ocean currents from island group to island group.

"I chose to live in the Pacific," Neale wrote toward the end of his life, "because life there moves at the sort of pace which you feel God must have had in mind originally when He made the sun to keep us warm and provided us with the fruits of the earth for the taking."

In 1943 the currents carried Neale from Moorea, near Tahiti, westward 800 miles to Rarotonga in the Cook Islands, then one of the most inaccessible island groups in the Pacific. He accepted a position as a keeper of a general store on Atiu, a small island with rounded hills and fertile valleys where orange trees, coconut palms, and papaya bushes grew in luxurious profusion.

"Each morning I would make my breakfast, open up the store, and wait for the first native customers in the square functional warehouse with its tin roof," Neale recalled later. "The walls were lined with shelves of flour, tea, coffee beans, tinned goods, cloth, needles—everything which one didn't *really* need at all on an island already overflowing with fruit and fish!"

On one of his rare trips back to Rarotonga, Neale met Robert Dean Frisbie, an American author and vagabond, who twenty-three years earlier in far-off Cleveland, Ohio, had heard the siren song of the South Seas islands. He had set out for the Pacific looking for solitude, so that he could develop his talent as a writer. He found it on the isolated atoll of Pukapuka in the northern Cook Islands. There he married an island girl, started a family, and began writing stories for American magazines.

Frisbie was to have a major impact on Neale's life. The New Zealander already knew the American writer from his books and by reputation. The two quickly became close friends. Frisbie talked at length about a three-month stay with his four children on uninhabited Anchorage Island in the lagoon of Suwarrow atoll. It was perhaps the happiest time of his life. They enjoyed a carefree, vagabonding existence, living off the reef fish, coconuts, birds, and eggs. And they survived the terrible hurricane of '42, the worst in a century. In his book *Island of Desire* he described how they had lashed themselves to the upper branches of tamanu trees and then watched in terror as the rampaging seas ripped away the island beneath them. One of his little girls slept through the great wind, until Frisbie woke her to make her drink a little rum, for apparently it was terribly cold with the wind and rain. Afterwards she told her father she was perfectly content until she drank that rum because she could not get back to sleep again.

Frisbie leaned across the cheap wooden table.

"Suwarrow is the most beautiful place on earth, and no man has really lived until he has lived there," he told Neale with great intensity.

Neale thought on it for a while.

"Suwarrow's the sort of place for me," he finally admitted.

"Well, if you feel that way about it, why don't you go there?" Frisbie urged.

Suwarrow quickly became the great obsession which was to consume Neale for the next thirty years.

Lying 513 islands northwest of Rarotonga, Suwarrow appears lost in an immensity of sea and sunlight, so fragile that one wonders how it ever survives the hurricanes which sweep the area with devastating regularity. The atoll consists of eighteen or so tiny chips of emerald islets scattered across the opal waters of an enormous shallow lagoon, snugly tucked inside a twenty-six-mile-long coral reef which encircles them all like a loose-fitting necklace. Some one hundred acres of land divided among five islets and a dozen or so brush covered sandbanks strung along the northeast side of the almost circular reef make up the total land mass. The southern side has no islands or sandbars to warn of its existence. The atoll is little more than a hazard to mariners.

Never permanently inhabited before Neale, Suwarrow nonetheless enjoyed a curious and sometimes gaudy history of shipwrecked mariners, pearl poachers, buried treasure, murder, and seduction. At least eight ships have wrecked on her outer reefs. American and Mexican gold and silver coins have been found buried beneath Suwarrow's sands as well as other artifacts indicating that the Spaniards had visited the island centuries before she was officially discovered and named by the captain of the Russian vessel *Suvarov* in 1814.

It was not until June 1945 that Neale, then an engineer on the copra boat *Tiare Taporo*, saw Suwarrow for the first time. Several coast-watchers had been stationed on Anchorage Island as part of the war effort against Japan. The sea that morning was as smooth as silk, stretching away to infinity, making the *Tiare Taporo* seem pitifully small. None of the islets in the vast lagoon were more than fifteen feet above sea level, and only the tops of coconut palms rising from a ring of surf proclaimed their existence. The trading schooner dropped anchor just off Anchorage Island. Frigate birds wheeled and screeched overhead.

Neale was deeply moved. "How puny the islets seemed in the vast emptiness of the Pacific!" he observed. "Frisbie had called them fragile but they were more than that. To me they almost looked forlorn, so that it seemed amazing they could have survived the titanic forces of nature which have so often wiped out large islands."

Neale eagerly went ashore at the first opportunity. The peace, beauty, and solitude of Suwarrow immediately captivated him. He walked around the island and then checked out the compound of the coast-watchers with its shack, water tanks, and garden with "the questing eyes of a man wondering if one day he would inherit it." The five coast-watchers, on the other hand, were desperately sick of their life on the remote atoll and eager to return to civilization.

The *Tiare Taporo* stayed at Suwarrow for three days, unloading supplies for the coast-watchers. At the end of his visit, Neale turned to the schooner's captain and told him, "Andy, now I know this is the place I've been looking for all this time."

Seven years passed before Neale realized his dream. He bided his time working at odd jobs, mostly as a storekeeper on Rarotonga, and growing increasingly restless and unhappy. He felt trapped and overwhelmed by civilization, even one organized as loosely as the town of Avarua, which in the 1940s was little more than an obscure South Pacific trading post. There were too many people, stores, and social conventions for him. Too much noise. Too much traffic. He was desperate to go to Suwarrow, but first he had to save enough from his meager salary to buy the necessary food, clothing, and tools he would need to survive. Then there was the difficulty of finding a boat heading in that direction, for the atoll was 200 miles from the nearest shipping routes. And finally there was the most difficult challenge of them all, securing official permission to settle on Suwarrow. And that the resident commissioner for the Cook Islands flatly denied.

But Neale persisted. In late 1952 soon after his fiftieth birthday events finally fell into place. An aunt died in New Zealand and left him a legacy of fifty pounds. The owner of an inter-island schooner agreed to detour to Suwarrow. And a new resident commissioner gave his permission for him to settle there.

Neale busied himself putting together the supplies he would need to survive. Several Cook Islands women offered to accompany him, but he quickly dismissed the idea. "I had been baching so long I really didn't need a woman," he wrote later. "And, perhaps most of all, the prospect of being cooped up with a woman who might eventually annoy me, of being imprisoned with her—like a criminal on Devil's Island without hope of escape—made me shudder. I would be better off as a middle-aged bachelor."

Neale decided against taking a battery-operated radio. He did not want to become dependent on something that would suddenly be valueless when its batteries gave out. He sought above all to be completely self-sufficient on his island paradise.

His neighbors in Avarua were skeptical. "All my friends said I was crazy and that I couldn't possibly stay alive on an atoll for two years alone," Neale boasted in 1954 to visiting yachtsman James Rockefeller. "They all said I'd be back damn soon."

On October 7, 1952, Neale finally reached Suwarrow and set about realizing that persistent and elusive dream of modern man, the escape to a deserted island with its palm-fringed beaches. At dawn following his arrival, the schooner *Mahurangi* chugged noisily out to sea. At this final break with the outside world Neale's only emotion was impatience that the boat took so long to get under way.

"I never felt so good," he admitted later. "I never felt so

free or more unlonely. It was one of the nicest moments in my life."

Soon there were only the natural sounds of the atoll—the thunder of the waves upon the distant reef, the faint rustle of the palm fronds, and the clamor of the frigate birds wheeling overhead. Fierce-looking red and blue coconut crabs, some weighing over five pounds, lumbered like miniature tanks through the nearby underbrush. Standing ankle-deep in the shallows, he surveyed the palm-lined horizon and said to himself, "Well, Neale, here you are after all these years. And it's all yours." Like Alexander Selkirk 250 years earlier, he had discovered the pleasures of absolute possession.

Neale had taken to heart the advice of the Australian beachcomber, Edmund Banfield, who had written fifty years before: "Small must be the Isle of Dreams, so small that possession is possible. A choice passion is not to be squandered on that which, owing to exasperating bigness, can never be fully possessed."

Neale took up residence near the entrance to the lagoon on Anchorage Island, a half-mile long and 300 yards wide, living in the two-room wooden building used by the coast-watchers. His furniture consisted of four homemade easy chairs and two beds with wooden slates. Three water tanks held 1,000 gallons of rain water caught from the roof of his hut. His only companions were two cats, Mr. Tom-Tom and Mrs. Thievery. He quickly learned the atoll had no mosquitoes, cockroaches, or rats.

"Haven't had a time for a proper look around but I can see miles of work sticking out," Neale wrote in his journal at the end of the first day. "There will be no time for sitting under a tree and watching the reef, not for a long time anyway."

His first action was to shed his shorts and replace them with a five-inch wide strip torn from an old *pareu*. He wore this native-style, one end fastened around his waist with the other end passed under his crotch, drawn up behind, and tucked under the waistband. From that day on he wore his shorts only when the occasional yacht anchored in his lagoon. Ten months would pass before he entertained his first visitors.

Before unpacking, Neale cleaned the shack thoroughly,

scrubbed the floors, and washed the walls. Then he spent four days tearing down the vines which strangled the hut and outbuildings under a profusion of tropical growth. He plaited the veranda roof using palm fronds, built some shelves, and strung a clothesline between two hibiscus trees at the rear of his yard. Although his nearest neighbors were 200 miles away, he refused to lower his standards. He was a fastidious housekeeper.

"He was the most house-proud man I ever met," Noel Barber, a senior reporter for the London *Daily Mail*, observed after a 1961 visit to Suwarrow. "Every cup and saucer was in its right place. When I dropped a bit of coconut shell on the veranda, he quickly kicked it away, and twice on that first day he swept out the hut with his home-made broom of palm fronds."

Neale quickly set about securing his food supply. The reefs abounded with a variety of fish—ku, parrot fish, cod, and eel—and lobster. These he caught easily with hand lines or his homemade spear. "Every fish in the lagoon seemed to queue up for my table," he wrote later. "Perhaps the easiest to catch was the reef cod which lay motionless in the pools as I approached. They never moved until my spear was within six inches of them. And once I had them quivering on the shore, I carried them back to the shack and steamed them in salt water."

One moonlit night Neale stood in two feet of water, fishing for ku with a bamboo rod and a lure made from the white feathers of a sea bird. A large fish took his lure in a whirl of spray. He worked it skillfully to the edge of the reef and leaned forward cautiously to grip it by the gills. Some instinct made him hesitate. Suddenly, while the fish struggled on his line, a great gray mass rushed on him like a torpedo. There was no time to move, no time even to panic. Before he could draw his hand away, a smashing blow whacked him across both legs, throwing him on his back.

Neale grasped for breath, spitting out salt water. The fish was gone, and the lure had vanished. His bamboo rod floated in the swell. The shark had missed his hand by inches as it took the fish and in passing had struck him with its tail. Stunned, he walked slowly back to his hut. The skin on his left leg was scratched, as though he had roughly rubbed sand-paper across it.

Neale's life on Suwarrow quickly settled into a comfort-able routine. He rose at daybreak and started a fire in his cookhouse. Then he shaved and took his breakfast which at first consisted of freshly brewed coffee, warm scones with jam and butter, and eggs. There was always enough work during the day to keep him busy. He rarely took lunch. In the late afternoon he caught whatever fish he needed for his din-ner. He spent his evenings reading. Aldous Huxley's novel, *Brave New World*, so depressed him that he wrote in his journal, "Neale, if *that's* what the world is going to be like, you can just stay where you are!"

A month after landing on his island, Neale turned fifty-one. He noted in his journal on that "beautiful warm day, the breadfruit is doing fine. Took my tea down to the beach after catching fish for the cats. Cooked them on the beach just before dusk and watched the night fall over the lagoon."

Neale did most of his cooking Polynesian style in an earthen oven inside a cookhouse located next to his living quarters. Sometimes the limited variety of foods wore down his spirits, "Breadfruit and coconuts sound all very well in adventure stories, but nobody can deny they are monoto-nous." He often experimented with new dishes. Once he cut several papayas in half, baked them in the oven, and served them hot with fresh coconut sauce. "They tasted like peaches," he observed proudly in his journal.

In mid-December Neale had his first omelet since his ar-rival on Suwarrow. Thousands of terns settled on the island, built nests, and started laying. To make certain he got only fresh eggs, he carried a tin full of water and dropped each one in. Fresh eggs sank to the bottom. Older eggs floated.

"For a month I ate eggs every day and fed the rest of my daily haul to the cats who loved them," he noted. "It is amazing how almost any bird or animal appreciates a change of diet. Not to mention myself. They were the best omelets I ever tasted."

The terns departed after several months, their nesting season concluded. By then, eggs had become a favorite item in Neale's severely limited diet. He had exhausted his supply of flour, sugar, and rice. The loss of his omelets quickly put

him into a minor depression. However, the coast-watchers
had left behind several chickens. These had gone wild and
multiplied over the years, scurrying noisily through the underbrush whenever he approached. Yet these wild fowls
proved incredibly elusive. He spent hours every day in futile
searches for their nests, each morning noting in his journal
his growing frustration:

August 5
    Wasted time following the hen that lays away.
She went in a wide semi-circle and finally eluded me.
I waited for half an hour to see if she would return.
Not a sign; nor did she cackle again. She was in the
yard when I returned. Am determined to find her
nest, besides now I've got to show something for the
time wasted looking.

August 6
    Tried to follow the same hen but a young rooster
upset her. I chased him and only managed to scare the
hen. She wouldn't go straight to her nest but hung
around in the bush.

August 7
    At last I discovered her nest with ten eggs. This
morning she started making a noise, so I followed her.
Suddenly, she disappeared. I couldn't believe my eyes,
so I waited a bit longer and investigated a coconut
stump about ten feet high. Damn me, if I didn't see
her head sticking out of a hole four feet from the
ground. Talk about pigs not thinking to look up—I'm
as bad! A lot of writing about nothing, but I feel I've
achieved a major victory . . . .

Neale saw that the only long term solution lay in domes-
ticating the wild chickens. To tame the fowls, he scattered
coconut meat in his yard and banged a gong to attract the
birds. Within a short time he had his chickens trained to
come on command. Then he constructed a fenced enclosure
from the ribs of coconut fronds, gathering them by the hun-

dreds and cutting off their leaves with his machete. He fastened these together with pieces of old baling wire and added a gate at one end. This project took him several weeks, but in the end he had his chickens safely in the pen. Now for the first time he had a steady supply of eggs and roosters for his Sunday meals to give him some relief from his usual diet of fish, fish, and more fish.

The most serious threat to Neale's survival during this period came not from sharks or the near hurricane-force winds that swept across Suwarrow in January 1953. Rather the danger lay with five wild pigs that rooted about the island, destroying his banana and papaya plants. His survival over the long term depended upon his successful cultivation of a garden. And that, he quickly perceived, was impossible while the pigs remained alive.

So Neale determined to kill the pigs. When a period of heavy rains confined him to his hut, he painstakingly filed a broken machete blade until it was razor sharp. This he lashed to the end of a stout pole. When the weather cleared, he spent three days constructing a platform twelve feet above the ground in a palm tree in the interior of the island and another two days clearing the brush from the tree's base.

The strategy appeared simple. All he had to do was lure the pigs into the clearing beneath the tree. At the first full moon he broke open a dozen coconuts and scattered the meat about the clearing. Then he climbed slowly into the tree and waited. For four nights no pigs appeared, only enormous coconut crabs which executed grotesque dances in the moonlight, their huge claws weaving in the air, and ghoulishly ripped at the nuts.

Then on the fifth night the first pig cautiously approached the pile of shredded coconut. Moonlight glinted along its tusks, accentuating the great bulk of its massive shoulders. "Suddenly, I was hardly able to breathe," Neale recalled later. "I felt cold but full of hatred and gripped my homemade spear more tightly." The pig paused directly beneath the platform. Neale aimed for just behind its neck and plunged his spear downwards with all his strength. The foot-long blade sank to the shaft. The pig gave a half-human scream, wretched away, and staggered off heavily toward a thicket. Neale chased after him, caught him as he reached cover, and cut his throat with a swift stroke of his machete, spilling the animal's blood over the coral sand:

"Staggering back, splattered with blood, I thought for a moment I was going to be sick, but once the gurgling and thrashing stopped, once the heavy body slumped into dark shadowed immobility and I could see it lying there, I was suddenly overwhelmed with a sense of melancholy. I suppose it was the reaction. All at once, I was no longer a hunter. I was just an old man of fifty-one, alone on an atoll."

The brutal, gory business had to be repeated four more times. By the late spring of 1953 Neale had killed the last animal. The death of the pigs brought an astonishing change on Anchorage Island. Papaya shoots sprang up everywhere. The wild bananas began to flourish.

Once the pigs were gone, Neale began to work in earnest on his garden. For several months he laboriously shoveled, sifted, and transported several tons of top soil from the opposite end of the island to his hut. He made his rakes of palm fronds. In the new layer of soil he planted tomatoes, shallots, rock melons, watermelons, pumpkins, cucumbers, and yams. Everything went splendidly, and he eagerly looked forward to the first fresh fruits and vegetables since his arrival on his island.

But the garden failed. The plants he had so confidently expected to see loaded with fruit produced nothing more than a couple of small tomatoes. He wrote gloomily in his journal: "Everything is growing vigorously and is full of flowers, but the fruit won't set; it just forms, then turns yellow and drops off. Must be the lack of bees."

There was only one thing to do. Since there were no bees, the blossoms had to be pollinated by hand. Neale set about doing exactly that, breaking off the male part of the flower and carefully rubbing pollen on the female parts of the flowers. It worked perfectly. Once he had fertilized the blossoms, he enjoyed excellent crops. Within three months, he was harvesting a bumper crop of tomatoes; within four months, pumpkins and melons.

Ten months after Neale had landed on Suwarrow, everything had finally settled into place as he had always imagined it would. By then he was almost entirely self-sufficient. He wrote proudly in his journal: "From this moment on I had more fish than I needed, plenty of fruit and vegetables, and a regular rooster for the pot." He had overcome the odds and managed to prosper on Suwarrow because he was, as he put it, "the handyman incarnate." Thirty years of life among the Pacific islands had given him the thousand and one skills he needed to survive on an atoll.

By then Neale had begun to feel an enormous affection for the atoll. He patched up a small sail boat the coast-watchers had left behind and named it the *Ruptured Duckling*. For the first time he had a means of getting about his lagoon and visiting the other islets. Most had been swept clean of palms in the fearsome hurricane of 1942 that had almost killed Frisbie and his family. To show his love for Suwarrow, he decided upon a plan of reforestation.

"The island was giving me happiness and contentment," he later told the visiting yachtsman James Rockefeller. "I wanted to do something to repay her. . . . I would set out early in the morning with thirty or forty spouting nuts, plant them, and return toward evening, thinking that I had speeded up evolution a hundred years."

Neale developed into a consummate beachcomber, scouring the island's beaches regularly for useful items that the breakers had washed ashore. One day he found several flat, yellowish blocks of paraffin wax. Another time he came across some bamboo which he reasoned had been discarded from a Japanese fishing boat. He had used up his kerosene, but here was a substitute. He cut the bamboo into short lengths, hung a string through each, and poured in the melted wax. Now he had candles and could once again enjoy the luxury of reading in bed each evening.

Throughout this time Neale found himself working harder than ever before. "And yet this was something I never resented because everything that cropped up seemed to come as a challenge. Every time I managed to find the answer, it was a new step forward that seemed tremendously worthwhile."

Not once in all this time had another ship called at Suwarrow. Finally, on August 4, 1953, ten months after his arrival on the island, Neale welcomed his first visitors, two American couples crossing the Pacific on their forty-foot sailboat. They, in turn, found a wiry, leather-skinned leprechaun with jug-handled ears who wore a pair of tattered shorts and a wide-brim straw hat to conceal his balding pate.

The Americans were keenly interested in Neale's Robinson Crusoe existence, and he graciously gave them a tour of his living quarters.

"What staggers me is the way you have everything fixed up," the captain put in. "It all looks so easy."

"Perhaps you'd all like a shower?" Neale offered.

"A bath!" the other man cried. "My God, I've been dreaming of a bath for a week!"

So Neale took them around to his bathhouse where he had rigged up a shower from a bucket. The two ladies went first. Afterwards he handed them clean towels.

"You do think of everything, don't you?" the captain's wife said admiringly.

That evening Neale took supper on their ship and enjoyed for the first time in many months roast beef, potatoes with gravy, bread with butter, and fruit with cream for desert. "I had long since accepted my rather monotonous diet as part of life and hardly worth a second thought. I don't suppose that I shall ever forget that supper as long as I live."

The visitors sailed for Samoa after two days on Suwarrow. Neale felt no apprehension whatsoever at seeing them leave. That evening after their departure he noted in his journal: "How vastly different their lives were going to be from mine once their pleasant cruise was over. There would be bright lights, cars, busy streets, cinemas, and hotels; so-called luxuries which, however desirable, exacted their own price in tensions, problems, and congested humanity."

What did Neale miss most about civilization? Apples! "There's no better fruit than an apple. But I tell myself, 'Neale, if you want an apple so badly, you can go where they are!'"

He rarely regretted the lack of human companionship and thrived on solitude. He recalled in 1966 that those were "very happy days. I was never lonely, though now and again I would walk along the reef wishing somebody could be with me—not because I wanted company but just because all this beauty seemed too perfect to keep to myself."

But life in paradise had its rough edges. The lack of variety in his diet, especially the absence of red meat, sometimes sent him into a slough of despondency that lasted for weeks. A major crisis started to build in time for his second Christmas on Suwarrow. It all began innocently several months earlier when a bedraggled wild duck suddenly landed on a nearby coral head. Neale stared in disbelief at such an unlikely sight. He slowly approached the bird. But when he was within a dozen feet, the duck panicked and flew twenty yards away to another coral outcropping. From there it eyed him with considerable suspicion.

A few days later Neale made a trip to the southern end of his island to collect more topsoil for his garden. He spotted the duck a second time. Once again he tried to approach, only to have the bird keep its distance. And so they fell into a routine, man and duck, with the bird keeping Neale company when he worked on the beach but never allowing him to approach closer than fifteen feet. He rose to the challenge and decided to tame her. He began by putting out shredded coconut for his migratory companion at the same time each day and then standing to one side while the duck cautiously approached and fed from the bowl. This lasted for several months. Finally, one time he broke open a coconut and impulsively held out his hand with some meat. The duck hurried over without hesitation and started to feed. From then on she would accept food only from his hand. Thus began a "long and curious friendship, complicated by a strange mixture of trust and temptation."

The duck became his constant companion, often following on his heels like an obedient and faithful dog. One evening he noted in his journal: "I really had to laugh today, for I was a bit late reaching the shack to prepare the duck's food and she came towards me with one solitary disapproving quack. . . . She was a creature of precise habit and never appeared in the yard before feeding time. Never once was there a note of disapproval so long as I was on time."

As Christmas of 1953 approached, Neale began to despair over the monotony of his diet. He longed for a slice of bread or a piece of chocolate. Work became difficult. He fantasized for long intervals about his favorite foods. Things got so bad, he started hallucinating about "big pot roasts of lamb in front of me, at the foot of the bed, or on the shelf where I kept my books." Visions of food filled his dreams each night.

Then one night he awoke suddenly in a cold sweat: "There on a great silver platter with, I remember, a highly ornate carving knife and fork, and surrounded by a mound of exotic vegetables, was the wild duck. . . . The impact was as terrifying as if a head waiter had lifted a silver cover to reveal the elaborately cooked head of my best friend."

The next morning Neale hurried to the lagoon to make certain his duck was safe. The bird flew to him and, as usual, waddled up to his outstretched hand to feed. But the dream had worked subtle changes in him. For the first time he started to think about eating the bird. After all, he reasoned, was he not desperate for a change of diet? Perhaps the duck understood this and wanted to sacrifice herself for her friend, he rationalized. The temptation grew with each passing day. His will slowly weakened. One evening he reached out and grabbed the bird gently around her neck. It would be a quick and painless death, he told himself. One sudden twist, a couple of hours spent plucking out the feathers, and then the duck would be ready for his pot. He withdrew his hand and hurried away drenched in a cold sweat.

"I had worked for weeks to gain her trust, and now at last she *did* trust me completely," he wrote later. "I am not a sentimental man and don't want to over-dramatise the situation but gradually it was borne in on me that I just couldn't bring myself to betray that trust."

At last Neale decided upon a course of action. When the duck approached the next evening, he refused to feed her by hand. Instead he put her food and water on the sand and walked back to his hut. She was a creature of habit. This was not her familiar routine. She refused to eat and flew off. The struggle between the two lasted a week. His depression hit a new low. Finally, one evening the duck failed to fly in at her usual hour. Neale never saw her again.

His spirits were restored on Christmas Day, 1953. Neale found a 300-pound turtle on his beach. He celebrated Christmas with an oversized turtle steak and proclaimed it the finest meat dish he had ever tasted! His spirits soared. "With plenty of good, nourishing turtle meals each day," he noted, "I discovered that not only my health but my whole outlook was taking a turn for the better. . . . My loneliness and depression vanished and I even forgot about the wild duck."

As the hurricane season approached, Neale began checking the barometer three and four times a day. He examined the tamanu trees Frisbie and his kids used for the big blow of '42 and planned how he would use them if another such hurricane swept over his atoll. At the foot of one tree buried in the sand he discovered an old bottle of Worcestershire sauce, a relic from Frisbie's stay on Suwarrow. "It was still good but every time I used it I had an urge to look at the barometer and in the end wished it had remained where it was," he told a later visitor.

Neale began the new year with a major project, the rebuilding of the island's coral pier. For six weeks he labored to move large coral blocks into place. By mid-February the job was completed. The pier stretched into the lagoon. On its far end he constructed a small thatched-roof shack for his night fishing. He reflected with pride that back home in New Zealand such a project would have required a crew of six men and a bulldozer. He declared the day a national holiday on Suwarrow and in a moment of whimsy wrote in his journal:

> Amidst scenes of great enthusiasm the new wharf was officially opened by the president of the island council, Mr. Tom-Tom. The trans-lagoon vessel *Ruptured Duckling* berthed at the end of the wharf while the band played, 'Oh, for a Slice of Bread and Cheese.'
>
> In his speech, Mr. Tom-Tom paid tribute to the contractor and his staff, who in the face of numerous difficulties successfully completed the colossal undertaking. He went on to say that with the great depth of twelve inches at the end of the wharf at low tide, the largest vessel could now berth with safety and that in the future we could hope to see many more vessels use this port.
>
> Afterwards tea was served by Mrs. Thievery and her able assistants. In the evening a dance was held at the pavilion after a fine supper of fish guts and rats' tails. . . . Dancing continued until the small hours and was concluded by the singing of the Suwarrow national anthem, "We Ain't Had a Ship in Years."

The next day the barometer suddenly fell sharply. A blanket of oppressive heat hung over Suwarrow's lagoon. Neale understood at once that these were the signs of an impending hurricane. He quickly checked his survival cache—a large box of tools with matches carefully packed in sealed tin cans—and then buried it in a deep hole in the compound. He gathered several days supplies of fresh fish, fruits, vegetables, and coconuts. He collected firewood. And finally he carefully checked the wires he had installed earlier to hold the roof in place. Neale was confident that he could withstand a siege of several days.

By mid-afternoon enormous waves were rolling across the outer reefs. Black clouds swept across the sky. The wind increased its velocity steadily and was shrieking through the palm fronds like a wounded animal. Suddenly, the first palm tree gave way, its roots tearing free, and crashed against its neighbors. "This could be another '42," Neale told himself, as he retreated into his hut. And he recalled Frisbie's warning: "Remember, Anchorage is damn fragile." Never before had he experienced such a terrible storm:

> More coconut palms were falling, nuts started flying through the air, and the tin roof vibrated like a buzz-saw. For it was the sound of the storm that was so incredible. I had weathered many a storm at sea, but there the sounds had been different and I had grown accustomed to them. But now the only resemblance to the wind whistling through the rigging came when the guy ropes twanged with each sudden gust. The wind was so strong that it blotted out almost all other sounds, though every now and then I could hear the crash of another tree falling. At any moment I expected the roof of the shack to be torn away. . . . As the night wore on, coconuts falling on the roof were to make sleep virtually impossible."

Early the next morning the storm had passed out to sea. The day dawned bright and sunny. Neale ventured outside to check for damage. The storm had blown away his chicken pen and toppled four large trees into his yard. Broken branches and palm fronds littered the compound. He hurried down to his beach. There he stood in stunned disbelief, staring at the ruins of the pier. The great waves had scattered the large coral blocks along the sandy beach. In just six hours the storm had destroyed what it had taken him six weeks of back-breaking labor to construct. "I was so downhearted," he wrote in his journal, "that I didn't even use any bad language, but walked slowly back to the house."

Neale's worst crisis came on May 22, 1954. He wrote in his journal in the morning that he had seldom felt better. The hurricane season was behind him. The weather was splendid. His garden was flourishing. "For once there was hardly a real care to worry me," he noted confidently. "Everything was perfect."

After breakfast Neale gathered some spouting coconuts, loaded them into the *Ruptured Duckling*, and rowed over to One Tree Island to plant them. His boat's bow slid gently into the coral sand and came to a halt. He leaped ashore. As he had done hundreds of times before, he lifted up the iron weight that served as his anchor and flung it up on the beach.

Suddenly, a sharp spasm of pain shot across his lower back, forcing him to double up and freeze in his tracks. He stood still, the sweat pouring off his face. The slightest movement sent shock waves of pain down his back and legs. Panic slowly built within him. "Neale, if you've got a dislocated back," he told himself, "then this is the end of you."

Neale slowly lowered himself to all fours and gradually made his way toward his boat. Intense pain spasms racked his body. The sun moved higher in the sky, and he began to worry about dehydration. His plight appeared desperate. Eventually, he managed to push the *Ruptured Duckling* off the sandy beach and climb on board. His compound on Anchorage Island was still three miles away. Somehow he made the trip across the lagoon, driven by the thought that if he was going to die he wanted to do so in his own bed. By late afternoon he finally reached his beach and dragged himself across the sand to his hut. He collapsed on the bunk, trembling with fear and pain. The two cats hurried over and curled up alongside him, purring contentedly.

Rescue appeared an impossibility. "I was horribly, almost

petrifyingly aware of the desperate fix I was in. Here I was, virtually paralyzed, two hundred miles away from the nearest human being. Nor was there any reason why a boat should unexpectedly call at Suwarrow."

As the days slowly passed, Neale's condition deteriorated rapidly. From two coconuts he got some drinking water. He urinated into a glass and then emptied the contents on the floor. His only hope was that in a week his muscles would relax and the pain spasms would pass. Slowly, he slipped into delirium, as his body dehydrated. Each day he grew weaker.

Then one afternoon Neale heard voices at a great distance. He thought he was hallucinating. The voices sounded again, closer and more distinct. Suddenly, he heard a footfall inside his house. A man's voice called out:

"Anybody home?"

"Who is it?" Neale asked weakly.

"Two fellows off a boat," the voice answered.

"Come in, come in," Neale pleaded.

Two men entered his bedroom. They stopped in amazement and stared down at his emaciated form. Every muscle, rib, and tendon showed under his mahogany skin. He lay on his back, his loins covered with a cloth. A glass of urine, two empty drinking coconuts, and a machete lay on the floor beside the bed.

"Christ! It's a white man!"

Neale smiled and weakly held out his hand in greeting.

"My name's Tom Neale. Dislocated my back. You'll have to help me up. What day is it?"

"Wednesday."

The two men stared down at him in utter disbelief.

"What's the date?" Neale asked.

"The twenty-sixth."

"I've been here four days, trying to summon the nerve to sit up."

"Good God, you must be starved," the one visitor insisted. "What can I get you?"

"I sure would like a cup of tea, thanks," Neale replied softly.

Neale's rescuers were two young Americans, James Rockefeller and Bob Grant. They were island-hopping their way across the Pacific on their sailboat, the *Mandalay*.

Rockefeller hurried back to his boat for supplies. Upon his return, he gently eased Neale into a sitting position and massaged his back with liniment.

"What you really need," Rockefeller insisted, "is a good meal. Every single rib you've got is showing."

That evening Neale told his story over a bowl of thick vegetable soup and a plate of tinned meat and vegetables. He enjoyed his first cigarettes in six months. The young Americans stayed on Suwarrow for two weeks and nursed Neale back to life. His back improved rapidly. And his strength returned on his diet of canned meats from the *Mandalay* 's pantry. Rockefeller and Grant, in turn, were happy to share in Neale's vegetables, fruits, eggs, and chickens. And they questioned him endlessly about his life on the island. At their request, he drew up a list of items he considered to be the bare essentials for life on an atoll:

1) Kerosene (light)
2) Soap
3) Matches
4) Knife and machete
5) Fish spear

6) Blanket
7) Sneakers for walking on the reef and some clothes

To make life easier, Neale recommended the following:

8) Tea and Coffee
9) Sugar
10) Flour
11) Baking powder
12) Lard
13) Beef
14) Rice

15) Tobacco
16) Butter or oleo
17) Salt and condiments
18) File
19) Hook and line for fishing
20) Reading matter

"With all these," Neale insisted, "and with what an island has to offer, one can live like a king."

Rockefeller read at length in Neale's journal.

"Didn't you get depressed after the storm destroyed your pier?" he wanted to know.

"It's impossible to feel downhearted long on Suwarrow,"

Neale chuckled. "The next day, to get away from the sight of those strewn blocks, I loaded the *Ruptured Duckling* with spouting nuts and took a trip to One Tree Island. I planted thirty nuts, sweating like a Turk. It was a beautiful day, and soon I felt very glad to be alive and the dock forgotten. I took a walk on the reef, speared three lobsters, found a glass ball used by the Japanese fisheries, a jar of honey only partly consumed, and a pirogue paddle of unusual design that must have floated from the Marquesas. I sailed home a rich man."

The Americans asked Neale if he had ever wanted to give up his solitary life and return to Rarotonga at any time during his twenty-month exile. He grinned and told them: "Naturally, now and again I would get depressed and wish I was back in civilization. But then I would think of all my friends saying, 'I told you so,' and just the thought of that makes me kind of mad. Besides, there was no way to leave even if I had wanted to, and those bad spells never lasted long."

But with his bad back it quickly became clear to Neale that now he would have to return to Rarotonga. Had he a companion, a Man Friday, then he could have managed on Suwarrow in spite of his back injury. Another person could have lifted him up each time the muscle spasms locked his back and massaged the pain away. But alone he stood no chance.

"It's one thing to be killed or drowned in a hurricane or storm—in a way, it's the sort of end that'd suit you, Tom," Rockefeller had gently advised him. "But it's something else to lie on your back, unable to move, all alone, slowly starving to death, alive but paralysed, knowing there's more food than you can eat just ten yards away."

Rockefeller sent a radio message to Rarotonga. Two weeks after the Americans had left his island, an inter-island steamer diverted to Suwarrow to collect Neale. As the atoll, his home of twenty-one months receded into the distance, he recalled an old Tahitian proverb:

"The coral waxes, the palm grows, but man departs."

Back in Avarua, Neale hurried to a doctor, who found no evidence of a ruptured disk and diagnosed his problem as an acute case of arthritis. He wrote a lengthy letter to James Rockefeller, which eventually reached him at his home in Maine. "Here in Raro I find myself discontented with civilization," he admitted. "Just too many people, so I am planning to go back to Suwarrow, this time with a twelve-foot sailing dinghy and a thirty-year-old Palmerston woman. In the meantime I'm working for a local firm, slowly building up a grub stake to last for the rest of my time on Suwarrow."

Six years passed before Neale saw Suwarrow again. They were years of continual frustration. The resident commissioner refused him permission to return to his atoll, insisting: "I represent the Government and Governments have responsibilities."

Neale loathed his job with the Cook Islands Trading Company. "Every moment in the warehouse found me nostalgically comparing this dreary commercial existence with the free and intensely satisfying life I had known on the island. For nearly two years my only clothing had been a strip of *pareu*; now long trousers encased and imprisoned my reluctant legs. Every time I drew breath I felt choked with petrol fumes from the cars outside my office window at the filling station."

But gradually Neale settled into his new routine. He rented for ten shillings a week a room in a house outside Avarua. Sometimes the wind brought him the faint boom of the surf on a distant reef. It was one of the few things in his new life that reminded him of his idyllic existence on Suwarrow. In 1956 he married Mrs. Sarah Haua, from nearby Palmerston Island. She bore him a son and a daughter.

Then his mother died in New Zealand and left him two hundred and forty pounds, enough to make him a rich man in Rarotonga. The day after he learned the news he gave notice at the Cook Islands Trading Company. Once again he made the rounds of the stores in Avarua buying the necessary supplies. This time he insisted upon a more substantial boat than the *Ruptured Duckling* and bought a twelve-foot sailing boat. The resident commissioner reluctantly agreed not to interfere. And Loren Smith, a visiting American yachtsman, offered to take him to his atoll on his ship, the *Tahiti*. Finally, in early March of 1960, Neale set sail for Suwarrow, abandoning without regrets his wife and children.

After eleven days the *Tahiti* reached Suwarrow and dropped anchor off Anchorage Island. An excited Neale waded ashore and stood again on his old beach, overcome with emotion: "In an instant the six years of waiting were wiped off the slate. It was as though they had never happened, and I felt just as if I were returning from an expedition to one of the motus and that Smithy's *Tahiti*, riding at anchor in the lagoon, was just another visiting yacht."

Neale hurried over to his compound to check on the condition of his buildings. A thick layer of vines covered his shack and tool shed. Weeds and spouting coconuts had reclaimed his garden. He quickly saw that he would have to start over, but this time he had better tools and a larger boat. When he walked through the rooms in his hut, he found everything just as he had left it. He noticed on a table two slips of paper, one white and the other green, under a piece of coral rock. The white paper was a note dated March, 1956. It said: "Don't know who you are or if you're returning, but I would like you to know my boat stayed here two weeks. We enjoyed the fruits of your well-kept garden and ate five of your fowls. Hope this will cover everything. Sincerely, Sid P. Thatcher, San Francisco." With the note was a twenty dollar bill.

Neale's second stay on Suwarrow lasted forty-two months. In that entire time only six yachts called. Once he went fourteen months without seeing another person's face. Yet he never found loneliness a problem. "I am free here!" he told one of his rare visitors. "I have freedom! I am a free man!"

This time Neale determined to avoid what he considered to be his major mistake during his first visit. "I rather ruefully came to the conclusion that I, who loved the leisurely pace of life on the islands, had failed when I reached Suwarrow the first time to put into practice the lessons learned during half a lifetime in the South Pacific," he admitted later. "I had been so proud of my island that I wanted to do everything in a rush. And so, in a curiously ironic way, I had unwittingly imposed on the timeless quality of the island the speed and bustle of modern cities from which I had been so anxious to escape."

One day the thought struck him that Robinson Crusoe

had built himself a second residence several miles from his stockade. Why should he not do the same? Why not, he asked himself, have a "summer house" on an outlying island where he might go for a "vacation" and a change of scenery? And this he did, constructing a rather substantial hut complete with kitchen on one of the smaller islets. Thereafter, whenever the pace became too "hectic" on Anchorage Island, Neale closed up shop and went on holiday to Motu Tuo.

In late November of 1960 the sound of roaring motors suddenly shattered the tranquility of Suwarrow. As an amazed Neale watched from the line of coconut palms, two helicopters slowly settled on his beach. Several men wearing military uniforms clamored out. Neale stepped from out of the shade, tipped his battered straw hat, and said, "United States Navy, I presume?"

The men stood there in stunned silence for several minutes. They were from the American icebreaker *Glacier*, bound for New Zealand and Antarctica. They had flown to Suwarrow to inspect an "uninhabited island."

An officer was the first to recover. He quickly stepped back, saluted Neale, and then said:

"Well, I'll be damned. What in the hell are you doing here?"

"I live here," Neale answered.

"Alone?"

"Yes, alone—you're the first person I've spoken to for six months."

"You don't look like a native, sir," the officer said.

"I'm not. I'm a New Zealander."

"Well, by God!" the man cried. "It's lucky for you we've called. Now we can get you off."

Neale patiently explained that choice, not bad luck, had brought him to Suwarrow.

"Well, I'll be damned!" the senior officer said. "Robinson Crusoe come true."

Neale gave his visitors a brief tour of his house and compound. They were dumbfounded to find a white man in the twentieth century who lived virtually in a natural state.

"Are you sure you don't want to string along with us?" the officer asked again.

Neale reassured them. Then the helicopters lifted off to rejoin the ship. That evening he wrote in his journal: "Their entire visit had occupied half an hour—the briefest visit anybody has ever paid to Suwarrow."

A much garbled account of the Americans' visit to Suwarrow appeared in newspapers in Australia and New Zealand. One of the readers was Noel Barber, a senior reporter for the London *Daily Mail*, who was then in Samoa. He and a photographer chartered a schooner in Pago Pago and hurried over to Suwarrow to interview "the man who had done what millions of us dream of doing but never seem to do." He brought Neale a generous supply of canned food, tea, tobacco, six bottles of whiskey, and a box of books. Neale was especially appreciative of the books. "The only thing I demand is an interesting book in bed the last thing at night," he told Barber.

Barber stayed several days and interviewed Neale at length.

"Why did you come here?" he asked the tall New Zealander with dark brown skin and a wardrobe consisting entirely of a pair of ragged shorts, a battered old hat, and tennis shoes.

Neale thought for a moment before answering.

"The real truth is, you don't make decisions like this all at once. I'd been growing towards the idea for thirty years. Don't go getting the wrong idea, though, and thinking I'm a hermit. Do I look like one? I like people. I honestly do. I'm not just evading responsibilities. I suppose really—honestly—I don't quite know why I did come here in the first place."

The pair talked far into the night. Barber watched the moon rise across the lagoon silhouetting his ship framed in the palms. Suddenly, the Englishman sensed an important truth about Neale and one that jarred his sensibilities.

"As he talked, I realised with something of a shock that though he was obviously pleased to see me and was delighted with the stores I had brought him, he would not miss me when I left," Barber wrote later. "He had not even bothered to inquire how long I intended to stay."

In May 1963 the American yacht *Tiburon* anchored in the lagoon with Ed Vessey, the owner, his Samoan wife, and their fourteen-year-old adopted daughter on board. They were bound from Pago Pago to Honolulu. Three days later the wind suddenly shifted abruptly and blew the *Tiburon* on to a coral reef. She sank in twelve feet of water at low tide. (A later visitor likened Suwarrow to a Venus fly trap, very alluring and easy to enter but once inside difficult to escape from because of the numerous coral heads studding the bottom of the lagoon.)

Neale found himself with three castaways on his hands. It was the only crisis he had never anticipated, not even in the wildest flights of his imagination. Later he wrote:

"From that night the four of us shared my bedroom. From that night forward my entire life was transformed. No longer was I the solitary inhabitant of an island occasionally unbending to welcome guests. I had become one of four people—three of whom I hardly knew. Moreover, my castaways might well have to endure their exile in my company for months, even years. They possessed virtually no clothes, no provisions—in fact, nothing but a guitar and the garments in which they stood. And though by now I was accustomed, even delighted, to welcome the occasional stranger from a visiting yacht, I had inevitably become so set in my ways that the prospect of sharing my life with these benighted strangers appalled me."

Neale's worst fears were never realized. Two months later as he took his morning walk he suddenly spotted the gray outline of a ship on the horizon. He knew at once it was a naval vessel of some sort. He ran excitedly back to his hut. Ed Vessey hurried to the beach with his wife's pocket mirror. Catching the sun's rays, he flashed a signal to the distant ship.

"She's spotted your signals!" an excited Neale shouted.

The ship changed course and steamed toward Suwarrow.

"We're saved, darling—do you realise it? We're saved!" Vessey cried, hugging his wife.

Within an hour the ship anchored in the lagoon. She was a New Zealand frigate, the *Pukaki*. A short time later the Vesseys were on board and steaming away from Suwarrow.

Neale's second stay on the atoll came to an abrupt end two months later on December 27, 1963. The reason this time was a group of eleven pearl divers from Manihiki Atoll.

They littered his beaches, partied every night, and drank most of his fresh water. His heaven now a hell, Neale took advantage of the first boat to call at the island and returned to Rarotonga.

This time he had no intention of going back to Suwarrow. He settled back in with his family, resumed his position at the Cook Islands Trading Company store, and began writing a book about his years on Suwarrow for a British publisher. His memoirs, *An Island to Oneself*, appeared in 1966. They are a lyrical and sensitive evocation of his experiences on the atoll. The book became a bestseller in Australia and New Zealand.

Neale's book demonstrates inadvertently a profound truth about his experiences as a beachcomber on Suwarrow. What begins as an adventure story ends in praise of a life of quiet domesticity and simple toil. Like Alexander Selkirk and his fictional counterpart Robinson Crusoe before him, he tamed the exotic and made it comfortingly familiar.

And this was the key to his success. Nature for Neale was less a subject for adoration than exploitation. The island's solitude became an exceptional occasion, not for undisturbed self-communion, but for strenuous efforts at self-help. What the literary critic Ian Watt wrote forty years ago about Robinson Crusoe is equally true of his modern counterpart:

"Crusoe observes nature, not with the eyes of a pantheist primitive, but with the calculating gaze of a colonial capitalist; wherever he looks he sees acres that cry for improvement, and as he settles down to the task he glows, not with noble savagery, but purposeful possession."

The writing of his memoirs made Neale nostalgic for Suwarrow. Once again he abandoned his family (all mention of which he had deleted from his book) and returned to his atoll in July of 1967, remaining this time for ten years. For this third stay he used the royalties from his book to set himself up in style, arriving on Suwarrow with forty boxes of personal belongings, drums of fuel, two boats, and a miscellaneous collection of building materials. He tidied up his island and resumed his former routine.

Once again Neale found himself obliged to entertain unexpected visitors. Carl Seipel and Hans Bernwall sailed their yacht into Suwarrow's lagoon in early September of 1972, carrying supplies from Rarotonga. They had read his memoirs a few months before and were eager to meet this Hermit of the South Pacific. He surprised them with his energy.

"All the photographs I had seen had revealed an ageless bony creature," Seipel admitted later. "If the rest of his body showed age, Tom's eyes were shockingly young. Small, brown, and lively, they seemed to be looking at everything for the first time. Even his body that had looked like a collection of tendons in the photos now gave the impression of power and ability to endure long physical effort. And this at the age of 70! His skin was deeply tanned with some dark brown spots and old scars here and there. "

Neale gave his visitors a tour of his two-room house, tool shed, chicken run, rain water tanks, and shower shed. In the cooking shed a fire smoldered at all times to avoid wasting matches—more difficult to replace than wood. They noted that he prepared his meals in ordinary cooking pots placed on a grating over a primitive brick oven. They inspected his small garden where papaya, bananas, tomatoes, beans, and sweet potatoes thrived under Neale's care.

"I try to make my own soil from leaves and garbage there," Neale told them, pointing toward a large bin, made from flattened drums. "The crabs are my biggest problem, all sizes of them up to the giant coconut crab. If they get past the fence, they eat everything I have. Months of work and waiting to no avail after one single night."

Neale had had no guests for four months and was eager to talk. That night over a bottle of rum and a meal of coconut crab and freshly baked scones he recollected his early life before his arrival on Suwarrow. Seipel and Bernwall listened intently to his tales of home brew parties that lasted for days, of hard work in the banana plantations, and the careless passion of the Polynesian women. He told them about what life was like in the French Polynesia of the thirties, of his simple happy life on Moorea, of the little Chinese girl who loved him but was sold by her parents to an old and ugly man. He admitted that what he feared most in his solitary existence on Suwarrow were not the sharks or hurricanes but being struck on the head by a falling coconut.

"Tom," Seipel asked, "what would you do if someone

came here and offered you a lot of money to appear on TV to talk about your life here? Would you go?"

Neale answered quickly, without hesitation.

"No, Carl, I could never leave Suwarrow for something like that. I love this island, and the years I have spent here have been the best of my life. Money? I have no use for it here."

His penchant for solitude had given Neale a reputation for being a recluse and a hermit. He bristled at the suggestion. "I'm not a hermit," he told another visiting yachtsman. "Hermits don't like people, but I do. I just live here because it suits me. I can do what I want to, when I want to, without being beholden to anyone. I'm free!"

But Neale's idyll would soon come to an end. Ironically, it was his own success in describing the beauty of his solitude that finally brought the outside world to him. The authorities in Rarotonga, anxious to promote tourism in the Cook Islands, declared Tom Neale a national resource, appointed him postmaster general of Suwarrow, and then advertised the island as the world's only one-man post office. Twice a year the inter-island schooner detoured to the island to cast up on the beach bulging bags of mail. The position of postmaster gave Neale a token income, enabling him to buy supplies in Rarotonga which were delivered by the occasional yacht.

The British newspapers sent in correspondents on chartered ships to interview the now famous Hermit of Suwarrow. A visit with Tom Neale became a badge of distinction among the yachtsmen crossing the Pacific. Whereas before no more than two yachts a year had called at Suwarrow, now a dozen or more would anchor in the lagoon. And each time Neale would have to disrupt his routine to show his visitors about, serve them tea, and suffer through countless sessions of picture-taking. Or worse. Once he welcomed an American yacht with an older couple and their dog. As soon as the dog came ashore, it chased down and killed his cat. Broken-hearted, he buried his pet in a secluded part of his compound and erected a small grave marker.

Then there were the fan letters. "You'd be amazed at the variety of stuff I'm asked to send along," Neale complained in a letter to an American friend. "Sand, dirt, leaves, coral—

and endless questions. To hell with 'em. It's a wonder someone doesn't ask for a turd from my old cat!"

The years of life on a deserted island had made Neale a
bit fussy. "Once a man sent me a tin of tobacco," he confided
to visiting yachtswoman Bette Thompson. "It took a year to
reach me. But it was too weak, and so I sent it back."

The yachts left behind their magazines and newspapers.
Copies of *Time*, *Newsweek*, and *The Economist* accumulated
regularly. Neale found himself growing increasingly concerned about the month-to-month problems of the world.
His letters from Suwarrow through the 1970s are filled with
expressions of concern about such issues as environmental
pollution, the oil embargo, the impending energy crisis,
Watergate, changing weather patterns, and even the Ford-
Carter presidential race of 1976. "The dollar seems to be taking a thrashing," he wrote to a friend in 1973, "and those
damned currency speculators ought to be shot, but I suppose
Watergate doesn't help any."

Neale had become a celebrity and not even the incredible
isolation of Suwarrow could give him back his privacy or his
peace of mind. His life had changed forever.

The idyll was coming to an end. In early 1977 Neale developed a chronic pain in his stomach. It grew worse as the
months passed. In May the crew of a calling yacht found him
seriously ill. The inter-island schooner diverted for the last
time to take Neale to the hospital on Rarotonga. The doctors
discovered he suffered from terminal stomach cancer. Early
in the morning of November 30, 1977, the man who had
once defined himself to James Rockefeller as "just an ordinary guy who wanted to go it alone" died. Later that same
day his body was laid to rest in a small cemetery by the sea.

When the author visited Neale's compound on Suwarrow
some years back, he found that Pacific yachtsmen had maintained the various buildings as a shrine to his spirit, repairing
the damage of time and the elements. A crushed coral path-
way led to a memorial inscribed "1952-1977, TOM NEALE
LIVED HIS DREAM ON THIS ISLAND."

Neale's two-room clapboard house was nearby. The pots
and pans were still neatly stacked in his kitchen. The book-
shelves still held his library. His worn straw hat hung from a
peg near his front door above his handwritten note asking

visiting sailors to respect his property and enjoy his vegetables. His chickens had gone wild and scurried nervously through the nearby bushes. Six yachts bobbed at anchor just off his beach. Scores of black and white terns and grey-headed noddies wheeled overhead.

Inside on the kitchen table lay a log which visitors to Suwarrow had signed since 1977. The captain of the French yacht, *Karak*, noted there in August of 1978 a sentiment shared by most of the island's visitors:

"We think this island is one of the last beautiful places where people can feel free, really free!"

FURTHER READING

Alexander Selkirk

The most authoritative and useful account of Selkirk's life before and after his stay can be found in John Howell's book, *The Life and Adventures of Alexander Selkirk*. Although writing over a century after the events he describes, Howell relies upon local documents and oral traditions in Largo regarding Selkirk's experiences there. The major contemporary accounts of Selkirk's years on Más á Tierra Island are Woodes Rogers' *A Cruising Voyage Round the World* and Richard Steele's 1713 essay in *The Englishman*. William Dampier's book *A New Voyage around the World* and William Funnell's account of that same cruise, *A Voyage Round the World, Containing an Account of Captain Dampier's Expedition*, are the major sources for Selkirk's passage to the Juan Fernández Islands.

Bryan Little's *Crusoe's Captain* is a reliable biography of Woodes Rogers, while Clennell Wilkinson's *Dampier: Explorer and Buccaneer* is solid in its scholarship on that other important figure. Christopher Lloyd's *Brethren of the Coast* and Alexander Winston's *No Man Knows My Grave* are both useful on the pirates and privateers of this era.

Captain Charles Barnard

Charles Barnard's book, *A Narrative of the Sufferings and Adventures of Capt. Charles H. Barnard*, is the principal source of information on this remarkable man's survival for over two years on the Falkland Islands. His account remains eminently readable, even after the passage of almost 170 years, thanks to a simple, straight-forward style. The original 1829 edition is virtually unobtainable, except through a handful of rare book rooms at major libraries. However, in 1979 Wesleyan University Press reprinted the good captain's book along with an outstanding introduction by Bertha Dodge, who also provided a host of supplemental documents she had uncovered in her research. (Barnard, by the way, drew all the fine ink illustrations.)

Two useful histories are Ian Strange's *The Falkland Islands* and M. B. R. Cawkell's volume by the same name. The latter is a lifelong resident of the islands.

The Crew of the Whaleship *Essex*

The tragedy of the *Essex* was well chronicled by the survivors. Owen Chase's book is the most important. A second lengthy account was written in 1880 by Thomas Nickerson, who was seventeen years old and at the ship's helm when the whale struck. (Interestingly enough, Nickerson cannot admit that he owed his survival to the cannibalism of his shipmates' bodies in Chase's boat.) The manuscript was lost for a century until it was discovered in an attic in Hamden, Connecticut, and donated to the Nantucket Historical Society. Both Captain George Pollard and crewmember Thomas Chappel left accounts, although much shorter than those of Chase and Nickerson.

Thomas Heffernan in *Stove by a Whale: Owen Chase and the Essex* reprints in their entirety the accounts of Chase, Pollard, and Chappel. He did extensive research into the subject and uncovered numerous important contemporary documents pertaining to the *Essex*. He includes these as well. His fine book is indispensable to the student of these events.

All four men are sparse in their descriptions of the daily activities on board a whaling ship of that era. To flesh out their accounts, I have relied upon Nelson Haley's *Whale Hunt: The Narrative of a Voyage on the Ship Charles W. Morgan, 1849-1853*. He was a harpooner on that ship. The journal of his voyage is a classic of whaling literature, worthy of standing alongside *Moby Dick*.

Henry Carlisle wrote *The Jonah Man*, a rather good novel based on the events surrounding the sinking of the *Essex* and the survival of its crew.

A.W. Brian Simpson's history, *Cannibalism and the Common Law*, is a full and provocative account of the controversy, legal and personal, surrounding the last voyage of the Victorian yacht *Mignonette.*

William Mariner

The major source for William Mariner's years on Tonga is John Martin's fine two-volume work, written in collaboration with the castaway himself. Although *An Account of the Natives of the Tonga Islands* enjoys a secure status as a classic of both anthropology and adventure, it has not been reprinted in over 150 years. Only one biography has ever been published, that by the English admiral Boyle Somerville in 1936. His scholarship is generally sound, even if his style is pedantic. Noel Rutherford's *Friendly Islands: A History of Tonga* and Edwin Ferdon's *Early Tonga: As the Explorers Saw It, 1616-1810* are two useful histories.

Herman Melville

I have used throughout this chapter the traditional spelling of "Typee" instead of the modern version "Taipi" common today.

The most comprehensive accounts of Melville's adventures in French Polynesia are his own books. *Typee* treats his adventures on the Marquesas, while *Omoo* details his experiences afterwards as a beachcomber in Tahiti. Both are readily available in modern editions.

Writing about Herman Melville has become a cottage industry among academics. Scores of books exist on the man, his life and works. The most useful for his years as a whaler and beachcomber is Charles Roberts Anderson's *Melville in the South Seas*, a brilliant study that resulted from four years of research on three continents into this period of his life.

Walter Herbert's fine academic study, *Marquesan Encounters: Melville and the Meaning of Civilization*, examines Melville's experiences in Typee within the context of two other Americans who had earlier impinged upon Marquesan society—the American Navy Captain David Porter, who seized Nuka Hiva as an American possession in 1813, and William Alexander, the head of the American missionaries who sought unsuccessfully to establish a presence there in 1833.

David Howarth's *Tahiti: A Paradise Lost* does an outstanding job of surveying the cultural genocide inflicted upon that island in the name of Christianity and European civilization. Gavan Daws' *A Dream of Islands: Voyages of Self-Discovery in the South Seas* covers some of the same territory; he also has a lengthy chapter on Melville.

Robert C. Suggs' *The Hidden Worlds of Polynesia* continues to be indispensable to the student of Marquesan archaeology and anthropology. He discusses in detail many aspects of Typee society that were beyond Melville's comprehension, given the brevity of his stay in the valley.

The Torres Strait

The stories of the survivors of the *Charles Eaton*, Barbara Thompson, and Mary Watson are virtually unknown outside Australia.

John Ireland authored a 64-page pamphlet about his experiences, *The Shipwrecked Orphans*, an excessively rare publication. I consulted the copy in the Hill Collection in the rare book room of the central library at the University of California in San Diego. Additional details can be found in the report of Captain Pasco to the Historical Society of Australasia on September 3, 1886. Pasco researched the subject extensively and conducted lengthy interviews with Ireland as well as with Captain Thomas Watson, who had led the official enquiry into the matter on behalf of the government.

The most authoritative and complete contemporary accounts of the story of Barbara Thompson can be found in John MacGillivray's *Narrative of the Voyage of H. M. S. Rattlesnake* and Thomas Huxley's *A Diary of the Voyage of H. M. S. Rattlesnake*, both of which have been reprinted in this century.

The Australian novelist Ion L. Idriess spent considerable time in the Torres Strait in the early 1940s and recorded the oral history of the natives about both John Ireland and Barbara Thompson. He incorporated this material into two fact-based novels, *Headhunters of the Coral Sea* (on the survivors of the *Charles Eaton*) and *Isles of Despair* (on Barbara Thompson).

Mary Watson's two diaries are preserved in the Oxley Memorial Library in Brisbane, Australia. Also there on display are photographs of her and her baby, some personal effects, and the small cast iron tank in which the three of them made their incredible sea journey.

Jillian Robertson's *Lizard Island: A Reconstruction of the Life of Mrs. Watson* is the only book on the subject. As the title suggests, the author fleshes out the historical outline with some fictional reconstruction. However, she does reprint virtually all the important documents associated with the story of Mary Watson, including her two diaries.

Excellent background on the history and culture of the Torres Strait can be found in John Singe's *The Torres Strait: People and History* and Bill Beatty's *Next Door to Paradise: Australia's Countless Islands*.

The Castaways of Minerva Reef

Olaf Ruhen's book *Minerva Reef* is a full account of the ordeal of the Tongans on Minerva Reef. He had lived for some time on Tongatapu and interviewed all the survivors at length. For the story of the Englishman on his rock off the Scottish coast in 1615, I relied upon the account in Edward Leslie's *Desperate Journeys, Abandoned Souls*.

Tom Neale

The fullest account of Tom Neale's adventures on Suwarrow is, of course, his own book, *An Island to Oneself*. (The title was changed to *An Island to Myself* in subsequent reprints.) A short account of his life with a full history of Suwarrow Atoll can be found in A.S. Helm and W.H. Percival's *Sisters in the Sun: The Story of Suwarrow and Palmerston Atolls*. Several of the yachtsmen and women who visited Neale on Suwarrow published accounts later. These include James Rockefeller, Jr., *Man on His Island*; Bette Thompson, "Suwarrow Atoll," in *Pacific Skipper* (January 1976) and "Sail to Suwarrow: In Search of a Hermit," in *Better Boating* (May 1976); and Carl Seipel and Hans Bernwall, "An Island to Himself," in *Spyglass* (1979).

BIBLIOGRAPHY

Adams, Percy G. *Travel Literature and the Evolution of the Novel.* Lexington, KY: University Press of Kentucky, 1983.

Anderson, Charles Roberts. *Melville in the South Seas.* New York: Dover Publications, 1966.

Anon. "Providence Displayed: Or A Very Surprising Account of One Mr. Alexander Selkirk," in *The Harleian Miscellany,* vol. V, pp. 429-433. London: John Murray, 1810.

Arvin, Newton. *Herman Melville.* New York: William Sloane Associates, 1950.

Barnard, Capt. Charles H. *Marooned: Being A Narrative of the Sufferings and Adventures of Captain Charles H. Barnard.* Bertha S. Dodge, editor. Middletown, CT: Wesleyan University Press, 1979.

Banfield, Edmund James. *The Confessions of a Beachcomber.* London: Unwin, 1908.

_____. *Further Confessions of the Beachcomber.* London: Unwin, 1911.

Bateson, Charles. *Australian Shipwrecks.* 2 vols. Sydney: A. H. & A. W. Reed, 1972.

Beaglehole, John C. *The Exploration of the Pacific.* London: Adam & Charles Black Ltd., 1947.

Beatty, Bill. *Next Door to Paradise: Australia's Countless Islands.* Melbourne: Cassell Australia Ltd., 1965.

Brown, Stanley. *Men from Under the Sky: The Arrival of Westerners in Fiji.* Rutland, VT: Charles E. Tuttle Co., 1973.

Carlisle, Henry. *The Jonah Man.* New York: Alfred Knopf, 1984. (On the Essex)

Carse, Robert. *The Castaways: A Narrative History of Some Survivors from the Dangers of the Sea.* Chicago: Rand McNally & Co., 1966.

Cawkell, M.B. R., D.H. Maling, and E.M. Cawkell. *The Falkland Islands.* London: Macmillan & Co., 1960.

Chase, Owen. *Narrative of the Most Extraordinary and Distressing Shipwreck of the Whaleship Essex.* Gloucester, MA: Peter Smith, 1972.

Daws, Gavan. *A Dream of Islands: Voyages of Self-Discovery in the South Seas.* New York: W. W. Norton, 1980.

De la Mare, Walter. *Desert Islands and Robinson Crusoe.* London: Faber and Faber Ltd., 1930.

Dening, Greg. *The Marquesas.* Papeete, Tahiti: Société Nouvelle des Editions du Pacifique, 1982.

Driessen, H. A. H., "Outriggerless Canoes and Glorious Beings: Pre-contact Prophecies in the Society Islands," in *The Journal of Pacific History,* vol. 17 (January 1982), pp. 3-27.

Edwards, Hugh. *Australia and New Zealand Shipwrecks and Sea Tragedies.* Sydney: Matthews and Hutchison, 1978.

Ferdon, Edwin N. *Early Tonga: As the Explorers Saw It, 1616-1810.* Tucson: University of Arizona Press, 1987.

Funnell, William. *A Voyage Round the World, Containing an Account of Captain Dampier's Expedition.* New York: Da Capo Press, 1969.

Furnas, J. C. *Anatomy of Paradise: Hawaii and the Islands of the South Seas.* New York: William Sloane Associates, 1947.

Golding, William. *Lord of the Flies.* New York: Coward-McCann, Inc., 1962.

_____. *Pincher Martin.* New York: Capricorn Books, 1956.

Heffernan, Thomas F. *Stove by a Whale: Owen Chase and the Essex.* Middletown, CT: Wesleyan University Press, 1981.

Haddon, Alfred C. *Head-Hunters: Black, White, and Brown.* London: Methuen & Co., 1901. [On the Torres Straits]

Haley, Nelson Cole. *Whale Hunt: The Narrative of a Voyage on the Ship Charles W. Morgan, 1849-1853.* New York: Ives Washburn, Inc., 1948.

Helm, A.S. and W. H. Percival. *Sisters in the Sun : The Story of Suwarrow and Palmerston Atolls.* London: Robert Hale & Co., 1973.

Herbert, T. Walter. *Marquesan Encounters: Melville and the Meaning of Civilization.* Cambridge: Harvard University Press, 1980.

Horder, Mervyn. *On Their Own: Shipwrecks and Survivals.* London: Gerald Duckworth & Co., 1988.

Howard, Leon. *Herman Melville: A Biography.* Berkeley: University of California Press, 1951.

Howarth, David. *Tahiti: A Paradise Lost.* New York: The Viking Press, 1984.

Howell, John. *The Life and Adventures of Alexander Selkirk.* Edinburgh: Oliver & Boyd Ltd., 1829.

Huxley, T.H. *Diary of the Voyage of H. M. S. Rattlesnake.* Ed. Julian Huxley. London: Chatto and Windus, 1935.

Huntress, Keith. *Narratives of Shipwrecks and Disasters.* Ames, IA: Iowa State University Press, 1974.

Idriess, Ion L. *Headhunters of the Coral Sea.* Sydney: Angus and Robertson Lt., 1941.

_____. *Isles of Despair.* Sydney: Angus and Robertson Ltd., 1947.

Ireland, John. *The Shipwrecked Orphans.* New Haven: S. Babcock, 1844.

Irvine, Lucy. *Castaway.* New York: Random House, 1983.

Langdon, Robert. *The Lost Caravel.* Sydney: Pacific Publications, 1975.

_____. *The Lost Caravel Re-Explored.* Canberra: Brolga Press, 1988.

Ledyard, Patricia. *The Tongan Past.* Tonga: Vava'u Press, 1982.

Leslie, Edward E. *Desperate Journeys, Abandoned Souls: True Stories of Castaways and Other Survivors.* Boston: Houghton Mifflin Co., 1988.

Little, Bryan. *Crusoe's Captain: Being the Life of Woodes Rogers, Seaman, Trader, Colonial Governor.* London: Odhams Press Ltd., 1960.

Lloyd, Christopher and P.K. Kemp. *Brethren of the Coast:*

Buccaneers of the South Seas. New York: St. Martin's Press, 1960.

MacGillivray, John. *Narrative of the Voyage of H. M. S. Rattlesnake.* 2 vols. London: T & W Boone, 1852.

Mackenzie, Margaret. "A Study of the Concept of Civilization: European Evaluations of the Tongans, 1616-1824." Unpublished doctoral dissertation. University of California at Berkeley, 1971.

Martin, John. *An Account of the Natives of the Tonga Islands.* 2 vols. London: John Murray, 1817. (In collaboration with William Mariner)

Maude, H.E. *Of Islands and Men.* Melbourne: Oxford University Press, 1968.

Melville, Herman. *Omoo: A Narrative of Adventures in the South Seas.* New York: Library Classics, 1982.

_____. *Typee : A Peep at Polynesian Life.* New York: New American Library, 1979.

Michener, James A. and A. Grove Day. *Rascals in Paradise.* New York: Random House, 1957.

_____ "Reflections of a Nesomaniac," in *Reader's Digest,* June 1978. pp. 189-194.

Moore, John R. *Daniel Defoe: Citizen of the Modern World.* Chicago: University of Chicago Press, 1958.

Morison, Samuel Eliot. *The Maritime History of Massachusetts, 1783-1860.* Boston: Houghton Mifflin Company, 1961.

Neale, Tom. *An Island to Oneself : The Story of Six Years on a Desert Island.* London: William Collins and Co., 1966.

Neider, Charles. *Great Shipwrecks and Castaways.* New York: Harper & Brothers, 1952.

Nickerson, Thomas. *The Loss of the Ship "Essex" and the Ordeal of the Crew in Open Boats.* Nantucket, MA: The Nantucket Historical Society, 1984.

Noonan, Michael. *A Different Drummer: The Story of E. J. Banfield, the Beachcomber of Dunk Island.* St. Lucia: University of Queensland Press, 1983.

O'Brien, Frederick. *Mystic Isles of the South Seas.* New York: The Century Co., 1921.

_____. *White Shadows in the South Seas.* New York: The Century Co., 1920.

Olson, Charles. *Call Me Ishmael: A Study of Melville.* San Francisco: City Lights Bookstore, 1958.

Pasco, Capt. "An Account of the Rescue of Joe Forbes from Timor Laut in 1839." *Transactions of the Historical Society of Australasia.* September 3, 1886.

Pettini, Marco and Roberto. "Rossel Island," in *Pacific Islands Monthly,* February 1984, pp. 23-25.

Poling, James. *The Man Who Saved Robinson Crusoe.* New York: W.W. Norton & Co., 1967.

Pomer, Henry F. "Herman Melville and the Wake of the *Essex,*" in *American Literature,* vol. 20 (1948), pp. 290-304.

Porter, Captain David. *Journal of a Cruise.* Annapolis: Naval Institute Press, 1986.

Robertson, Jillian. *Lizard Island: A Reconstruction of the Life of Mrs. Watson.* Richmond (Australia): Hutchinson, 1981.

Rockefeller, James S., Jr. *Man on His Island.* New York: W. W. Norton, 1957.

Rogers, Stanley. *Crusoes and Castaways.* London: George Harrap & Co., 1932.

Rogers, Capt. Woodes. *A Cruising Voyage Round the World.* New York: Dover Publications, 1970.

Root, Jonathon. *Halliburton, the Magnificent Myth.* New York: Coward-McCann, Inc., 1965.

Ruhen, Olaf. *Minerva Reef.* Boston: Little, Brown, and Co., 1963.

Rutherford, Noel, editor. *Friendly Islands: A History of Tonga.* Melbourne: Oxford University Press, 1977.

Seipel, Carl and Hans Bernwall, "An Island to Himself," in *Spyglass* (1979), pp. 53-60. [On Tom Neale]

Sahlins, Marshall. *Islands of History.* Chicago: The University of Chicago Press, 1985.

Simpson, A.W. Brian. *Cannibalism and the Common Law : The Story of the Tragic Last Voyage of the Mignonette and the Strange Legal Proceedings to Which It Gave Rise.* Chicago: University of Chicago Press, 1984.

Singe, John. *The Torres Strait: People and History.* Brisbane: University of Queensland Press, 1979.

Somerville, Boyle T. *Will Mariner: A True Record of Adventure.* London: Faber and Faber Ltd., 1936.

Stackpole, Edouard A. *The Sea-Hunters: The New England Whalemen During Two Centuries, 1635-1835.* Philadelphia: J.B. Lippincott C., 1953.

_____. *Those in Peril on the Sea : Great Adventures: from the Shipwreck of St. Paul to the Atomic Submarine.* New York: The Dial Press, 1962.

_____. *Whales and Destiny: The Rivalry between America, France, and Britain for Control of the Southern Whale Fishery, 1785-1825.* Amherst, MA: The University of Massachusetts Press, 1972.

Steele, Richard. "Alexander Selkirk," in *The Englishman*, No. 16, December 3, 1713.

Strange, Ian J. *The Falkland Islands.* Harrisburg, PA: Stackpole Books, 1972.

Suggs, Robert C. *The Hidden Worlds of Polynesia.* New York: Harcourt, Brace & World, 1962.

Swaney, Deanna. *Tonga: A Travel Survival Kit.* Berkeley, CA: Lonely Planet Publications, 1990.

Theroux, Paul. *The Happy Isles of Oceania: Paddling the Pacific.* New York: Putnam, 1992.

Thompson, Bette. "Suwarrow Atoll," in *Pacific Skipper* (January 1976), pp. 31-35.

_____. "Sail to Suwarrow: In Search of a Hermit," in *Better Boating* (May 1976), pp. 24-28. [Both on Tom Neale]

Vason, George. *An Authentic Narrative of Four Years' Residence at Tongataboo.* London: Longman, 1810.

Watt, Ian. "*Robinson Crusoe* as a Myth," in *Essays in Criticism: A Quarterly Review of Literary Criticism*, (April 1951), pp. 95-119.

Weaver, Raymond M. *Herman Melville: Mariner and Mystic.* New York: George Doran Co., 1921.

Whipple, Addison. B. "Three-Month Ordeal in Open Boats," in

Life, November 10, 1952, pp. 144-156. [On the survival of the *Essex* crew.]

_____. *Yankee Whalers in the South Seas.* New York: Doubleday, 1954.

Wilkinson, Clennell. *Dampier: Explorer and Buccaneer.* New York: Harper & Brothers, 1929.

Winston, Alexander. *No Man Knows My Grave: The Great Age of Privateers and Pirates, 1665-1715.* Boston: Houghton Mifflin Co., 1969.

Wood, A. H. *The History and Geography of Tonga.* Auckland, NZ: 1972.

Zweig, Paul. *The Adventurer.* New York: Basic Books, 1974.

INDEX

About the Author

James C. Simmons is the author of seven books and over 400 magazine articles on travel, history, and wildlife. Raised in Cincinnati, he received his bachelor's degree from Miami University, Ohio, and a doctorate in nineteenth century British literature from the University of California at Berkeley. Before becoming a freelance writer, he taught courses on British and American literature at Boston University and San Diego State University. His last book, *Americans: The View from Abroad*, won first prize as Best Travel Book of 1990 in the Lowell Thomas Competition of Travel Journalism. He has been a member of the Society of American Travel Writers since 1983. His travels over the past two decades have taken him to almost every island mentioncd in *Castaway in Paradise*. He lives in San Diego.